RELIGION AND GANDHIAN PHILOSOPHY

RELIGION AND GANDHIAN PHILOSOPHY

MANISHA BARUA

AKANSHA PUBLISHING HOUSE
NEW DELHI-110 059 (INDIA)

AKANSHA PUBLISHING HOUSE
R 37-B, Vani Vihar, Uttam Nagar
New Delhi - 110 059
e-mail : ektabooks@yahoo.com

Religion and Gandhian Philosophy

First Edition 2002
ISBN 81-87606-11-8

PRINTED IN INDIA

Published by M.P. Misra for Akansha Publishing House, New Delhi and Printed at Mehra Offset Press, Delhi.

CONTENTS

PREFACE

Mahatma Gandhi (1869-1948) was not a philosopher nor a religious preacher in the accepted sense of the term. He did not expound a system of philosophy. Neither did he preach a religion of his own, nor did he organize a religious community. He is often described as a saint turned into a politician. Gandhi was at once a successful politician, a radical social reformer and one who formulated economic principles without himself being an economist. But behind all these diverse activities of Mahatma Gandhi there lies hidden the religious fervour which like a magic stone radiated his activities with the greatest brilliance.

In every field of activity Gandhi was concerned with the ultimate Reality or Truth which he did not hesitate to call God. His passion for truth was almost terrifying. This is true about Ahimsa as well, which he called the other side of the medal which is Truth. Gandhiji has faith in the essential goodness of man. He wanted ever individual to develop this goodness so that a better world order could be achieved.

Gandhiji in his religious views acknowledges his indebtedness to the spirit of various other scriptures like the *Bible*, the *Quran* and to the writings of Tolstoy, Ruskin and others. But above all he is greatly influenced by Hinduism. He never accepted anything if it did not conform to reason. In that way "he represented in himself the loftiest virtues of Hinduism and showed to mankind the way to achieve the final goal of life". Like other great apostles of religion he was an inspired devotee of God. He himself confessed that "He did hear like a voice....It was as unmistakable as some human voice definitely speaking to me". (*Harijan* 8.7.1933).

Gandhiji towards the end of his autobiography (My Experiments with Truth) remarks with a certain amount of emphasis, "I can say without the slights hesitation and yet in all humility, that those who say that religion has nothing to do with politics, do not know what religion means". (Autobiography up. 404-405). This applies not only to politics but to every sphere of his activities, social, economic, education etc. He used to say that what he preached were nothing new, they were as old as the hills, he only tried to put them into everyday practice. Thus essentially Gandhi was a religious man. Had he been born in the sixteenth or seventeenth century he would have passed as a religious saint like Kabir, Nanak etc. But the need of the age turned him into a politician. With his religious zeal, he come to save India at the most crucial period of her history.

Gandhiji's concept of Ideal racial relationship, his insistence on non violence and peace, his idea of satyagraha, his dream of Saraj and Ramarajya, cannot be understood apart from the philosophy and religion that he preached. Social reforms such as abolition of untouchability, temple entry, service to the Harijans, concept of equality were all based on what Gandhiji taught and preached. His idea about capitalism, his theory of trusteeship, his insistence of the development of cottage industries in village reorganization, above all what he called Gandhian socialism are fundamentally rooted in what may be allied the philosophy and religion of Gandhi.

The purpose of this study is to correlate his philosophical and religious views with his thoughts in other spheres or national life. It will be profitable and interesting to examine how Gandhiji's ideas of Truth, Non-violence and the essential goodness of men which are basically religious ideas are reflected in his thoughts and actions in the political, economic and social fields.

The preset work is divided into six chapters. The first chapter is the introductory one where the nature of the problem is discussed. The second chapter deals with the general philosophical and religious principles of Gandhiji. In the third chapter it is shown how his ideas in the political field are influenced by religion. In the fourth chapter we have discussed the economic ideas from the standpoint of religion. The fifth chapter deals with the social problems in the background of religion. In the last chapter we have the relevance of Gandhian thoughts in modern times.

Though there is no such thing as 'Gandhism' or Gandhian philosophy in the true sense of the term because Gandhi did not formulate any new system of philosophy. For our convenience we have used the terms 'Gandhism' or 'Gandhian' on many occasions. Again, though we have discussed the impact of religion in general and not any particular religion, we have mainly dealt with the Hindu religion, because Gandhi was a Hindu first and then an advocate of universal religion.

I am proud to have two renowned Professors of Philosophy to write foreword to my book.

I express my sincere gratitude to Professor S.P. Banerjee Ex-Vice Chancellor, Burdwan University who has been kind enough to write the foreword. Professor K.K. Bagchi, former Head, Dept of Philosophy, and a great philosopher has written another foreword for my book. I am fortunate to have the two philosophers of international repute to review my book. I also express my sincere gratitude to my worthy teachers Prof. Dilip Kr. Chakravarty, Prof. Nilima Sharma and Prof. Sib Nath Sarma who had always been my constant source of inspiration and guidance. It would be ungrateful on my part if I do not express my thanks to Mr. Bordoloi who has taken enough pains to type the manuscript of the book. Latly I thank the publisher and all those associated with the publication of this book.

Guwahati **Manisha Barua**

FOREWORD - I

Whether Mohandas Karamchand Gandhi, more popularly and widely known as Mahatma Gandhi, is the best exemplar of our species—*homo sapiens* in the century we just left behind has not been universally settled as yet; but that he was one of the very best has been accepted uniformly. I feel tempted to quote Albert Einstein in this context. He wrote: "Generations to come, it may be, will scarcely believe that such a one as this ever in flesh and blood walked upon this earth."

What was Gandhi's speciality? Why is he regarded as a politician of a different type who dared shun the common pragmatic saying that religion and politics should never be mixed up? It appears that he tried to not only humanize Politics but he intended to moralize and regionalize Politics so that no gap is created between preaching and politics. Politics is a human affair and a human being is basically a moral agent based on Truth and *Dharma* (The first *Purusartha* to start with). Ahimsa (Non-violence) is not only a traditional Indian virtue but it also naturally stems from human nature. Gandhi's steadfast devotion to Truth, which for him is God, and the application of Non-violence as a method even in politics are perfectly in accord with human nature. Non-violence is not for the weak, it is for the mentally strong who can face violent attacks with perfect mental composure and equanimity. Non-violence goes hand in hand with Satyagraha and Sarvodaya. They are all basic human virtues which are to be established through translating them into action. The test of success of a theory lies in its application into practice. And Gandhi's speciality lies herein, he practised what he preached. He expected the human community to rise upto its moral standard, to fulfil the dictates of its conscience. Judith Brown, the famous Oxford Professor of History, seems correct when she entitles her near classic book—*Gandhi: Prisoner of Hope*. And it is also time that the rare phenomenon like Gandhi, the transvaluer of values, will always remain visionaries of a Ramarajja-prisoners of hope.

It is but natural that there will be hundreds of books within on such a personage each trying to study Gandhi with a special focus of the author. Manisha Barua's book *Religion and Gandhian Philosophy* is an attempt at a comprehensive and cogent presentation of Gandhi's philosophy taking religion as the principal moving force behind Gandhi's vast field of activities. It has a claim to novelty in the sense that instead of fighting shy of Gandhi's "dabbling with politics by mixing up and confirming issues with religion she starts by according primacy to religion as the basic standpoint behind Gandhi's thinking and actions. To my mind, she has done her job admirably.

The book justifically deserves carefully consideration. I shall be only happy if this addition to our commonwealth of letters receives that attention it is entitled to.

S.P. Banerjee.

Acharyya Brajendra Nath Seal
Professor of
Mental & Moral Philosophy,
University of Calcutta (Rtd.)
Formerly Vice-Chancellor
University of Burdwan
West Bengal

FOREWORD - II

To add one more book to the existing legion on Gandhi's thought may call for an explanation. And Dr. Manisha Barua's book is its own explanation: it is out and out a philosophical work on Gandhi's thought and action and, more importantly, on Gandhi's philosophy of action. Ever bit philosophical, it is a refreshing departure from other works on Gandhi's thought which claim to be works on Gandhi's philosophy, but understand philosophy, in an all-too-bald sense. Dr. Baruah makes a philosophy, in an all-too-bald sense. Dr. Baruah makes a philosophical scrutiny of Gandhi's many reflections on 'nonviolence', 'truth', 'God', 'religion', 'moksha', 'peace', 'ramarajya', 'trusteeship,' *et al:* spread over her numerous writings, fixes those reflections in a conceptual framework (which Dr. Barua constructs Quite in conformity with her philosophical task—for herself), and helps the philosophic researcher conceive Gandhi in a logical map and assess for himself the philosophical merits (or shortcomings) of Gandhi's thought.

Influence of Hinduism, Jainism, Islam, Christianity, of the Buddha and Tolstoy on Gandhi have been detailed in Dr. Barua's work. Gandhi's revulsion to the polities- better, politicking- of his days has been made explicit; Gandhi's attitude to government has been rightly traced to Thoreau's famous essay on 'Civil Disobedience'; and Gandhi's reflections on world-peace have been set in their cosmic dimension; and so on and on.

But Dr. Barua's historical scholarship, commendable as it is, has not got the better of the philosophical task to which she has addressed herself in the work. She brings out the conceptual lineaments and the conceptual interlacing of Gandhi's reflections on 'truth', 'nonviolence', 'Ramarajya', 'trusteeship', 'God', 'religion', 'peace', and, whatever. At the same time, Dr. Barua is also conscious of her responsibility—as a philosophical researcher though—to Gandhi who gave the world the 'moral equivalent of war' (Joan Bondurant). And so in the end Dr. Barua weave the stray reflections of Gandhi into the great *philosophy of man* which was Bapu's perennial gift to humanity.

It is indeed heartening to find that Dr. Barua combining, as she does, critical acumen with deep philosophic sensitivity has repaid the debts of India's philosophic community to Gandhi.

Kalyan Kumar Bagchi

Rtd. Prof. & Head Dept. of Philosophy
Visva Bharati
Santiniketan

1

INTRODUCTION

Every nation like an individual has its own soul. And the soul of the nation manifests itself in its institutions, social structure, political framework, economic policies, its laws, customs etc. Religion which is the soul or the very breath of Indian life similarly gets exemplified in its various fields of human activity. The prosperity of a nation depends upon the extent to which the people cling to these ideals. The decline of a nation is due to its retreat from the ideals for which its stands.

India is a country where people are predominantly religious. Religion and spirituality are firmly rooted in the minds of her people. It is this feature which has attracted men from all parts of the world to her.

Etaddesa prasutasya sakasadagra

Janmanah svam svam curitram

Sikseran prithivyam sarvamanavah.[1]

Some countries are well known for their political institutions, others for their economic prosperity while some others for their social advancement. India is great for her philosophy and religion. The life of an Indian from the cradle to the grave is dominated by Religion. In India, religion is not merely a 'Japanese vase' as Swami Vivekananda calls it.[2] It is practical attitude which the people translate into action in their own lives. According to Max Muller the study of religion is incomplete unless it is studied with reference to India. To quote him, "Take religion and where can you study its true origin, its natural growth, and its inevitable decay better than in India, the home of Brahmanism, the birth place of Buddhism and the refuge of Zoroastrianism even now the matter of new superstitions and why not, in the future the regenerate child of the purest faith, if only purified from the dust of nineteen centuries?"[3] To others, Religion is one condition among so many other conditions, but to the Indian people it is one great sustaining force, pertaining to all the spheres of their lives. Mahatma Gandhi who was born and brought up in India could not escape this strong influence of religion in all his activities.

But gradually the glory and power of India began to fade. India's downfall was regarded as a demonstration of the theory that highly religious, moral or philosophical ideals should not be allowed to meddle with practical politics. Hence during some stage of India's freedom struggle terrorism, political assassination and the like were adopted by some as the sane methods of liberation. Even Bal Gangadhar Tilak adopted a similar method. Tilak's commentary on the *Gita* could be taken as an interpretation by which even violence for the sake of India's swaraj could be defended. But the revolution which Gandhi sought to bring about was different—it was a non-violent revolution. His was the glory of leading an unarmed people against the most powerful empire the world has every seen. But he did so not as a matter of policy to fight a powerfully armed nation but as a matter of creed. Gandhi did not take non-violence as a weapon although we call it a weapon. Critics point out that Gandhi seeing that it was impossible to fight the powerful British by means of any arms took resort to non-violence as a powerful weapon to arose sympathy of the opponents. But he took non-violence as a way of life which ultimately took the form of a weapon.

Mahatma Gandhi found that the chief causes of India's slavery were the cowardice of the people, communal dis-harmony, backwardness of women and the minority classes, economic disparity among people, economic dependence on foreign countries in respect of its basic needs of food and clothing and the lack of a proper system of education. To remove these Gandhiji started certain organisations for social and economic upliftment of the masses. He led non-violent political campaigns against the rulers and encouraged disobedience of morally unjustifiable laws. But he did all this with the twin weapon of Truth and Non-Violence. Gandhi believed that individual perfection and political emancipation go hand in hand. Gandhiji put his concept of swaraj beautifully as follows- "The swaraj of the people is the sum total of the swaraj of the individual."[4] The statement lays emphasis on individual swaraj. For the attainment of individual swaraj he prescribed the famous set of twelve fold vows (Dawadasha-Vrata). Gandhiji made it clear that truth and non violence which were primarily religious virtues could be employed as means to achieve political and social ends. Religious reformers before Gandhi have taught that truth and non violence were purely religious ideals fit to be practiced by only selected individuals. But Gandhi revolutionized the very conception of these two religious virtues and used them as means to a perfect political, economic and social life. Gandhi himself chose the path of politics as a means to his own spiritual perfection. He showed to the world the politics need not necessarily be a dirty affair as is commonly thought to be but could be as sacred as any path leading to God provided it had religion and religious virtues at its background.

In the book *'Mahatma Gandhi-100 Years'*, there is an essay by Toynbee in which he has compared Gandhi with Christ, Buddha, Ashoka and Muhammad and remarked that Gandhi excels all of them. Ashoka and Buddha were born kings but they kept aloof from active politics because they thought that politics corrupts people. Gandhi here is an exception since he tried to spiritualize politics. To quote Toynbee "Two of Gandhi's greatest fellow countrymen, the Buddha and Asoka could not escape contact with politics.

Both of them were born in the spiritual slum of politics. The Buddha jumped clear of politics. Asoka on the other hand entered into his political heritage and used it as an instrument for the practice of the spread of knowledge and practice of the way of life that the Buddha had worked out. Like Jesus and Muhammad, Gandhi was not committed by the accident of birth to a political career.... Unlike Muhammad, Gandhi did not take this step under the pressure of crisis. Gandhi's objective was to raise the spiritual level of life in a spiritual slough of politics. Gandhi waded into the slough, showed how the slough could be purified, and remained personally uncontaminated by his immersion in it."[5]

Mahatma Gandhi's ultimate aim of life was 'moksha' i.e. to free himself from the bondage of the flesh. This is the ultimate aim of man according to most of the important religions of the world. But Gandhi was not prepared to accept the ancient religious ideal of withdrawal from the world. Gandhi said "My service to the people is part of the discipline to which I subject myself in order to free my soul from the bonds of flesh...for me the path of salvation leads through unceasing tribulation in the service of my fellow countrymen and humanity."[6] Gandhi gave a practical colour to the lofty principles of religion not only in individual life but in the social plane also. He believed that spiritual sadhana was not an escape from the worldly demands but greater involvement in it. In a letter to Premabehen Kantak, he distinguishes between speaking of and fulfilling the congress programme and said: "The real worshippers of Sri Krishna are not those who shout 'Krishna, Krishna', but those who do his work. Our hunger is not appeased if we keep shouting 'bread, bread'. It is appeased by eating bread."[7] In his *Discourses on the Gita*, Gandhi explains his idea of Karmayoga in the light of th e teachings of the Gita in the following words, "Sanyasa means wisdom and Karmayoga means selfless action. Both of them are good but it I had to choose between the two, I would say that yoga or selfless action is better....A man who has purified himself by means of selfless action, who has his mind and his senses under control and who has identified himself with all beings, loving them as himself, such a man stands apart from action although he is acting all the time."[8]

According to Gandhi life could not be divided into watertight compartments some spiritual and others secular. "Politics, religion, social reform, economic uplift all those form parts of a whole."[9] Thus, Gandhi developed Hindu religion by modifying the concept of "Sanyasa', according to his own ideas and insights. In the following words Gandhi gives his opinion that there are two aspects of Hinduism "there is on the one hand the historical Hinduism with its untouchability, superstitious worship of stocks and stones, animal sacrifice and so on. On the other hand we have the Hinduism of the Gita, the Upanishads and Patanjali's *Yoga sutra* which are the acme of ahimsa and the oneness of all creation, pure worship of one, immanent and imperishable God. Non-violence which to me is the chief glory of Hinduism has been sought to be explained away by our people as being meant for the sanyasin only. I do not share that view. I have held that it is the way of life and India has to show it to the world."[10]

Gandhi said, "Man without religion is man without roots. Therefore religion is the basis on which life structure has to be erected if life is to be real."[11] Therefore he dedicated all his work whether social, political or economic in the name of God. Public life, social life, political and economic life would be much purer if we do it in the spirit of religion. That Gandhi was inspired by religion in different fields of human life like social, political and economic is evident from the fact that he had used such terms and concepts which unmistakably points out to its religious overtones. 'Harijan', 'Ramrajya,' 'Swaraj', 'Swadeshi,' 'Satyagraha', 'Varnashrama dharma', 'Ahimsa,' 'Satya', 'Brahmacharya,' all these have their reference to the Hindu religion. These are appealing to the Indians because they are very well acquainted with such principles of religious life. But in spite of these terms being Hindu in origin, they are applicable to any society confessing any religion.

A glance at the history of India from Vedic times upto the time of Mahatma Gandhi will show that most of the socio-political movements were connected with religion. Those movements that were backed by religion could succeed very easily. Even a bad practice like the caste system could continue because it had the support of religion. Buddhism thrived because it was a religious reaction to the existing religion. This is true also of the Jaina movement of the same period. Later historical events such as the Mahabharata wars were described as 'Dharma Yuddha'. All these show that anything could get the support of the people if it has a religious sanction and support. Mahatma Gandhi understood the mind of the Indian people. That may be a reason why he expressed his social, political and economic ideas in religious term.

Mahatma Gandhi's movement for Independence was not based on religion. It was a secular movement. His conception of satyagraha was based on religion. His insistence on fasting, Brahmacharya, truth and Ahimsa are all derived from the Hindu scriptures. It is for this reason that initially his movement could not attract the Muslim population in general. Although there were some Muslim followers, majority of the Muslims kept away from the movement. This was perhaps due to the Hindu character of the movement. The movement in South Africa, however is to be judged from a different point of view. Indian independence movement took a turn only when the Khilafat movement was attached to it so far as the Muslims are concerned. It attracted Hindus in spite of the efforts of the British government against it because the Hindus found here everything that was in their religion. Even the *Srimad* Bhagavat Gita was made indispensable to a satyagrahi. Thus religion was one of the prime factors which guided the Indian movement for independence.

It will be appropriate here to give a brief account of the development of religion in general.

DEVELOPMENT OF RELIGION

In the most primitive societies religion was not much above material wants. The interests which prompted man to be religious were mainly the want of food, the problem of sickness, death, war, security etc. Religion was thus purely selfish in nature and not clearly differentiated from the other human interests.

The next advancement in religion, was that of the conception of 'mana'. Man in this stage conceived of a living spirit which was analogous to the spirit of man within himself. The next important step was reached when man believed that the various objects of nature for example the rock, the tree, the cloud, the stream etc. were bound up with those spirit. Thus this paved the way for the religious spiritualism which was expressed in the beautiful saying, "God is a spirit, and whoever worships Him, must worship Him in spirit and in Truth. And thus, though in childlike and unsophisticated form, it has proclaimed a great truth."[12]

Herbert Spencer, defined evolution as a movement from an indefinite, incoherent homogeneity to definite heterogeneity. Biological and social evolution is characterised in passing from the homogeneous to the heterogeneous. The same process also manifested itself in the religious field. In the primitive societies, religion was not differentiated from other activities like social organisations, laws, magic, art, morality etc. Gradually religion came to be differentiated and treated as a separate activity. Religion developed into a separate system of ideas, rituals, customs, sacrifices, prayer, temples etc. This development, however, seemed to be a danger to religion for it became too departmentalised and institutional. The result was that religion gradually separated itself from other aspects of human life which were outside the religious field. Thus it introduced a sort of dualism in human life creating a barrier in the way of unification of life into a harmony. All the different branches of life science, art, ethics etc. tried to free itself from ecclesiastical control. Commerce, industry, social organisations and political institutions tried to cut off themselves from anything associated with religions. People habitually acted on the principle that the industrial life, for instance, is a separate sphere governed by purely economic laws which operate in their own right and cannot be interfered with by religious principles, which belong to quite another sphere—an assumption which crystallises in that last word of worldly wisdom, "business is business."[13]

Later on, however, men realized the fact that true religion must aim at the ultimate unification of life. Religion is not one thing among many existing things but should be the life force or that guiding factor of all human activity. It was realised that all human activities—social, economic or political should have to be reinterpreted and re-valued under the light of religion. In the words of Schliermacher, "a man's special calling is the melody of his life, and it remains, a simple, meagre, series of notes, unless religion with it endlessly rich variety accompany it with all notes and raise the simple song to a full voiced harmony."[14]

Religion in essence, is the individual's conscious aspiration for the realisation of an ideal intuitively felt. An analysis of intuitive feeling would reveal that this is just another name for the numinous element of our religious consciousness. It can be further shown that this is the non-rational counterpart of our idea of the infinite. This idea of the infinite comprehends everything, thus creating in the individual a sense of his unity and oneness with all. It is this that acts as a binding force among all and probably is at the basis of many of our higher social and political institutions. In the individual this aspiration functions like an inner thrust or as Nikos Kazantzakis says,[15] 'a great cry' which forces the individual to move onward, to visualize religious ideal in intelligible forms and to devise ways and means to achieve the goal.

Religious ideas and practices are thus consequence of this religious consciousness and not the cause of religious consciousness or of religion. In other words, religious consciousness is prior to religious ideas and practices. Religion as expressed in human life involves all faculties of man. Historical religions are born when some enlightened person formulates these religious aspirations of men in intelligible terms using contemporary idioms and when people at large willingly subscribe to these formulations as they appear to be reasonable and satisfying to them. These enlightened persons are accepted as Messiahs or messengers of God or as incarnations by their followers. Probably they find in them the embodiment and fulfillment of their religious aspirations. The Messiah thus satisfies the natural religious need of man: what the many vaguely grope for: the messiah sets before them by precepts and practices.

It was a common belief that religion is a matter of individual experience. But modern psychology has shown that there is no such thing as a merely individual experience. A man is always a member of a social group. In other words, human life is always both individual and social. There is an important element of truth in the views of Durkheim and other members of the French Sociological school, who maintain that religion is essentially a social phenomenon. Religion strengthens individuals against society, and it is this fact that makes religious progress possible. "Society on the whole is conservative, it conserves the values which have already been discovered, by embodying them in customs, traditions, institutions and creeds. But initiative, the will to progress, the impetus to fresh discoveries, emancipations, expansions,—these come mainly from prophetic and original souls who have the courage to break from conventions. It must be recognised, however that these prophets and pioneers are themselves largely the products of society, and represent largely the community itself as its growing point. The conclusion of the whole matter is that the individual and society are necessary to each other, and that behind both social and individual religion there is the same vital impulse, the same craving for the realisation of life."[16] Self realisation of the 'self' in isolation from the society is an abstraction of thought. The individual can realize his true self in so far as he participates in the life of the society. Modern religions have shown that the best way of self realisation is through self sacrifice. The modern religions of the world teaches us to attain a true way of life by which the individual rises above his selfish desires for the larger interest of the society. Mahatma Gandhi, keeping himself in tune with the present religious ideals, dedicates his entire life to the service of the community. His long life of sacrifice and whole-hearted devotion was itself the product of religion.

The religious and social condition of India before the advent of Gandhi

Indian philosophy, religion and culture became stagnant and dead due to the Muslim and British rule of India for centuries. The Muslim domination followed by British suppression destroyed India's fabulous heritage. The Indians were subjected to mental slavery. Consequently the orthodox Indians in order to safeguard the purity and sanctity of their faiths created walls of customs, rites, ceremonies and many social taboos. The sense of fear and insecurity forced them to have a conservative outlook in matters of religion. Their first and foremost concern was to preserve their traditional philosophy and religion. So they had little or practically no time at all for creative adventures in the realm of thought. In such a rigid society of separation, distinction, hard rules and customs lay the dead spirit of India.

But at the end of the eighteenth century, the history of Hinduism saw some important developments. Towards the end of the eighteenth century, the Hindu society had learnt to adjust itself to the presence of foreign powers and different religious communities. The long period of Muslim rule in India had left an indelible impression on Indian religion and society, but it failed to shake the Hindu religion as such. The religious practices and social institutions of Hinduism went on as before, though in a somewhat subdued spirit.

But the most serious challenge to the Hindus came during the British rule, from the impact of English education and European thought. The contact with the new ideas and thoughts had a powerful effect on a section of educated Indians. This was primarily responsible for the birth of the renaissance. It left to the revival of the past and the evolution of new thoughts and systems of philosophy. The ancient thoughts and ideals that were in a crude form were given a new outlook by the different thinkers. It changed the form and texture of the ancient truths and set it in a new light.

The age of the renaissance began with Raja Ram Mohan Roy who is often described as the inaugurator of the modern age. In 1822, he opened a Hindu College at Calcutta, a secular college where Bengalis could receive English education. This institution infused European liberal ideas in the mind of some young Hindus which resulted in their renouncing the whole system of Hinduism and declaring themselves as free seekers of truths. In 1827, Raja Ram Mohan Roy founded the Brahmo Samaj. The greatest social reform that he initiated was the abolition of Sati (the voluntary immolation of the Hindu widows). Unlike most of the westernised Hindus who took an active part in the struggle for Indian independence, he believed very strongly in the virtues of British rule.

Debendranath Thakur sought to give the Brahmo Samaj movement a more Indian basis by eliminating the Christian influence. The Brahmo Samaj was, however, not in any way a mass movement. It was an association of those persons who were influenced by liberal ideas of early nineteenth century.

Then we have Arya Samaj, formed in 1875 by Dayananda Saraswati. This movement was an attempt to restore the ancient Vedic religion and to reject all the later developments of the post Vedic Hinduism. It pointed out the fact that Hindu religion and culture stood in need of reforms, but the inspiration to such reforms could come from the ancient Vedic religion. It was not necessary to Europeanise Hinduism. Dayananda Saraswati stood against untouchability, idol worship, child marriage and other corrupt features of Hinduism on the ground that such practices were not to be found in the Vedas. The Arya Samaj, though confined to a small minority, had it far reaching influence in the reassertion of Indian's own Vedic heritage which coincided with the distrust of British imperial rule.

Gradually Hinduism was recovering from the excessive influence of European thought. People were getting immune to the constant exposure and acquiring the skills of adjusting themselves to meet challenges in the religious field. In some places the activities of the Christian missionaries were increasing alarmingly. They tried every possible means to point out the shortcomings of Hinduism and the superiority of Christianity. The missionary activities finding little or no response amongst the cultured and influential people of India, turned to the lower castes of society and to the less sophisticated tribal people of the remote hill and jungle areas where a large number of people were converted. But the long term propaganda of the Christian missionaries was also responsible for developing a Hindu resistance to Christian beliefs and ideas.

During this period India also witnessed the rise of another great movement in the Ram Krishna Mission, which was founded in 1897. Ram Krishna's philosophy was, in brief, the Hindu affirmation that all the different forms of faith in God are different paths to the same goal. This was the spirit of Hindu Universalism and the essential teaching of the great Advaita philosophy. This was an attitude distinguishable from the Christian and Muslim exclusiveness on the ground of its tolerance and catholicity. This Ram Krishna Mission was a clear manifestation of the spirit of a new awakened Hinduism. Hinduism at this stage laid greater emphasis on toleration and charity works. In India there grew up a large number of dispensaries, welfare centres, public libraries and lecture halls. Swami Vivekananada is mainly remembered for his efforts to popularize Hinduism. The message he delivered at the Parliament of World Religions at Chicago in 1893 found unprecedented appreciation among the western people.

The more aggressive aspect of Hindu India's awakening was witnessed in the activities of Bal Gangadhar Tilak. His primary aim was to unite the Hindus in every part of India and form a mighty Hindu nation. This was an attitude with a striking contrast with the ideals preached by Ramkrishna Mission in respect of its catholicity. Tilak's doctrine found a wide appeal in his native land of Maharashtra and in some areas of Bengal. He advocated militancy as a Hindu virture and was not at all hesitant of fanning hatred against non-Hindus. To gain the desired end, Tilak even justified taking resort to violent means, if circumstances demanded it. This was a glaring contrast to the principles of Mahatma Gandhi. Tilak wrote a long commentary on the *Bhagavad Gita*. His interpretation of it emphasised the necessity for political action in the name of religion, and that in such a cause the most violent act was fully justifiable.

The history of modern Hindu renaissance should include a number of other names. Among them are M.G. Ranade and G.K. Gokhale who were the source of true inspiration to Mahatma Gandhi. Then we have Aurobindo Ghose and Rabindranath Tagore, the renowned poet, philosopher who believed that man's spiritual regeneration should come from Asia which was the cradle of worlds' great religions. Tagore's work is a synthesis of both religion and philosophy and was deeply influenced by the catholic and dynamic views of Raja Ram Mohan Roy.

Thus we have seen that the age before the advent of Gandhi presented certain basic characteristics. One notable point of this period was that the different thinkers of this time had a positive attitude towards the world. This was in contrast to the predominant philosophical view that the world is illusory and unreal. The twentieth century thinkers emphasized the philosophy of humanism and well being of the society which reaches its culmination in the philosophy of Mahatma Gandhi. The modern Indian philosophers are very liberal and dynamic in outlook. They all advocated toleration in religious matters, save and except Tilak. The age of the renaissance was opposed in general to sectarian religion, dogmatism, casteism and ritualism. Ramkrishna Paramhamsa, Tagore, Vivekananda and others advocated the ideals of equality, brotherhood and catholicity and visualized a dynamic, universal and all embracing religion.

Mahatma Gandhi who came to India's rescue at the most critical period could not escape the influence of the age. Consequently the life and philosophy of Mahatma Gandhi was a clear reflection of the ideals prevalent in that period. But one point needs special mention there. All the different thinkers we have mentioned, represented, or appealed to, special sections of the Hindu society. None of them could reach all sections of the Indian community and herein lay the distinction of Mahatma Gandhi. From the time of Tilak's death in 1920, Gandhi became the indisputed moral leader of Hindu India, not only of the intellectuals or of the nationalists, or of the middle class, or of the poorer section, or of the rich class, but of all of these, Mahatma Gandhi's ideas embraced the whole of India. To the Indian people he was a saint, at least to the harijans and the weaker sections, an incarnation of God who has taken birth to set right the evils of this world.

As has been said that Gandhiji's success was due to his insistence on the principles of Truth and Non-violence. Hence it will be interesting to examine the significance of these two concepts in the light of ancient India's background.

Truth and Ahimsa in the light of ancient Indian background

As has been said the two important pivots of religion

on which rested the philosophy and teachings of Mahatma Gandhi are Truth and Non-violence. It is believed that at the beginning of the great battle of Kurukshetra, Arjuna found himself in utter confusion whether to fight his own people or remain content in the position he and his brothers were thrown into. Arjuna was of opinion that there cannot be real peace in fighting with arms and therefore fighting can be described as a 'ghora karma' (ferocious work). It is more so when a fighting is between one's own people. According to Arjuna "I do not see any good in killing our own people. I do not desire for victory nor kingdom and pleasures."[17] Here there has been a conflict between the two maxims. One is when violence is justified when there is an atatayi (an atatayi is one which administers poison, sets fire to a living house, comes to kill with arms and ammunitions, takes away money and possesses illegally cultivated land or forcibly carries away one's wife). The Kauravas committed all these crimes against the Pandavas and they are atatayis in the true sense of the term. Therefore they deserve to be killed without consideration, according to the teachings of the political works. Such works say "Atatayinam ayantam hanyad eva vicarayan."[18] The other maxim is that one should not kill any living being.

Arjuna in his utter confusion could not take as a real dharma to kill one's kith and kin though they are atatayis. He placed more importance to the second maxim of the dharmasastras "Na himsyat sarvabhutani" (Do not kill any living being). He does so because when there is a conflict between the dharmasastra and the Arthasastra, dhamasastra reigns supreme.

"Arthasastrat balavaddharma sastramiti sthithih"[19]

Lord Krishna had to take sufficient pains in explaining that killing does not mean complete destruction of the soul and therefore there can be no sin in killing in a rightful battle (dharma yuddha).[20] The battle of Kurukshetra was a rightful battle for a Kshatriya. Therefore it was the duty of Arjuna to fight and not to throw away his arms because

Arjuna threw away his bow and arrow and sat down in his chariot refusing to fight.[21] The destruction of the race which brings power and culture to an end, was considered by Arjuna, to be a great sinful act. An act which ultimately produces destructive effect is sinful for whatever is harmful in result is adharma.

There are two ways of doing things. In one the doer is concerned only with the end. The means are of no importance. The other one is that the end alone is not justifiable if the means to perform it are not acceptable ethically. Krishna had to take sufficient labour in order to convince Arjuna that it was his duty to perform his own duty as a Kshatriya prince and he adduced spiritual reasons in justification of the killing.

This introduction of the Gita as its background has a special significance. It points out two sides of human activities, including social and political. One is adherence to absolute dharma (duty), the other is dharma as a limited individual achievement. The other activities may be justified without adhering to spiritual teaching in its entirety. This background of the Gita has a political meaning because the battle of Kurukshetra was fought to gain a lost kingdom from the Kauravas and all means including fighting between brothers had to be resorted to. Arjuna's contention and Krishna's justification of violent battle represent the two traditional thoughts of national activities in India. The *Mahabharata* of which the *Gita* is a part represents the Krishna's point of view that one has to perform his duties whether social, individual or political without caring for its results. The other one which places Truth and to some extent non violence and absolute Good represents the point of view which is embodied in the *Ramayana*. The whole of the story of the *Ramayana* developed from adherence to absolute Truth in all affairs. These two traditions we may call for our purpose Ramayanic and Mahabharatic.

In the Indian political thought beginning from Kautilya the latter is followed mostly (i.e. the end justifies the means).

But specially after the advent of Buddhism and Jainism justifiable means as well came to be regarded as equally important. Asoka tried to follow the maxim that a good end should be achieved by good means, after witnessing the devastation that was created in the Kalinga battle. He took a vow to shun warfare and after that whatever he did, he tried to achieve it by rightful means. Some of the Jaina kings also tried to follow Truth and Non-violence as far as practicable for a king.

Even in the Vedas specially in the Brahmanas numerous sacrifices were prescribed. Animals were sacrificed in large number. The sacrifices were called 'Posuyajna.' These sacrifices were performed very often. This was a clear instance of violence towards the animals which most certainly offended thoughtful and kind persons of the age. Even in the tenth century Jaideva has declared in clear terms that Buddha was born as an avatara (incarnation) out of compassion to oppose animal sacrifices.

Nindasi yajnavidherahahasruti jatam

Sadaya hrdaya darsitapasughatam

Kesava dhrta Buddha sarira

Jaya jagadisa hare.[22]

The animal sacrifices were carried out by many acts of violence. There has been attempts even before the advent of the Buddha to explain sacrifices as an act of non-violence because the animal sacrificed finds a place in heaven. Yaska (of 6th century B.C.) explains it as follows:

Dhvaratiti himsa karma, tatprati sedhah

'Advara' means where there is no himsa (violence).

There is a case of clear compromise on the part of the Vedic interpreters who considered ahimsa as the highest value.

Thus, we see that Truth ad Ahimsa were regarded as the highest value from the Vedic times but these were not always applied in practical life. The virtues however were given the highest place. In general the Dharmasastras stand for highest values while the *Arthasastra* and other political work do not hesitate to prescribe ways and means of performing political works which cannot be justified if considered from the highest ethical standpoints. Thus we see there were two parallel traditions governing Indian life and the two epics (*Ramayana* and *Mahabharata*) stand for these two traditions. Let us examine them in detail.

The two epics (*Ramayana* and the *Mahabharata*) though generally regarded as religious scriptures, may be considered as political works also in the form of stories of two royal families. Although outwardly both the works stand for the great maxim yato dharmah tato jayah' (virtue begets victory) the ways and means they prescribe are of different nature. In the *Ramayana*, truth reigns supreme whereas in the *Mahabharata* truth is subservient to the exigencies of political gain.

The story in the *Ramayana* begins with observance of Truth on the part of Dasaratha which as a son, Ramachandra had to carry out. The whole story is only the elaboration of satya palan (observance of truth). Kaikeyi herself in whatever light she may be depicted insists on the observance of Truth and she wanted to bind Dasaratha to his original promise, which in other words means an insistence to Truth. The next step in the story that is Rama's friendship with Sugriva is also the second phase of carrying out of his truth of his promise to kill Bali. The promise was uttered before the sacred fire and Rama by all means had to fulfil it. *Ramayana* is not a work which may be called a work preaching non-violence to its fullest extent. But in many places it decries violence to living beings without any cause. Sita forbid Rama to kill the denigens of the forest for no reason and create havoc among them. Throughout the *Ramayana*, Rama and the main characters have not transgrassed Truth or have not indulged in unnecessary violence. The description of Ramarajya in the work itself is based on Truth, justice and establishment of universal peace for all.

The story of the *Mahabharata* on the other hand practically begins with the burning of the lac house (jatugriha daha). It was devised by the Kauravas to burn the Pandavas to death, and the story of the disputes between the Pandavas and the Kauravas begins here. In this connection Dhritarastra's minister, Kanika's advise to root out enemy by any means reveals the attidue of a set of political person in those days.[24] The *Mahabharata* deals with every topic relating to the society and the general saying that whatever is not found in the *Mahabharata* is not there in Bharata (India) is true. But in the story the characters take resort to untruth, injustice and unnecessary deceitfulness. During the whole of the battle of Kurukshetra, the Pandavas and the Kauravas, both the parties take course to deceitfulness whenever they find an opportunity. Even Bhisma was fought keeping Shikhandi in between the two so that Bhisma may desist from shooting arrow to an eunuch. Drona also was killed in the same way, when he was shedding tears at the false news of Aswatthama's death. The line of tears on the bow string was pointed out as a snake riding upwards by Lord Krishna and Arjuna shot his arrow on that string resting on Drona's neck. Drona was thus killed. In the same way all the commanders in the battlefield on the Kaurava's side were killed in a deceitful manner. Duryodhana was hit below his belt by breaking the thigh bone which was not allowed in a club fighting (gada yuddha). Thus we see that the Mahabharata did not care much for truthful behaviour in political affairs.

These two great works served as political guidance for royal families to conduct themselves in the affairs of the state and as such they played the role of political handbooks to the royal families for centuries in India. So we see that throughout the political history of India great royal persons like Asoka, Chandra Gupta, Shivaji, Rana Pratap, Krishna, Raja Rai of Vijaynagar followed primarily one of these works in conducting their affairs. It is doubtful whether *Ramayana* and the *Mahabharata* were complete during the reign of Asoka but the traditions embodied in these two works were already taking form. Asoka who turned a Buddhist royal monk created the tradition of dhamarajya. If we turn to Shivaji we see that he followed the tradition of the *Mahabharata*, who in the true Mahabharatiya fashion played political tricks against the Mughals and vanquished Aurangzeb and his empire while Rana Pratap a contemporary king was a person straight as an arrow, so far so that he refused to lower down the umbrella from his horse to hide himself from his enemies charge. Thus we see that the Ramayanic tradition was partially followed alternately by kings.

Even in the nineteenth century we have two great political persons in Bal Gangadhar Tilak and Mohandas Karamchand Gandhi. Lokmanya Tilak placed the country above Truth. While Mahatma Gandhi placed Truth above everything else. The former followed the Mahabharatic tradition while the latter was a product of the Ramayanic tradition. Tilak's commentary on the *Gita* which is known as *Karma Yoga shastra* places final motive of action as of primary importance and his works served as a political handbook of the revolutionaries of Bengal and Maharashtra. On the other hand Gandhiji's commentary on the Gita known as *Anasakti yoga* has tried to emphasise Truth and non-violence as teachings of the Gita. Gandhiji's *Anasakti yoga* was the most important picture to his followers during the non cooperation movement.

Truth and non-violence had their proper place in the individual sadhana (spiritual practice) down from the days of the Buddha and Mahavira. The Upanishads also gives the highest place to Truth but that was for the spiritual progress of an individual. They were however never applied in political, social and other organizational matters in full. Even in the *Ramayana* which places Truth above personal pleasure and kingdom, which has given much importance to Non-violence also in places could not adhere to non-violence in all matters. Non-violence was tried only in the individuals who devoted their time to spiritual pursuits, for example the sages in the forests. They were given the highest place and practical shape by Mahatma Gandhi not only as personal sadhana of spiritual life but as a means of achieving political, social and economic ends. He took Satya and Ahimsa as means for the establishment of Rama Rajya.

In the following pages our endeavour will be to show in what way Gandhiji had used Truth and Ahimsa in his nation building work and how religion plays its part in every sphere of his activity.

REFERENCES

1. *Manusmriti,* chapter IV. 20.
2. P.B. Vidyarthi, *Early Indian Religious Thought,* p. 11.
3. Prof. Max Muller, *India, What can it teach us,* p. 13.
4. U.S. Mohan Rao (ed.), *The Message of Mahatma Gandhi,* p. 86.
5. Dr. Radhakrishna (ed.). *Mahatma Gandhi-100 Years,* pp. 379-90.
6. Albert Schweitzer; *Indian Thought and its Development,* p. 238.
7. *Young India,* 13, 10.1921.
8. *The Selected Works of Mahatma Gandhi,* Vol. IV, p. 284-86.
9. *Young India,* 2.3.1922.
10. D.G. Tendulker, *Mahatma,* Vol. VII, p. 320.
11. *Harijan* 21.7.46.
12. C.P. Tiele, "The Science of Religion,' *Gifford Lectures,* 1896 Vol. 1, p. 74.
13. D. Miall Eiwards, *The Philosophy of Reigion,* p. 158.
14. Caldecott and Mackintosh, Selection, p. 293.

15. Nikos Kazantzakis, Reportot Greco, p. 291.
16. D. Miall Edwards, *The · Philosophy of Religion*, pp. 74-75.
17. *Gita*, ch. 1, sl. 31.
18. Sridhara Swami, *Commentary of the Gita*, 1, 36.
19. *Ibid.*
20. *Ibid.*
21. *Gita*, ch. II, sl. 31.
22. *Gita Govinda of Jayadeva-Dasavatara stotram*-Buddha
23. *Yaska*-Nirukta 30.9.
24. *Mahabharata*, 1-140, sl. 1-93.

2

PHILOSOPHICAL AND RELIGIOUS PRINCIPLES OF GANDHI

INTRODUCTION

Mahatma Gandhi did not formulate any philosophical principle and religious doctrine of his own. To put it in his own words: "I do not claim to have originated any new principle. I have simply tried in my own way to apply the eternal truths of our daily life and problems.... Well, all my philosophy, if it may be called by that pretentious name, is contained in what I have said. You will not call it Gandhism, there is no "ism" about it. And no elaborate literature or propaganda is needed about it."[1] Thus, Mahatma Gandhi cannot be regarded as originating any new system of philosophy or any new religion in the academic sense of the term. He learned simply the principles or eternal truths from the greatest traditional philosophical and religious teachers of the world. But Gandhi's contribution lies in the fact that he tried to assimilate in his own way the teachings that appealed to him and to apply these not only in his personal life but also to social, political and economic problems. In this sense Gandhi could be called an applied Philosopher.

The basis of human life according to Mahatma Gandhi is not material but spiritual. The aim of human life therefore is to realize this spiritual basis which is the attaintment of moksa (liberation). He believed in an unseen power that shapes the destiny of man but at the same time he did not deny the part played by human effort. The code of human life, social and political that go by the name Gandhian are related to this basic concept of the spiritual nature of man.

Now this faith in spiritualism in Gandhi can be traced to the influences that shaped his outlook.

GANDHI'S VIEW OF RELIGION

Mahatma Gandhi's view of religion is highly practical. "You must watch my life, how I live, eat, sit, talk, behave in general. The sum total of all those in me is my religion."[2] Religion which takes no account of practical affairs and does not help to solve them, according to Gandhi, is no religion. He further says, "If any action of mine claimed to be spiritual is proved to be impractical, it must be pronounced to be a failure. I do believe that the most spiritual act is the most practical in the true sense of the term."[3] According to Gandhi life is a unity. It cannot be divided into watertight compartments called social, political and religious. All act and react upon one another."[4] Therefore Gandhi believed that one could reach God by service to man. So Gandhi could not find God apart from humanity. Consequently he dedicated his entire life to the cause of the human race-their day to day problems whether it be in the political, economic or social field.

Mahatma Gandhi's mission was not only to humanise religion but also to moralise it. He would reject any religious doctrine that was in conflict with morality. It is a tragedy to allow religion to mean nothing more than restriction on food and drink and adherence to a sense of superiority or inferiority. According to Gandhi true religion and true morality are inseparably bound with each other. "There is no religion higher than Truth and Righteousness."[5] For Gandhi "God is Truth, Love, ethics and morality."[6] If religion in the sense of spiritual realisation along with social advancement and freedom is the end; morality is the means. In other words, Sarvodaya requires adherence to moral principles and moral ways of life. This brings us to the problem of ends and means. Impure means cannot result in good end. The theory that the end justifies the means is dangerous in the view of Gandhi, since it warrants the use of violence, fraud, opportunism and others which lead to moral degradation. Gandhi believed in the Indian Law of Karma and Gita's view of Niskama karma regarding the means. So Gandhi was convinced of the fact that if one takes care of the means, the end will take care of itself.

Regarding the question of the criterion of the moral nature of means Gandhi takes resort to non-violence. Ahimsa or non-violence is the supreme virtue and the guiding factor of all affairs of life. The non-violence is the means for attaining Truth which is another name for God. Gandhi says, "If it is possible for the human tongue, to give the fullest description of God.... I have come to the conclusion that for myself, God is Truth. But two years ago I went a step further and said that Truth is God."[7]

Mahatma Gandhi's religious beliefs were largely the product of his Hindu heritage. He has inherited the belief and practices of the Hindu way of life and consequently he understands the meaning of the term religion from its use in his own form of life. According to the Hindu view Religion is not so much a revelation to be attained by us but an effort to unveil the deepest layers of man's being and get into an everlasting contact with it. "The religions of the world can be distinguished into those which emphasise the object and those which insist on experience. For the first class religion is an attitude of faith and conduct directed to a power without. For the second it is an experience to which the individual attaches supreme value. The Hindu and the Buddhist religions are of this class. For them religion is salvation. It is more a transforming experience than a notion of God.... In theistic systems the essential thing is not the existence of the deity, but its power to transform man."[8] Mahatma Gandhi's view of religion was perfectly in accordance with this view.

Mahatma Gandhi subscribes to the view of monotheism.

He refers to the charge against Hinduism that it is polytheistic in nature. According to Gandhi "They do say there are many gods, but they also declare unmistakably that there is one God, God of Gods. It is, therefore, not proper to suggest that Hindus believe in many gods. I believe that I am a thorough Hindu but I do not believe in many Gods."[9] The world is a reality and God is its creator. According to Gandhi self surrender to God is essential for spiritual realisation. Like a strong theist, Gandhi had an avowed faith in the efficacy of prayer.

Gandhi has no anthropomorphic conception of God. In other words he does not worship God as a human being. Gandhi says, "My Rama is not the historical Rama. He is the eternal, the unborn the one without a second. Him alone I worship."[10] Again he says, "My Krishna has nothing to do with any historical person. I would refuse to bow my head to the Krishna who would kill because his pride is hurt, or the Krishna whom the non Hindus portray as a dissolute youth. I believe in Krishna of my imagination as a perfect incarnation, spotless in every sense of the word, the inspirer of the Gita and the inspirer of the lives of millions of human beings. But if it is proved to me that Mahabharata is history in the same sense that modern historical books are, that every word of the *Mahabharata* is authentic and that the Krishna of th e *Mahabharata* actually did some of the acts attributed to him, even at the risk of being banished from the Hindu fold, I should not hesitate to reject that Krishna as God incarnate."[11]

Like Swami Vivekananda and Rabindranath Tagore, Gandhiji's religion was not confined to Temples, churches, books, rituals and other outer forms. In the words of Swami Vivekananda, "Temples and churches, books and dogmas, forms are simply the kindergarten of religion to make the spiritual child strong enough to take higher steps....Religion is not in doctrines, in dogmas, nor in intellectual argumentation; it is being and becoming, and it is realisation."[12] According to Gandhi also religion does not mean a set of dogmas nor does it mean conformity to rites and rituals. As Nehru observed, "Gandhiji's conception of religion had nothing to do with any dogma or custom or ritual."[13]

The root meaning of religion or dharma comes from 'dhri' which means 'to sustain'. Dharma is therefore the sustaining force of the universe which binds or holds together. In Gandhiji's conception also religion is the law, the dharma, which sustains the universe. Gandhi was however opposed to religion which was not supported by reason. He had all respect for the scriptures provided it stood the test of reason. He would reject all authority if it was in conflict with reason or the dictates of the heart. Gandhi was certain of the fact that the greatest challenge to religion came from ritualists and dogmatists. "Hence any tradition, however ancient, if inconsistent with morality, is fit to be banished from the land."[14] Mahatma Gandhi was undoubtedly the greatest social reformer. His opposition against untouchability, child marriage, child widowhood, inferiority by birth, animal slaughter etc. is a glaring proof of the importance he attached to reason.

The one, true and all perfect Religion, according to Gandhi is not capable of being realised within finite existence. No particular religion can ever claim to have the monopoly of Truth. Yet these particular religions, are necessary to convey the meaning of the one Perfect Religion just as particular truths are necessary to realise the Absolute Truth. Gandhi describes religions as human constructs which underlies and gives them reality but all of them are to some extent liable to error. "Even as a tree has a single trunk, but many branches and leaves, so there is one true and perfect Religion, but it becomes many, as it passes through the human medium."[15] Just as Gandhi had glimpses of absolute Truth through instances of relative truth, similarly he had glimpses of the Absolute or Perfect Religion through particular historical religions which transcends Hinduism, Christianity, Islam and all other religions, yet it harmonises them and gives them reality."[16] Therefore Gandhiji rejects any claim for the superiority or inferiority of status in matters of religion. He enjoins an attitude of respect and reverence towards all religions since they all contain an element of truth. Gandhi also maintains that a study of other scriptures might well lead to the extension of one's regard for one's own religion and at the same time, provide a better understanding of one's own faith.[17] Gandhi was fortunate to have as his colleagues, persons belonging to different religions and creeds. Two striking examples are those of Abul Kalam Azad, a devout Muslim and Rev. C.F. Andrews, who was a Christian missionary.

In India Gandhi dedicated his entire life to the cause of Hindu-Muslim unity. He expressed his friendly attitude towards the Muslim in early 1921 by identifying himself with the Khilafat cause. This was possible due to Gandhi's Catholic attitude and his liberal views in matters of religion.

To be brief, everything that Gandhi wrote, said or did bears witness to his faith in Truth, God or Spirituality which are only another names for Religion. Thus in his unique way in the language of simple, daily life, Gandhi brings him to everyone the spirit of religion.

INFLUENCES

Mahatma Gandhi was like the proverbial swan which had the capacity to separate milk from water. Gandhi also had the capacity to separate the good from the bad. What he took as good, he not only assimilated, but also put into practice.

In the formative period of his life he was exposed to all kinds of influences. In his childhood days he was influenced by the Vaishnova and Jaina ideas. He was also exposed to the missionary work done by the Christians. During his stay in England and South Africa he was strongly influenced by the doctrines of Christianity. But these influences only helped him to take more interest in understanding his own religious tradition. Gandhi realised that in essence all religions are one and it is better to practice sincerely one's own religion than follow the religion of a different tradition. Gandhi remained a staunch Hindu but kept an open mind. Enabling ideas from other religion to come he only reinforced his beliefs, and helped him to be a better Hindu.

In the remaining part of this section an attempt will be made to indicate some of the major influences that affected Gandhi's thought.

The Family Influence

Mahatma Gandhi's belief that religion is the main spring of all human activities is the result of his acceptance of the teachings of the great religions of the world and views of some great men. That Gandhi came to accept a religious view of the world is due to the influence of the family.

Mahatma Gandhi's family belonged to the traditional theistic faith called Vaishnavism which believed that salvation could be attained by devotion to God and service to humanity.

Being brought up in a Vaishnava household, Ahimsa (Non-violence) was in his blood. Mercy and non-killing was in him and he would never be able to give up these things. It is this Vaishnava spirit that made him to champion the cause of the depressed classes or the 'Antyajas.' Against this many wrote threatening letters to him. To them, Gandhi would frankly say that if Vaishnavism did not want to have anything to do with the untouchables then they were not fit to be called Vaishnavas but only godless and sinful people. Vaishnavism was a religion which was full of love and sympathy for mankind. It was against killing anybody or injuring any living being. If Vaishnavism taught the people to despise their fellow creatures, then he for one could not call it a religion but a monstrous perversion of religion. Gandhi feelingly appealed to the Vaishnavas to give up such hatred for the untouchables. The holy *Bhagavat* on which Vaishnavism was based taught what their true religion should be. It was not "tough-me-notism." It was essential that they should have love and feeling for the poor, and unless they had those qualities in plenty they could not call themselves true Vaishnavas. For what was religion without love for the oppressed and the depressed? It was only a godless and perverted religion.[18]

Gandhiji from his early childhood adored his mother who a pious lady and was considerably influenced by her ideals and virtues. She would fast on Ekadashi and other holy days and sometimes she would go without food even when she could not have a glimpse of the moon due to bad weather.

Gandhiji read the *Ramayana*, the *Bhagavat* and other religious texts. The *Ramayana* left a deep impression on the young mind of Gandhi. He said "what however left a deep impression on me was the reading of the *Ramayana* before my father....The reader was Godha Maharaj, a great devotee of Rama...That laid the foundation of my deep devotion to the *Ramayana*."[19]

The play Harischandra which was based on a story from the *Mahabharata* had aroused the mind of young Gandhi. The ordeals undergone by Harishchandra for his devotion to truth made a deep impression on him. He asked himself, "Why should not all be truthful like Harischandra?"[20]

The great principle of non-violence of the Manu (Ahimsa paramo dharma) formed the key stone of Gandhiji's life and teachings. A study of the *Manusmriti* revealed to Gandhi that morality should be the basis of all activities and that truth is the substance of all morality.

The Influence of the Bhagavadgita

Gandhiji refers to the Gita as his mother. In Mahatma's own words "Today the Gita is not my Bible or my Koran, it is more than that—it is my mother."[21] Whenever Gandhi felt that he was in distress he used to take refuge in the bosom of the Gita and find consolation there.

For Gandhi the Gita was a book par excellence for the knowledge of Truth. Moreover, Gandhi looked upon life as the battleground where the eternal conflict between right and wrong goes on. To him the battlefield of Kurukshetra was not simply a historical place of war but it had a far greater significance. According to Gandhi Kurukshetra points out to the battlefield in the heart of man and the constant battle that goes on there between the forces of good and bad. Gandhiji himself wrote that the Gita under the guise of a physical warfare suggested the conflict in the heart of an individual. He was also convinced of the fact the Gita did not encourage warfare but instead it has proved its futility by showing the amount of bloodshed, and wastage that a war brings about.[22] Consistently enough with the teaching of the *Gita* Gandhiji tried his utmost to discard warfare be it against a society or nation.

The slokas 62 and 63 of the second chapter of the *Gita* impressed him most.

> *Dhyaya to vishayan punsah sangaste shupjayate*
> *"Sangat sanjayate kamah kamat krodhabhijayate*
> *Krodhat bhavati sammoha sammohat smritivibhramah*
> *Smritivibhranshate buddhinash buddhi nashat pranasyati"*[23]

> Ponders on objects of the sense, there springs
> Attraction, from attraction grows desire,
> Desire flames to fierce passion, passion breeds recklessness
> Then the memory-all betrayed-
> Lets noble purpose go, and saps the mind,
> Till purpose, mind and man are all undone.

Gandhi himself wrote: "The verses in the second chapter made a deep impression on my mind, and they still ring in my ears. This book struck me as one of priceless worth. The impression has ever since been growing on me with the result that I regard it today as the book par excellence for the knowledge of Truth.[24]

Gandhi in accordance with the Gita followed the golden mean of Anasakti yoga which was a synthesis between action and inaction (Karma and akarma). Anasakti means disinterestedness. So action without attachment to its fruits is to be sought. The Gita exhorts Arjuna to fight without attachment towards its result.

"Tasmat asaktah satata karyam karma samachara

Asakto hyacharan karma paramaponyati purusha."[25]

Therefore "perform all your actions in a detached manner. A man performing actions in a detached manner can attain the summom bonum of life."

Anasakti Yoga implies perfect surrender at the feet of God. The Gita says that if a person dedicates all his actions to Brahman (the supreme deity) and performs all his actions without asakti (attachment) then sinfulness of his actions cannot cleave to him just as water cannot cleave to the leaves of a lotus plant.[26] Anasakti is not therefore renunciation of action but renunciation in action. Gandhiji strongly appreciated and himself practised the doctrine of anasakti as advocated by the Gita in all aspects of his life.

Influence of Jainism on Gandhi

Jainism had a profound influence on the life and thought of Mahatma Gandhi. This may be attributed to the fact that he was brought up in early period of his life in the formative stage, in Kathiawad a place where Jaina traditions were strongly preserved. As Dr. Devanesan says, "Gandhi could not escape the influence of Jainism since the atomosphere of Kathiawad was impregnated with its teachings and spirit."[27]

Gandhi's own conscious interest in Jain ethics and philosophy dates from his days in South Africa. The source from which he acquired a good deal of knowledge, not only of Jainism but also of his own religion (Hinduism), was from a deeply religious Jain, Jeweller of Bombay, Raichand with whom he maintained a regular correspondence.

For Gandhi Jainism, with its doctrine of syadvada or Anekantavada, was the most logical of all faiths and its most remarkable characteristics was the scrupulous regard for all things that lived. Jaina influence was clearly visible in his conception of Satyagrah and the practice of non-violence. Similarly his respect for other religions could be attributed to the Jain teaching or Anekantavada. Gandhi also refers to this in his writings.

Influence of Buddhism

In some important aspects the teachings of Gandhi resembles that of Gautama Buddha. Mahatma Gandhi himself has emphasised the part played by the eightfold path of the fourth noble truth of Lord Buddha for the salvation of the human race.[28] The futility of caste distinctions, rites, rituals and dogmas were recognised by both Buddha and Gandhi.

Gandhi was influenced by Gautama Buddha in many ways. Buddha refused mere speculation on the nature of transcendent reality; nor was he interested in metaphysical discussions for their own sake. Buddha found that the Vedic philosophers of that age interpreted the Upanishadic teachings in their own way which led to confusion amongst the ordinary men. Buddha therefore discarded such unnecessary discussions. He was concerned with providing practical remedies for the ills and sorrows of life. Mahatma Gandhi had a similar mission in life. The teachings of both these great men were therefore simple, direct and practical. Gandhi was moved by the emphasis on morality by Buddhism. Buddha was the first to rebel against the tyranny of the caste system. Buddha also gave the world the message of human dignity and equality which was followed later on by Mahatma Gandhi.

Other Influences

Mahatma Gandhi was also influenced by two other men, Dadabhai Naoroji and Gokhale. Dadabhai was the founder of the Indian National movement. As Romain Rolland writes, "It was Dadabhai who, in trying to moderate Gandhi's youthful ardour, gave him, in 1892, his first lesson in Ahimsa by teaching him to apply heroic passivity—if two such words may be linked—to public life by fighting evil, not by evil, but by love."[29]

Again it was due to Gokhale that he was able to bring politics and religion nearer to each other. Gandhiji said, "Gokhale taught me that the dream of every Indian who claims to love his country, should be not to glorify in language but to spiritualize the political life of the country. He inspired by life and is still inspiring, and in that I wish to purify myself and spiritualize myself. I have dedicated myself to that ideal.

I may fail, and to what extent I may fail, I call myself to that extent an unworthy disciple of master."[30] It was Gokhale who for the first time introduced the principles of religion into political and public life. No wonder, Mahatma Gandhi accepted Gokhale as his "political guru."

The other great Indians who stimulated the young mind of Gandhiji were Sir Pherozeshah and Lokmanya Tilak. Gandhiji, on his return from South Africa, chose Bombay as the first city to educate public opinion in regard to the problem of the Indians in South Africa. He tried to ventilate their grievances through pamphlets. On this occasion he met several Indian personalities such as Justice Ranade, Justice Badruddin Tyabji, Sir Pherozeshah, Lokamanya Tilak and Gokhale. Among them, he was impressed most by three only, he himself said "Sir Pherozeshah had seemed to me like the Himalaya, the Lokmanya like the ocean. But Gokhale was as the Ganges. One could have a refreshing bath in the holy river. The Himalaya was unscalable, and one could not easily launch forth on the sea, but the Ganges invited one to its bosom."[31]

Swami Vivekananda was another person to have exercised a considerable influence on Gandhi. His concept of 'daridranarayana' or the poor as God had been used by Vivekananda also. Ramkrishna Paramhamsa, the guru of

Vivekananda, believed that all religions are true and led to the realistion of God. He proved this in his own life by practicing the disciplines of Islam and Christianity. Gandhi wrote, "The story of Ramakrishana Paramahamsa's life is a story of religion in practice. His life enables us to see God face to face. No one can read the story of his life, without being convinced that God alone is real and all else is illusion. In this age of skepticism Ramakrishna presents an example of a bright and living faith which gives solace to thousands of men and women who would otherwise have remained without spiritual light. Ramakrishna's life was an object lesson in Ahimsa. His love knew no geographical limits."[32]

The Brahmo Samaj which was supported by a great spiritual genius Maharshi Devendra Nath Tagore also influenced Gandhi. Its greatest service lay in liberalising and rationalising Hinduism. Mahatma Gandhi had a great respect for Arya Samaj also but he had a belief that they took a somewhat narrow view of Hinduism, which was the most tolerant and liberal religion in the world. Apart from these we have the theosophical society with one of the most outstanding figures Mrs. Annie Besant. Mahatma Gandhi appreciated the role of the theosophical society thus: "Whatsoever critics may say against Madme Blavastsky, or Col. Olcott or Mrs. Besant their contribution to humanity will always rank high."[33]

Influence of Christianity

Gandhiji also had a profound respect for the teachings of Jesus Christ. He read the *New Testament* and found immense pleasure in its lofty principles. The saying "If thou smite thee on thy right check turn to him the other also" greatly moved Gandhi. Gandhi said "I have not been able to see any difference between the *Sermon on the Mount* and the *Bhagavadgita*. What the Sermon describes in a graphic manner, the *Bhagavadgita* reduces to a scientific formula...Today supposing I was deprived of the Gita and forgot all its contents but had a copy of the sermons, I would derive the same joy from it as I would do from the Gita."[34]

The life and character of Mahatma Gandhi is also similar to that of Jesus Christ. The martyrdom of Mahatma Gandhi was due to his preaching a liberal view of religion. Mahatma Gandhi tried his best to save the Hindu religion at the most critical period. In this way we have much resemblance in the life of Jesus Christ and Mahatma Gandhi.

The cross is the symbol of sacrifice and Satyagraha stands for supreme sacrifice. It infuses the spirit to suffer and to overcome any dangerous situation. In all the campaigns of Mahatma Gandhi from the boycott of foreign cloth to the march against salt tax, manifest the spirit of the Cross. As S.K. George observes, "for fasting unto death in obedience to an inner conviction is, Gandhi himself says, only the final form, the crown of satyagraha, from the picketing of a foreign cloth shop to the starving of oneself to death...the Cross of Christ can yet be a working principle of conquering love and overcoming evil everywhere."[35] Thus Satyagraha can be taken to be the practical application of the teaching of Christ. The greatest teaching of Jesus Christ consists in suffering death while following righteous path. "Satyagraha is the Christian weapon in the fight for Truth and Justice in the individual and in society, to which the Christian is committed by his profession."[36]

Both Christ and Gandhi were concerned with the individual's inner purity and perfection. Their aim was to moralise the society, purify the political atmosphere and spiritualise the laws of the state.

But here a special point deserves mention. Though Gandhi was an admirer of the Christian religion, he did not agree to all its conceptions. Gandhi did not accept the sin inherent in all simple acts of man. For Gandhi it is better to suffer the consequence of one's own sin than wish for redemption from it by God. He expresses his basic conception thus: "If this be the Christianity, acknowledged by all Christians, I cannot accept it. I'd not seek redemption from the consequences of my sin. I seek to be redeemed from sin itself, or rather from the very thought of sin. Until I have attained that end, I shall be content to be restless."[37] Again, Gandhi did not believe that Jesus Christ was the only incarnation of God. To him, Krishna, Rama, Mohammad and Zoroaster were equally incarnated divine persons. Moreover, Gandhi did not accept the view that Christianity is the only true religion, for no religion can be absolutely perfect.

Tolstoy and Ruskin

Gandhi was greatly influenced by Tolstoy's famous book *The kingdom of God is within You*. It offered to him his first belief in Ahimsa. Gandhiji was fascinated by the new outlook that Tolstoy gave to Christianity. Gandhiji accordingly tried to change the face of Hinduism by some important reforms. The importance of manual labour came to Gandhi's mind from Tolstoy. For Tolstoy, the man who abstains from manual labour is a thief. Mahatma Gandhi is indebted to Tolstoy for his philosophy of bread-labour. He says, "The Law, that to live man must work, first came home to me upon reading Tolstoy's writing on bread Labour."[38] Only those men deserve to eat bread who are actually tilling the ground, spinning cloth and producing things. All men, great or small, high or low, rich or poor must earn their bread by physical labour.

Mahatma Gandhi and Tolstoy both do not undermine intellectual pursuit. There must be persons whose devotion on pure academic studies is quite essential and necessary. Gandhiji observes, "Intellectual work is important and has an undoubted place in the scheme of life. But what I insist on is the necessity of physical labour. No man, I claim, ought to be free from that obligation. It will serve to improve even the quality of his intellectual output. I venture to say that in ancient times, brahmins worked with their body as with their mind. But even if they did not, labour is a proved necessity at the present time. In this connection I would refer to the life of Tolstoy and how he made famous the theory of bread-labour first pronounced in his country by the Russian peasant, Bondaref."[39]

Secondly, the philosophy of non-violence preached and practised by Mahatma Gandhi has been derived from Tolstoy's teaching. Tolstoy asserts, "The more I live—and specially now that I am approaching death, the more I feel inclined to express to others the feelings which so strongly move my being, and which, according to my opinion, are of great importance. That is, what one calls non-resistance, is in reality nothing else but the discipline of love underformed by false interpretation."[40] In his celebrated book, *"The Kingdom of Gods is Within You"*, we find the great torrential force creating an indelible mark on Gandhiji. All doubts, hesitations and wavering as regards the efficacy of non-violence disappeared from Gandhi by reading this book. Gandhiji confesses that its reading cured him of his skepticism and made him a firm believer of ahimsa. Tolstoy perceived the truth, love and non-violence and Gandhiji made it the motto of his life and all future action.

Ruskin was another thinker to whom Gandhi owes a great deal. He translated Ruskin's book *'Unto the Last'* under the title of 'Sarvodaya.' Ruskin's writing made Mahatma Gandhi realise the dignity of labour and the ideal of not 'the greatest good of the greatest number' but 'the greatest good of all."

Influence of Socrates

The ancient philosopher Socrates exercised an incalculable influence on Gandhiji, as a seeker after Truth. Gandhiji said, "Socrates would not refrain from preaching what he knew to be truth to the Athenian youth, and bravely suffered the punishment of death. He was, in this case, a satyagrahi"[41] he admired the moral courage of Socrates who preferred the cup of poison to giving up his pursuit of truth and stood against the superstitious ideas of the people in a non-violent way. Gandhi considered Socrates to be his hero and himself wrote a book on Socrates named "Vir Sukrant' in Gujarati.

Influence of Thoureau

In addition all these persons Gandhi was also influenced by the well known American anarchist, Thoureau. He read Thoureau's 'Civil Disobedience' with great interest while he was in jail as a result of the satyagraha campaign in South Africa. This offered a valuable suggestion to Gandhi regarding his own Civil Disobedience movement, the name of which was later changed on to 'Civil resistance' or 'non violent resistances'. In Gandhiji's word, "Thoureau invented and practised the idea of civil disobedience in Concord, Massachussetts, by refusing to pay his poll as a protest against the United States Government, he went to jail too. There is no doubt that Theoreau's idea greatly influenced my movement in India."[42]

Islamic Influences

Gandhiji was also influenced by the Persian and Islamic teachings to a great extent. This was obvious from the fact that in his prayer meetings, he would often refer to the *Holy Koran* and *Zend Avesta*. His acquaintance with the Holy Koran was due to a Muslim friend of his, Seth Abdullah. As Gandhi said "Contact with him gave me a fair amount of practical knowledge of Islam. When we came closer to each other, we had long discussions on religious topics."[43] One of his friend recommended a book of Carlyle *Hero and Hero Worship* and was struck by the prophet's (Muhammad) greatness, bravery and austere living. Gandhi learnt that "The very word Islam means peace which is non violence. The Sword is no emblem of Islam."[44] Though Muslims are too frequent with their swords, *Quran* does not preach violence.

The surrender of ego to God and self-denial are preached in the Bhagavadgita as well as in the *Quran*. Mahatma Gandhi cites many parallel passages from the *Gita* and the Quran. Both scriptures promulgate self-denial, self-sacrifice and self-surrender. The *Holy Quran* says, "Whosoever surrendereth his purpose to Allah while doing good, he verily hath grasped the firm hand hold.[45] The follower of Islam is that man who does righteous actions, puts his life into danger and is prepared to sacrifice his life for truth. He does moral acts in order to annual his evil deeds done in the past.

Mahatma Gandhi accepts the Quran's faith in a supreme God. God is infinite Power and Truth. He is the creator and destroyer of the universe. He is immanent and transcendent to the universe. Like Gandhi, Mohammed also taught the religious principle of toleration, the brotherhood of man and absolute self-surrender to God.

A combination of all these influences helped Gandhiji, to have a new religio-philosophical outlook which helped him to find solution to all problems confronting man.

GOD

The nuclear element of Gandhiji's thoughts and activities is belief in God. His idea of God is largely the product of the Hindu conception of God. As Gandhi says "I am surer of His (God's)" existence than of the fact that you and I are sitting in the room. Then I can also testify that I may live without air and water but not without him. You may pluck out my eyes but that cannot kill me. You may chop off my nose, but that will not kill me. But blast my belief in God, and I am dead. You may call this a superstition, but I confess it is a superstition that I hug." Such was Gandhi's faith in God.

Gandhiji claimed that if we have a little faith in God we will see him and his love everywhere about us. But it is very difficult for a finite individual to describe the nature of God. Man is an imperfect being. He is made in the image of God but he is far from being God. (Adam Khuda nehi, lekin khuda ke nurse Adam juda nehi.)[47] Regarding the nature of God Gandhi says: "To me God is Truth and

Love, God is ethics and morality, God is fearlessness. God is the source of life and light and yet he is above and beyond all those. God is conscience. He is even the atheism of the atheist. For in His boundless love God permits the atheist to live. He is the searcher of hearts. He transcends speech and reason.... He is a personal God to those who needs His personal presence. He is embodied to those who needs His touch. He is the purest essence...he is in us and yet beyond us..and withal he is ever forgiving for he always gives us a chance to repent. He is the greatest democrat the world knows, for he leaves us imfettered' to make our choice between good and evil. He is the greatest tyrant ever known...therefore it is that Hinduism calls it all His sport—Lila, or calls it can illusion—Maya. We are not, He alone Is. And if we will be, we must eternally sing His praise and do His will. Let us dance to the tune of his bansi (flute) and all would be well."[48]

The above description of God points out that Gandhi's view is essentially the echo of the view of God given by the Hindu religious texts such as the Upanishads and the *Gita*. To cite an example we may take the Upanishads where the nature of God is stated. "Not by speech, not by mind, not by sight can he be apprehended. How can He be comprehended otherwise than by one's saying "He is!"[49]

According to Gandhiji God is invisible, beyond the reach of the human eye. All that we can do therefore is to try to understand the words and actions of those whom we regard as men of God. Man can only conceive God within the limitations of his own mind. God is vast and boundless as an ocean and it is therefore impossible for man to imagine what He is like. Man can only experience God being merged in Him with faith and devotion. God according to Gandhi is the vital force which is all pervading and all embracing.

God is Truth

In Gandhiji we find the age old teaching of the Upanishad

that God is *Sat* or Truth (sat, cit, Ananda). In saying that God is Truth it does not mean 'is truthful. Truth is not a mere attribute of God but He is simply That.. The word Satya (Truth) is derived from sat, which means "being' or 'is. Nothing' is or exists in reality except Truth. Therefore the more truthful we are the nearer we are to God.

There is another justification why Gandhiji prefers the word Truth or calls God as Truth. God may be denied. There are people who do not believe in God. But there is no denial of Truth. Even the atheist belives in truth. Gandhi said "I would say with those who say God is love, God is love. But deep down in me I used to say that God is Truth above all. I found that love has many meaning in the English language and that human love in the form of passion could become a degrading thing also. I found too that love in the sense of Ahimsa had only a limited number of votaries in the world. But I never found a double meaning in connection with Truth and even the atheists have demurred to the necessity or power of Truth. Prophets and seers have identified Truth with reality."[50] The *Gospel* says "Ye shall know the truth and the truth shall make you free."[51] This is also cited by Tolstoy at the very beginning of his book *The Kingdom of God is Within You*. The sufis of Islam and the Upanishadic seers who declared Brahman to be Sat, Cit and Ananda identified Truth with reality.

To the question 'What is Truth?' Gandhiji replies, "A difficult question, but I solved it for myself by saying that it is what the voice within tells you. How, then, you ask, do different people think of different and contrary truths? Well seeing that the human mind works through innumerable media and that the evolution of the human mind is not the same for all, it follows that what may be truth for one may be untruth for another and hence those who have made these experiments have come to the conclusion that there are certain conditions to be observed in making those experiments...therefore we have the belief based upon experience, that those who make individual search after

God must go through several vows, as for instance the vow of truth, the vow of brahmacharya...the vow of non violence, of poverty and non possession...if you swing in the bosom of the ocean of Truth you must reduce yourself to a zero."[52] This concept of God as Truth although not a new invention, is a somewhat unique approach to the meaning of God.

THE WAY TO GOD

Gandhiji's ultimate spiritual goal is moksa or salvation which means freedom for the cycle of births and deaths. Gandhiji himself confessed that his utmost desire was to merge himself in the absolute. The body persists because of egoism. The utter extinction of this egoism therefore leads to moksa. This is the basic teaching of Indian philosophy and religion. Gandhi believed in the necessity for ceaseless effort in this spiritual endeavour. This also require grace of God. The *Bhagavadgita* which was Gandhiji's best guide devotes a long part in showing the way to the ultimate self realisation or Moksa.

The main cause of our attachment to this world is ignorance. But there is a way out of this ignorance. The attainment or right knowledge leads to its destruction. Almost all the systems of Indian philosophy believe that the evil of Samsara (this world) carries with it the seeds of its destruction and it will ultimately lead to the right. This has infused a sense of optimism in Gandhi who had a deep faith in God. Faith in God is a dispensable element to a seeker after truth. "But for my faith in God I should have been a raving maniac" was the first sentence Gandhiji uttered at the evening prayers on the day news of the death of Maganlal Gandhi was received at Sabarmati in 1928.[53]

With regard to the three paths leading to God—jnana, bhakti and karma Gandhiji laid more emphasis on Bhakti and karma, of devotion and complete self surrender to God. Here Gandhiji is influenced by the *Gita* which sings the glory of devotion. In the *Gita* it is said that the Lord is ready to forgive even the most dreadful sinner provided he surrenders himself with the greatest devotion at the feet of God.

> *"Ksipram bhavati dharmatma sasvat santi nigaschati*
>
> *Kaunteya pratijanih na me bhaktah pranasyati."*[54]
>
> ["Though a man be soiled with the sins of lifetime,
> Let him but love me, rightly resolved in utter devotion.
> I see no sinner. that man is holy. He shall not perish."]

Commenting on the allegory of Gajendra and Graha, the elephant king and the alligator what is found in the Bhagavad, Gandhi writes: "The moral of the story is that God never fails his devotees in the hours of trial. The condition is that there must be a living faith in and the uttermost reliance on Him. The test of faith is, having done our duty we must be prepared to welcome whatever he may send-joy as well as sorrow, good luck as well as bad...A man of prayer will be in the first place be spared mishaps by the ever merciful providence but if the mishaps do come he will bear it with an undisturbed peace of mind and joyous resignation to his will."[55]

This again bears resemblance to the Gita's teaching 'Karmenyeva dhikaraste maphalesu kadacana'[56] — Your concern is only with the duty and never with the fruits. The highest wisdom therefore is never to worry about the future but do our duty and resign ourselves completely to the will of God. Hence it is necessary for us to offer our prayer to God to protect ourselves from evil. Prayer is the most important part of one's religion and a man who is yearning for communion with the divine should take the greatest help of prayer.

Besides prayer and worship Gandhiji relies on karma in the form of selfless service of the poor as way to supreme God realisation, Gandhi believes that there is no worship more pleasing to God then selfless service of the poor. To serve the poor is therefore to serve God. In short Gandhi approaches the whole problem in a compromising spirit.

He realised the fact that karma and bhakti are complementary to one another. Thus Gandhi is successful in creating a mutual connection (samavaya) among the different paths leading to the realisation of God.

PROOFS FOR THE EXISTENCE OF GOD

Mahatma Gandhi who was brought up in a Vaishnava family adopts the theistic views like that of Ramanuja. God is the creator and also the ruler of the universe. Gandhi believed that belief in God is essentially a matter of faith. But his existence may also be rationally proved. "Seeing God face to face is to feel that He is enthroned in our hearts just as a child feels a mother's affection without needing any demonstration. Does a child reason out existence of a mother's love? Can he prove it to others. He triumphantly declares 'It is.' So must it be with the existence of God. He defies reason."[57]

Gandhi, however believes that it is possible to reason out the existence of God to a limited extent. The causal proof is based on the view that everything has a cause. Logically, the entire cosmos depends on the ultimate cause which is God. Gandhi says, "If we exist, if our parents and their parents have existed then it is proper to believe in the Parent of the whole creation."[58] Gandhi offers teleological argument for the proof of existence of God. It is based on the observation that there is an underlying unity and purpose, adjustment and order in the cosmos. It is governed by some law. It is moving towards some purpose or goal. If nature is unconscious and its activities are blind, the teleological process of the world must be traced to some intelligent Supreme person. Mahatma Gandhi observes, "That there is orderliness in the Universe, there is an unalterable law governing everything and every being that exists or lives. It is not a blind law; for no blind law can govern the conduct of living beings. That Law then which governs all life is God."[59]

Again Gandhi puts forward another argument. Everything

around us is ever changing and dynamic. Underlying all this change there is a power which is unchangeable and this power is nothing but God.

Moreover such testimony according to Gandhi is found in the experiences of great prophets and seers of the world. He testifies that his own experience of God gives him direct evidence of His existence. He says, "there is an indefinable mysterious Power that pervades everything. I feel it, though it I do not see it. It is this Unseen Power which makes itself felt and yet defies all proof, because it is so unlike all that I perceive through my senses. It transcends the senses."[60]

Mahatma Gandhi attaches great importance to the moral proof. According to him the so called voice of conscience is God's command and direct intimation to man. If the moral conscience is accepted, as a command then we have to accept the source of this command and this is God. Mahatma Gandhi observes, "This can only be done through a definite realisation more real than the five senses can ever produce. Sense perceptions can be, often are, false and deceptive, however, real they may appear to us. Where there is realisation outside the senses it is infallible. It is proved not by extraneous evidence but in the transformed conduct and character of those who have felt the real presence of God within. Such testimony is to be found in the experience of an unbroken line of prophets and sages in all countries and climates. To reject this evidence is to deny oneself."[61]

Thus, Mahatma Gandhi offers a number of proofs for the existence of God. But above all faith, Gandhi believes precedes all evidences. There is no argument to convince one who does not have faith in God. Faith transcends reason. Like Lotze, Gandhi believes that 'The so called proofs for the existence of God are so many pleas put forward for the justification and conviction that God does exist."[62] Logical proofs only succeeds in attaining the husks to the neglect of the kernel. Thousands of lectures cannot convince a blind man as to what colour is like. He will see colour only if vision is restored to him. Same is the case with God.

WAS GANDHI AN ADVAITIN?

We may discuss here one very important point regarding Gandhi's view about the ultimate reality—whether he was an advaitin or visistadvaitin. Philosophers differ with regard to this view. Though in accordance with the traditional Vaishnavism he show his leanings towards visitadvaita, at other times he appears to be out and out an advaitin like Shankra, believing that everything in this world is the manifestation of one ultimate principle or Reality.

Gandhi like Shankara says that nothing exists except Truth which Shankara calls Brahman. And where there is Truth there is also true knowledge (cit), and where true knowledge is there is also bliss (ananda). Truth then is Saccidananda, existence, consciousness and bliss. This is why Gandhi seems to have been strongly influenced by the advaita philosophy of Shankara.

It should be noted however that the descriptions given by Gandhi regarding the nature of the ultimate reality leaves all the ways open, to call him either an advaitin or a dualist, or a visisadvaitin—all the three major philosophical schools of Vedanta. The statement of Gandhi 'God is Truth' seems to simply that truth is an attribute of God. Later, however Gandhi found it more accurate to call Truth is God' than it was to say 'God is Truth'. This means that Gandhi thought it better to take God to be equal to Truth rather than to take Truth as an attribute of God. Thus the statement Truth is God was more accurate or appropriate from the standpoint of an advaitin. In Gandhi's view this Truth need not take any form or shape and can do very well without it but if required it can be made to do so in order to meet the demands of the finite human beings, when it may be called God or Isvara having personal attributes.

For Gandhi, however, the primary connotation of the term 'God' is not personal. He describes God as the essence, pure consciousness, as force, as truth, goodness and love. God according to Gandhi is undefined power pervading all life, the spirit, the indefinable, formless and nameless. These descriptions point out to the idea of an impersonal ultimate Reality or Absolute like the Brahman of Shankara, and hence Gandhi himself does not hesitate to express his idea of God as formless Truth.[63] Yet he does not forget to mention that God is personal to those who feel his presence and embodied to those who need his touch.[64] Gandhi therefore is not much concerned with the fact whether the devotee conceives God as personal or impersonal, so long as he is true to his devotion. Gandhi thus freely gives us personal and impersonal descriptions of God and therefore he is described by many as an anekantavadin or the one who subscribes to the view of many sidedness of reality. It may however be pointed out that when he describes God in both impersonal and personal terms, he may be described in the traditional advaitin manner between higher and lower levels of truth or reality. But Gandhi does not have preference for either the impersonal or personal description of God.

No doubt, a careful observation reveals the fact that Gandhi was very much drawn towards the advaita philosophy of Sankara. As he himself said: "I believe in advaita. I believe in the essential unity of man and for that matter of all that lives."[65] Gandhi believed in the fact that the inner oneness pervades all life. The forms are many, but the informing spirit is one. Gandhi explained his own views as such: "When we descend to the empirical level, we descend to the world of duality. In God there is no duality."[66]

This indicates that God is not personal in the sense that He has human forms or limitations. But He is personal in the sense that He is approachable to man and is in close relation with him. This is clearly indicated by the opinion which he gives about God. Gandhi speaks of God either as Rama or Krishna or as Allah or Ahuramazdah. These different names according to Gandhi are nothing but man's attempt to define the all pervading, invincible force. According to Gandhi Hinduism teaches that God has a thousand names but he also was sure, according to the teachings of Hinduism,that beyond those thousand names by which we call God, there is an indefinable Power which is nameless and formless. It is nothing but the same power or brahman which Sankara calls 'neti neti'—not this, not this and therefore is Indefinable, indescribable. For Gandhi the best way to describe this power would be to call it Truth (Satya) which is derived from sat, which means being or to exist. Thus what Gandhiji wants to say is that God in reality is formless. But he assumes forms of a person for the good of his devotees. This reminds us of the saying:"

"Bhaktanam anugrahthaya Brahmana rupa kalpana"

[Brahman assumes forms for the sake of his devotees or bhaktas.]

Therefore though at times Gandhi makes an attempt to describe God as just, benevolent, merciful, all pervading and so on, in the long run he admits that God cannot be described in his fullness and any description of Him would fall short of reality. So God is best described as neti neti (not this, not this).

Now, our point is how Gandhiji translates this belief in advaita or oneness in actual life. It should be noted that Mahatma Gandhi's belief in truth, non-violence and his insistence on the brotherhood of all men are all rooted in such a monistic belief. Thus all his thoughts and activities of his life—the constant battle against colour prejudice, racial discrimination class conflict, religious rivalries, the campaign against untouchability are all the result of this strong sense of oneness with all.

In South Africa he was very much grieved to see the prevailing racial discrimination. The advaita which was latent in him had become a living force guiding his thoughts and moulding his activities and in a city of Johhensburg that denied the brotherhood of man he learned how to affirm that all men are brothers.

According to Gandhiji, if the virtuous deserve our respect and adoration, the sinners also require our sympathy. This sense of identification with the sinful as well as the virtuous fellows necessarily form the doctrine of non-difference, or the universality of spirit (Sarvatmatva) as Sankara called it. Gandhiji always wanted that we should hate the wrong but not the wrongdoer.

This sense of oneness was always manifested in whatever he said or did. Gandhi said: "I believe in the absolute oneness of God and therefore also of humanity. What though we have different bodies, we have but one soul."[67]

The concept of Sarvodaya which aimed at the welfare of all is also the outcome of Gandhiji's belief in non duality. 'Sarva' means all and 'udaya' means prosperity. So the concern of this maxim is the welfare of all. Again Gandhi's conception of Ramrajya where everyone works for other's welfare out of moral sense of duty is ultimately traceable to the sense of advaita. In such a state there is no scope for violence, inequality, unhealthy competition and the like.

The individual soul Gandhiji believed was but a part and parcel of this Almighty Spirit. To abide in that supreme consciousness in every moment of his being was Gandhiji's endeavour. He would sing with Mira and call upon God.

"Jyotame jyot milaja" saying—'Oh God, see that this little flame of my soul merges in the flame of flames and the light of lights."[68]

Thus we have seen that the activities of Gandhi whether it be social, political or economic is basically rooted in the fundamental religious belief of monism.

GOD AND EVIL

The existence of evil in the world is a fact which cannot be denied. It is only the other side of the medal which is good. Gandhiji offers his own explanation with regard to the problem of evil because it is a difficult task for a theist to accept evil along with the goodness of God.

Gandhi defines evil as follow:

"Evil is good or truth misplaced. It has no separate existence at all." [69] If there is good there must also be evil just as where there is light there must be darkness.

But the question arises: If God is free, why does he not free us from evil? Gandhiji in accordance with his religious belief describes God as an all inclusive reality which include the diverse phenomena of the world. Gandhi tries to explain like the Christian theists that evils, sins, etc. are due to the wrong acts of man who are endowed with free will. He also tries to bring in the Indian law of karma according to which actions of men are responsible for both good and evil. Natural evil according to Gandhi, is the affect of man's deeds upon nature. Gandhi says, "I share the belief with the whole world—civilised and uncivilised—that calamities come to mankind as chastisement for their sins. Such calamities are not a mere caprice of the Deity or Nature. They obey fixed laws as the planets move in obedience to laws governing their movement. Only we do not know the laws governing these events and, therefore, call them calamities or disturbances."[70]

According to Gandhiji, there is no doubt that God could have prevented evil but he allows man to remove evil by himself in order to train himself and grow morally strong. The theory of the "vale of soul making" of Christian theology holds that God could have created a perfect universe and perfect men but He did not do so for some reasons. God has arranged the universe and men in such a way that they would develop in the spiritual path slowly and reach salvation. The world is created by God in such a way that man can mould his character amidst all pains and sufferings. Happiness would have no meaning in a world full of happiness where there is no suffering.

Gandhiji's view of evil can also be compared to the

visistadvaitin view of Ramanuja. According to Ramanuja only baddha (bound) souls suffer, not the nitya mukta (eternally free) and mukta (freed from bondage). Evil are therefore for the souls in bondage and not for the liberated ones. The general Indian explanation for evils, sins and sufferings is karma and ignorance. Ramanuja also explains evils with the help of these and Gandhiji also seems to have been influenced by this traditional Hindu explanation. Man suffers because of his own bad actions which is due to ignorance about the truth of this universe, God and himself.

But on the whole Gandhiji feels that a complete explanation of the problem of evil is a difficult task. So he confesses: "I cannot account for the existence of evil by any rational method. To want to do so is to co-equal with God. I am humble enough to recognise evil as such."[71] Like all other theists Gandhi believes that the evils of the world are inspired by some unknown good motives and not due to any evil intention of God who is all good, all just and all merciful.

Gandhi also believed in the identity of spirit or universality of spirit as put forward by Sankara. If we worship and adore the virtuous, we must also be sympathetic towards the sinners. "Hate the wrong but not the wrongdoer", was the famous maxim of Gandhiji. Therefore we should not hate men but we should hate only their evil ways. Explaining this Gandhi says: "I believe in the absolute oneness of God and therefore also of humanity. What though we have different bodies? We have but one soul. The rays of the sun are many through refraction, but they have the same source. I cannot therefore detach myself, from the wickedest soul, nor I may be denied identity with the most virtuous....If we are sons of the same God and partake of the same divine essence, we must partake of the sin of every person whether he belongs to us or to another race."[72]

Gandhi himself practised the above maxim. When Gandhi was in gaol in South Africa, he prepared a pair of leather sandals, the product of his own labour for his opponent General Smuts and presented it to him. This was a demonstration that the Indian bore no ill will personally against General Smuts but only against the government or institution which he represented.

TRUTH, LOVE AND AHIMSA

In no other philosophy of the world perhaps save that of the Jaina has Truth and Ahimsa found so much importance. Truth, love and ahimsa are the guiding principles of Gandhian philosopy and religion. Human happiness and welfare is based on Truth. Ahimsa or non-violence is only another name of truth. According to Gandhi truth and non-violence are only the two sides of the same coin. Ahimsa is the practical expression of truth. Gandhiji defines truth in a variety of expressions. He calls it God, and also calls it sat, cit and Ananda. He explains this very clearly in the chapter on Truth in his book called *"Mangal Prabhat"* translated into English called 'From *Yervada Mandir*.'

Generally speaking, observing the Law of Truth is merely understood to mean that we must speak the Truth. But the word 'Satya' or Truth is issued in a much wider sense. The word satya is derived from the word 'Sat' which means 'being.' And where there is truth there is also knowledge and also bliss (ananda). Hence we know truth or God is sat, cit and Ananda, one who combines in himself Truth, knowledge and bliss.

Gandhi considers devotion to truth to be the only reason for our existence. Truth should be the very breath of our life. When once this state of progress is reached all other rules of correct living will follow naturally. There should be truth in thought, word and action and one who has realised it becomes perfect, as all knowledge is included in it. Gandhiji often used to quote a Sanskrit verse which said 'satya nasti paro dharma, or there is no religion higher than truth.

But the question before us is: how is one to realise this truth? Gandhiji replies in accordance with the *Bhagavadgita*, that it can be realised by single minded devotion (adhayas) and indifference to every other interest in life (Vairagya). The quest for truth involves also tapas—Self suffering, sometime even unto death. In it there is no place for cowardice, for this path leads to the realisation of God—the supreme being.

Gandhiji repeatedly said that all his activities whether social, political or humanitarian is directed to the end of the search of Truth. The discovery of truth requires self analysis and self purification. One cannot see the Truth so long as one is under the influence of lust, anger, greed infatuation and so on. One who is morally strong alone can see the Truth. Gandhi was deeply moved by the ancient Indian dictum 'Satyam eva jayate' —'Truth alone prevails,' which is now adopted by India as her official motto.

Thus Gandhi holds that truth is the ideal of life. It is a goal towards which we must all strive. But what is the way to approach Truth? It is nothing but ahimsa. Therefore for Gandhi Truth is the end and non violence is the means.

Gandhiji's assertion that Truth is God carries with it a great value in our religious and practical life. He insisted on the fact that religion is based on Truth. The object of devotion should be truth. The end for which we should strive for, is Truth. This has helped to create a sort of universal brotherhood in respect of religion. It can do away with the rivalries in the religious field to a great extent because worship of Truth can unify persons belonging to different castes, creeds and religions. So all persons including the atheists can be brought under the religion of Truth because even the atheists find it difficult to ignore Truth.

One may raise objection to Mahatma Gandhi's identification of God with Truth. How can Truth be identified with Reality? Truth is the characteristic of some propositions or symbols which express true meanings. It may be argued that there is a gulf of difference between knowing and being. How can one ignore the fundamental difference between the two? the simple answer to this question is that it is a difficulty experienced by the logicians but it is no difficulty for the seers, mystics or a man of religion. Such a difference is felt at a level of sensuous and rational knowledge but at the intuitive stage this distinction no longer remains. J.H. Muirhead says, "There is a higher level in which these two are not only united but also transcended, in a sense of an immediate vision and absorption in what is seen."[73]

From the logical point of view also Mahatma Gandhi does not find it difficult in converting the sentence from "God is Truth" to "Truth is God." Logic provided that in cases where the subject and the predicate have equal extension we can have conversion and in this case also the subject and the predicate having equal extension or denotation allows for conversion.[74]

This concept of Truth is an important feature of all religions especially Hinduism. It is said that Yuddhisthira was denied heaven because he was untruthful on only one occasion.

Ahimsa

Ahimsa or non-violence has been a salient feature of the important religions of India like Hinduism, Buddhism and Jainism. But it was rarely applied to social and political matters save and except that which shines glaringly in the reign of Asoka in Indian history. Ahimsa in Indian thought was a part of the spiritual discipline. Gandhi transferred the ethics of Ahimsa from the individual to the social plane.

But an important point needs mention here. In his concept of Ahimsa, Gandhiji was greatly influenced by Jainism because it is the Jaina religion which preached ahimsa in the true sense of the term. So though Gandhi was influenced by Hinduism and Buddhism also in his concept of ahimsa, the contribution of Jainism was somewhat greater. The Vedic concept of ahimsa is not perfect or comprehensive. It excluded the enemies from the application of ahimsa. In the *Yajurveda*[75] and also in the *Atharvaveda*[76] there are hymns which allow some form of violence. "Sumitriya na apa osodhyaha santu dumitriya tasmay santu Yo asmandesti yam cha vayam dvismaha."[77]

"Water and crops be helpful or favourable for us. The same should be unhelpful or injurious to those who think ill of us or whom we think ill of." This clearly shows that even the natural gift was denied to the enemies.

Buddhism too did not preach non-violence in its extreme form as the Jainas because in Buddhism there was no bar to killing of animals for food. It is Jainism alone which preached non-violence in its perfection.

According to Gandhi, Truth is God and non-violence is the way of realising Him. Ahimsa or non violence is the practical expression of Truth. Ahimsa however is not a negative virtue. The Jaina philosophy explains it as 'Pranatipata Viramana' that is 'to abstain from killing any living being.' Gandhi however does not remain confined to this negative aspect of Ahimsa. According to him one cannot be perfectly non-violent by merely keeping away from violence. Ahimsa consists in not bearing any ill will towards any living creature. In other words Ahimsa in its perfection means Truth. Gandhiji also seemed to have been influenced by the ancient teaching 'ahimsa paramo dharma.' Our Shastras seems to teach that a man who really practices Ahimsa in its fullness has everything at his command. He acquires the power of affecting even his surroundings and even the snakes and other venomous reptiles does not harm him.

As has been said the Bhagavadagita is the guide book in Gandhi's life to which he often refers. At times his political opponents challenged him on the point of the problem of violence and non-violence in the Gita. To Gandhiji there was no contradiction in his devotion to the Gita and his belief in non-violence over violence can be easily deduced from the Gita, though the Gita was not written to establish Ahimsa.

According to Gandhi, the *Mahabharata* is not a historical work in the accepted sense of the term but only a religious work. Moreover the battle between the Kauravas and the Pandavas which the *Gita* illustrates is a battle between the forces of good and evil which become personified in us as virtues and vices. Further the author of the Mahabharata has not established the necessity of physical warfare but on the contrary he has proved its futility as he had made the victors shed tears of sorrow and repentence and has left them nothing but a legacy of miseries.[78]

The Gita's central teaching, according to Gandhi is the renunciation of the fruit of action which cannot be cultivated without Ahimsa. Renunciation of the fruits of action is possible only for a selected few who are above the petty consideration of hatred, anger, jealousy and so on which are the main source of violence. To quote Gandhiji "After forty years of unremitting endeavour fully to enforce the teaching of the Gita in my own life. I have in all humility, felt that perfect renunciation is impossible without perfect observance of Ahimsa in every shape and form."[79]

Again Gandhi feels that the object of the author of the *Gita* is not to exhort Arjuna to fight but only to get rid of his cowardice which is the result of his attachment toward his relatives. Moreover, according to Gandhi, the Gita is mainly concerned with the discussion of questions relating to ethics, religion and metaphysics than with physical warfare. it tells us the characteristics of a perfect man. The Gita shows us the path of self realisation, hence its object is mainly spiritual. Gandhi felt that *Niskama karma* and Ahimsa were so closely knit together that one cannot separate the two. It implies that a man who has renounced fruit of action has not been left with any ground to commit violence.[80]

Non-violence according to Gandhi is not a philosophical principle but it is the very breath of his life. Gandhi says "I have been practicing with precision non-violence and its possibilities for an unbroken period of over fifty years. I have applied it in every walk of life—domestic, institutional, economic and political. I know of no single case in which it has failed. Where it has seemed sometimes to have failed I ascribe it to my imperfections...In the course of the search for Truth, non violence came to me. Its spread is my life mission. I have no interest in living except for the prosecution of that mission."[81]

Gandhiji believed that Ahimsa is a natural virtue of the human soul. Man is essentially spiritual in nature and in course of civilization the progress is essentially moving towards Ahimsa. In its positive aspect ahimsa is love, which can be realised only when the mind is free from anger, hatred, jealousy, revenge etc.

In his *Autobiography* Gandhiji has explained how one is moved by an act of Ahimsa and what force it can have on oneself. While at school Gandhi under the influence of some older boys learned to eat meat and smoke cigarette; which he was strictly forbidden to do. Gandhi went so far as to steal money and gold from his parents to meet such expenses. But soon he realises his mistake and confessed before his father. Gandhi apprehended severe punishment but to his utter surprise his father forgave him with silent tears. This was for him the first lesson on the powers of truthfulness and ahimsa—how truthfulness can arouse love and how love can transform the heart. As Gandhi said in his *Autobiography*: "This was for me an object lesson in ahimsa...When such ahimsa becomes all embracing, it transforms everything it touches. There is no limit to its power"[82]

But it should not however, be thought that ahimsa means cowardice. Gandhiji has said clearly that when there is a choice between cowardice and violence, he would prescribe violence. Thus an individual or a nation could take resort to arms in order to defend its honour rather than be a helpless witness in a cowardly manner. The practice of ahimsa calls for the greatest courage and determination.

Mr. Zacharias once criticised Gandhi on the ground that the Khilafat which Gandhi supported was against the principle of nonviolence. Mr. Zacharias put the question thus: "How could one find an apostle of the principle of Ahimsa, upholding its very contradiction—the principle of the Khilafat? ... Will he not remain true to himself, rather than compromise himself, for the sake even of so precious a thing as Hindu Muslim friendship is, with this antithesis of his, the principle of Khilafat?" To this question Gandhi replied thus; "Mr. Zacharias argues, that the Khilafat is based on force. The Khilafat is the earthly representative of Islam pledged to defend it even with the sword. And how can I, a believer of non-violence, fight to sustain an institution that is permitted to resort to physical force for its defence.

Mr. Zacharias is right in his description of the Khilafat. He is wrong in his estimate of the function of a votary of non violence. A believer in non violence is pledged not to resort to violence or physical force either directly or indirectly in his defence of anything, but he is not precluded from helping men or institutions that are themselves not based on non-violence...Mr. Zacharias' proposition will reduce all commerce by a believer in non violence to an impossibility. And there are not wanting men who do believe that complete non-violence means complete cessation of all activity.

Not such, however, is my doctrine of non-violence. My business is to refrain from doing any violence myself. But I would be untrue to my faith if I refused to assist in a just cause any men or measures that did not entirely coincide with the principle of non-violence. The robbed man has justice on his side, even though he may be preparing to regain his lost property by force. And it would be accounted as a triumph of non-violence if the injured party could be persuaded to regain his property by methods of satyagraha that is love or soul force rather than a free fight."[83] This gives us a clear idea of Gandhi's concept of non-violence as opposed to violence.

A Comparison of Gandhi and Marx on Truth and Non-Violence

Gandhi's concepts of Truth and Non-Violence were not principles to be merely 'known' but they were to be practised in everyday life. Gandhi's chief message to man was to concentrate all his efforts in the discovery of Truth. He believed that through such discovery man would be able to change himself and by changing himself, he would change society and remove the negative consequences of modern civilisation resulting from the misuse of violence and force throughout history.

From this point of view there is a kinship between the philosophy of Gandhi and Marx. For Marx also, truth is something that we do not fully know but towards which we are continually moving. They believe that truth is infinite; we are getting closer to it but we shall never know the full truth. According to Gandhi one has to struggle hard to discover the truth. As it is, we follow a slow and difficult process and it is only through a better knowledge of truth that we can transform man and society, and through truth alone we can achieve progress. Of course, for Gandhi—and this is where his ideas are different from Marx—this transformation can be brought about by the personal effort of the human individual. Although he spoke of the transformation of society, his goal was to address himself to man, to educate individual man in the spirit of non-violence.

Gandhi's non-violence was not fatalism, in that one had merely to forgo violence and things would happen as they should happen. He wanted to see a change brought about, and that is why his concept of non-violence has to do with the notion of freeing man from fear and hatred, and of transforming the attitude of man towards society and towards other members of the society. Through this transformation of man, the individual, he hoped would free himself from the negative aspects which had appeared throughout history. By freeing himself man would be in a better situation and thereby change the environment in which he lived, so as to lead to the social revolution which was the main goal of his action."[84]

MEANS AND END

Mahatma Gandhi believed in the spiritual nature of human existence and therefore his unshakable faith in Truth and ahimsa naturally led him to equate the means with the end. The end, however great it may be does not justify the means if it is bad. In order to achieve a good end the means must also be good. Bad means even if successful for the time being in carrying us to a good end ultimately nullify the very purpose for which they are employed. Gandhiji said that a tree sprouting up of a seed of poisonous tree cannot bear fruits with juice of nectar. Gandhiji accordingly practised non-violence in every walk of life. He led his non-cooperation, Civil Disobedience and Quit India movements according to the principles of non-violence which added a new chapter to the history of human civilization.

According to Marx the ultimate aim was the creation among men of an association in which the free development of each is the condition for the free development of all. This aim could not be realised without the overthrow of all those conditions in which man is a degraded, servile neglected, contemptible being. Hence, to him, the abolition of capitalism and the establishment of a socialistic order of society was the precondition and the means for the realization of human freedom.

To Gandhi Truth was the end and Ahimsa was the means. Relative truths were conceived as means to Absolute Truth. From this understanding he began his pursuit of experiments with relative truths and the testing of their validity in practice. Experiments involved imperfections, in effectiveness, limitations, errors and even Himalayan blunders under certain conditions. But they also meant improvements and corrections to make them more and more effective and as perfect as possible.

SARVODAYA

The principle of Ahimsa also led Gandhiji to practice the ideals of Sarvodaya. According to the Western thinkers a state should aim at the greatest good of the greatest number and they think it well nigh impossible to deliver good to the last person. This did not appeal to Gandhiji. In this respect he was influenced by Tolstoy's *'Unto this Last.'* He translated the book in to his own mother tongue Gujarati under the title of 'Sarvodaya' meaning prosperity to all. Sarvodaya conveys that it is not the greatest number but all should be able to enjoy what good the life has to offer—Sarva (all), Udaya (prosperity). The ideal of sarvodaya is the base of the Gandhian society. In other words when we aim at the welfare of all including the meanest person of the society, question of exploitation and tyrannical attitude of the rich and powerful cannot arise.

GANDHI'S SADHANA AND VOWS

Gandhiji's spiritual discipline was a synthesis of the three yogas—Bhakti, jnana and karma. He has himself remarked as follows:

"The Gita contains the gospel of karma or work, the gospel of bhakti or devotion and the gospel of jnana or knowledge. Life should be a harmonious whole of these three."[85] Knowledge of identity or oneness by prayer and meditation and a life of selfless service was the way he preferred than argument or logic. Another important feature of Gandhiji's concept of knowledge was that he understood God not so much as an abstract reality but as a Truth which one experiences in his daily life.

Gandhi was one of the greatest bhakta, the world has

ever known. He said "The identification of the worshipper with God should be still close than that between the lover and the beloved."[86] Gandhiji believed that God revealed Himself through humanity and therefore the service of humanity was the highest worship of God. In addition to service his other side to a spiritual life were Ramanama, prayer and fast.

Gandhiji was the greatest karmayogi known to us. He always believed in the maxim that example is better than precept, hence his concern was always to put thought into action and translate ideas into practice. He fought with his best effort against all forms of injustice in any sphere of human life.

Mahatma Gandhi is also well known for the vows that he undertook as part of his spiritual endeavour. He believed that the vows are essential for the strength of one's character. The observance of eleven vows formed an important part of Gandhiji's religion. The Yoga system prescribed five vows or yamas for a student of yoga. To these existing five, Gandhi added six more. The five vows are as old as the Upanishads and later followed by the Jainas and Buddhists. Gandhi gave these views a new outlook and a socio- religious content. The eleven vows of Gandhiji are as follow:-

1. Ahimsa—Non-violence or active love
2. Satya—Truth in thought, word and deed
3. Asteya—Non-stealing
4. Brahmacharya—Continence and control of the senses
5. Aparigraha—Non-possession
6. Shrama—Bread labour
7. Aswad—Non-attachment to taste or palate.
8. Swadeshi—Use of the product nearest to one's place
9. Sarvatra bhaya varjana—Fearlessness

10. Sparsha bhavana—Removal of all kinds of untouchability by birth or race.
11. Sarva dharma samanatva—Equal respect for all religions.

Now let us explain the significance of these different vows which are at the same time the cardinal moral principles.

1. *Ahimsa:* We have already discussed Ahimsa as the fundamental religious principle of Gandhiji. In fact ahimsa is the key stone on which the thoughts and ideas of Gandhi in the economic, political and social aspects rest.

2. *Truth*: We have also discussed Truth as the basic guiding principle of Gandhi's thoughts. In fact the whole of Gandhi's philosophy and religion revolves round the principle of Truth.

3. *Asteya (Non-stealing):* Asteya or achaurya seems to be a deduction from the Jaina religion. The Jain thinkers believe that property is 'the outer life of a person and to rob him of property is to rob him of his life'.[87] By this we mean that since a person cannot live with some of the basic necessities, to rob him of such necessities means injuring his life which is contrary to the principle of Ahimsa. This virtue also follows from love towards one's fellow beings. So Gandhi takes *asteya* to be an important vow. It not only signifies keeping one self away from committing theft but it also urges one to desist from all kinds of exploitation in the economic field for example, the exploitation of the labourers by the capitalists.

Gandhi goes to the length of saying that taking or keeping things more than what we require is a form of stealing. It the words of Gandhi: "it is theft to take something from another even with his permission if we have no real need of it. We are not always aware of our real needs, and most of us improperly multiply our wants, and thus unconsciously make thieves of ourselves...One who follows the observance of non-stealing will bring about a progressive reduction of his wants. Much of the distressing poverty in this world has arisen out of breaches of the principles of Non stealing."[88] At the same time Gandhi says, 'One who observes the principle of non stealing, will refuse to bother himself about things to be acquired in the future. This evil of anxiety for the future will be found at the root of many a theft."[89]

4. *Brahmacharya:* Etymologically the word 'Bhrahmacharya' means a life dedicated to, or practice of, Brahma, God or Truth. However, the word is mostly used to denote a life of celibacy or renunciation which is regarded as essential for the realization of God, Brahmacharya, as a vow is the foremost requirement of a student life. It does not merely mean the control of the sex organs but all sense organs. Gandhi says, "If we practice simultaneous self control in all directions; the attempt will be scientific and possible of success.[90]

Gandhiji also emphasised the need for maintaining Brahmacharya in married life. According to him marriage should be an instrument of discipline and sublimation and not indulgence. The ideal of marriage is the union of the spiritual through physical. The law of marriage is justified or sanctified only when it is done for the purpose of procreation. Following the *Manusmriti*, Gandhi considered the child born of righteousness as 'Dharmaja' and others as 'Kamaja' or born of lust.

Gandhi has the following instructions for practising brahmacharya in one's life:

(a) Remember if you are married that your wife is your friend, companion and co-worker, not an instrument of sexual enjoyment.

(b) Self control is the law of your being. Therefore the sexual act can be performed only when both desire it.

(c) If you are unmarried you owe it to yourself, to society and to your future partner to keep yourself pure. If you cultivate this sense of loyalty, you will find it as an infallible protection against all temptation.

(d) Think always of that unseen power which though we may never see we all feel within us as watching and watching every impure thought and you will find that Power ever helping you.

(e) Laws governing a life of self-restraint must be necessarily different from a life of self-indulgence. Therefore, you will regulate your society, your reading, your haunts of recreation and your food.

   (1) You will seek society of the good and the pure.

   (2) You will resolutely refrain from reading passion breeding novels and magazines and read the works that sustain humanity.

   (3) You will avoid cinemas and theatres. Recreation is where you may not dissipate yourself. You will, therefore, attend bhajan mandal where the word and the tune uplift the soul.

   (4) You will eat not to satisfy your palate but your hunger. A self-indulgent man lives to eat, a self restrained man eats to live. Therefore, you will abstain from all irritating condiments, alcohol which excites the nerves and narcotics that deaden the sense of right and wrong.

(F) When the passion threaten to get the better of you, go down on your knees and cry out to God for help. Ramanama is my infallible help. As extraneous aid take a hip bath i.e. sit in a tub full of cold water with your legs out of it, and you will find your passions have immediately cooled.

(g) Take brisk walking exercise in the open air early in the morning and at night before going to bed.

(h) "Early to bed and early to rise, makes a man healthy, wealthy and wise", is a sound proverb. 9 O' clock to bed and 4 O' clock to rise is good rule.

(i) Remember that man is a representative of God to serve all that lives and thus to express God's dignity and love. Let service be your sole joy and you will need no other enjoyment in life.[91] This we shall discuss again in the social aspect.

Though brahmacharya as a religious vow is known to India from times unknown yet Gandhi recommended it at a time when these values were nearly forgotten.

5. *Aparigraha*: The principle of aparigraha is also one of the important principle of Jaina religion. It is interpreted as the vow of not possessing anything (akinchan vrata). This was meant only for the hermits who would depend on natur's fruits, and roots for their survival. But even Gandhi admits that absolute non-possession is an impossibility. So Gandhi allowed the possibility of the minimum bodily necessities and comforts but Gandhi was against any enjoyment of luxury. Gandhi realised that exclusive possession was against the law of Love, and so he wrote, 'Theoretically when there is perfect love, there must be perfect non-possession. The body is our last possession. So a man can exercise perfect love and be completely dispossessed, if he is prepared to embrace death and renounces his body for the sake of human service.

But that is true in theory only. In actual life, we can hardly exercise perfect love, for the body as a possession will always remain with us. Man will ever remain imperfect and it will always be his part to try to be perfect. So that perfection in love or non possession will remain an unattainabe ideal so long as we are alive, but towards which we must ceaselessly strive."[92] On this principle of Aparigraha rests the most important economic ideas of Mahatma Gandhi.

6. *Abhaya (Fearlessness):* Abhaya or fearlessness is an addition to the five cardinal principles of ancient Hindu religion. Fearlessness is a virtue that is prized highly by scriptures such as the Upanishads and the *Gita*.[93]

A man of religion, according to Gandhi, fears only God and no one else besides Him. To tread the path of religion, it is essentially required that a person be free from all kinds of fear—disease, injury dispossession or even death. As Gandhi said, "You will find that God is always by the side of the fearless. Therefore, we should fear Him alone and seek His protection. All other fears will then by itself disappear."[94] According to Gandhi, cowardice is possibly the greatest violence than bloodshed. And where there is fear and violence, there cannot be truth and non-violence. Hence the stress on fearlessness which Gandhi considers as an important sign of self-purification.

A Satyagrahi should always possess this quality of fearlessness, for he should be ready to face any danger for the sake of his country and his fellow beings. Mahatma Gandhi's life itself is a glaring proof of such fearlessness. He stood undaunted even in face of the greatest opposition and this alone helped him to resist the British who ultimately had to leave India.

7. *Aswad (Control of the Palate):* Control of the palate forms a part of Brahmacharya or control of the senses. In other words control of the palate is an important aid to the practice of Brahmacharya. Gandhi describes it in the following way: "I have found from experience that the observance of celibacy becomes comparatively easy, if one acquires mastery over the palate.[95] The food that we take,therefore, should be extremely simple. We should not live in order to eat, but we should eat in order to live and the amount of food should meet the requirement of the body.

Gandhi has insisted on the avoidance of condiments or stimulating food and drink. Gandhi had himself made a series of experiments on diet to find the most conducive one to the religious pursuit of an individual. And he found that the best way is to live on fruits and vegetable. He, therefore, believed that a vegetarian diet whether raw or prepared in a simple way was the best for a man or religion.

8. *Sarira Srama (bread labour):* By bread labour, we mean that everyone should contribute in the form of physical labour towards earning his own bread. It is believed that

Gandhiji was influenced by Tolstoy and Ruskin in his concept of bread labour. This vow is related to the vows of non-violence and non-possession. Violence in the society arises due to inequality. In order to maintain this quality, it is imperative for every individual to do some kind of physical labour in return for his food. Gandhi believed that the observance of this principle everywhere, would establish equality among men, none would starve and the world will be free from many a sin. We shall describe later, how this principle of bread labour forms the basis of Gandhi's economic ideas and programmes.

9. *Sparsha Bhavana (untouchability):* Untouchability means pollution by the touch of certain person by reason of their birth in a particular caste or community. This practice has greatly hampered the progress of the Hindu society, by its narrow outlook. Mahatma Gandhi had a life long war against this malpractice of Hinduism. In the words of Gandhi: "None can be born an untouchable, as all are sparks of one and the same.fire. It is wrong to treat certain human beings as untouchables from birth."[96] This vow of the removal of untouchability stands for social equality and seeks to eradicate all sorts of distinctions made on the basis of caste, creed, race or religion. With this end in view, Gandhiji strove hard to gain the right of free entry to the Harijans in Hindu temples. Removal of untouchability means, love for the service of the fellow beings and thus it paves the way for ahimsa. Removal of untouchability seeks, therefore, to establish justice in the social field which we shall discus separately in the social aspect.

10. *Sarva dharma samanatva (Equality of religion):* Gandhi's belief in advaita or oneness led him to believe in the equality of all religions like the equality of man. Just as the one soul is manifested through the medium of many bodies, so there is one religion which is manifested in different ways when it passes through the medium of human beings. Gandhi was convinced that the different religions are but different ways leading ultimately to the same goal of the

Supreme Being. But no religion can claim absolute finality or perfection. Every religion, however, has certain merits. Gandhi therefore insisted on having equal reverence to the scriptures of different religions.

11. *Swadeshi:* Swadeshi is another important moral vow and a fundamental concept in Gandian philosophy and religion. This vow consists in the use of things produced in one's own country. Gandhi regarded swadeshi as a sacred law of human beings and should be practised even it means utter physical discomfort.

Gandhi also had the glimpse of the law of Swadeshi in the *Gita* which says: "It is best to die performing one's own duty or svadharma. Paradharma or another's duty is fraught with danger.[97]

What the *Gita* said with regard to svadharma equally applies to swadeshi. Swadeshi is svadharma applied to one's immediate environment.[98] In its ultimate and spiritual sense, swadeshi stands for the final emancipation of the soul from her earthly bondage. A believer of Swadeshi, therefore, in his striving to identify himself with the entire creation, seeks to be emancipated from the bondage of the physical body. In Swadeshi, according to Gandhi, there is no room for selfishness, and in its purest form is the same as universal service.

Gandhi took the Khadi or the spinning wheel, which forms an important part of the economic principles, to be the most important application of the principle of swadeshi. Gandhi realised that khadi or the spinning wheel would help the millions of the semi-starved people. But it should not be forgotten that a true follower of Swadeshi should not bear ill will towards anyone on earth. He should harbour no ill feeling against a foreigner. It is, according to Gandhi a doctrine of selfless service, and has roots in the purest ahimsa that is love.

The above are the important vows of Mahatma Gandhi. It is clear that in the formulation of these vows, he was influenced by the scriptures of Hinduism, Vedas, Upanishads, Gita, Manu and the like, Buddhism and Jainism. Tolstoy's interpretation of the ten commandments of the Bible influenced and strengthened Gandhi's interpretation of the five vows to a great extent. "For the perfect practice of the cardinal virtues or any other principle Gandhi accepted the general Indian formula in thought, in speech and in action (manasa, vachasa, kayena). There is no wall dividing the different levels of human life. Purity cannot be fully attained until the entire life of thought, speech and action becomes pure."[99]

Another important aspect of Gandhiji's spiritual discipline was Ashram life. Ashram life had its beginning in South Africa where the Phoenix Settlement and the Tolstoy Farm were founded. Later on in India Gandhi set up the satyagraha ashram in Sabarmati and the Sevagram Ashram in Wardha. It should be noted that this concept of ashram life formed an important part of ancient Hindu religion. Similarly life in monasteries is an important element of Christianity. Such ashrām life which calls for the strict observance of austerities is an important aid to the attainment of religious ideals.

It should be noted that Mahatma Gandhi with due regard to the ethical and religions ideals conceived of the superiority of quality over quantity of actions. He holds that the one good or meaningful action is better than hundreds of bad and meaningless actions. To quote Gandhi's own words: "I attach the highest importance to quality irrespective almost of quantity...one virtuous son is better than a hundred loafers. Five Pandavas were more than a match for one hundred Kauravas."[100]

GANDHI AND MYSTICAL EXPERIENCE

Mysticism is a common feature of almost all the great religions of the world. The ancient Vedic seers cried out:

"Vedahmetam Purusam Mahantam

Aditya Varnam Tamasati Parastat."[101]

[I have known the Great God who is as brilliant as the sun and far beyond darkness']

Mahatma Gandhi too, we are told had some form of mystical experience which gave him certain message. Such religious experience in the form of communion with God moulded his thoughts and influenced his activities in different ways. Gandhiji has told us again and that he yearned to see God face to face which he did realise to some extent. One such communication of the inner voice came to him for instance in the year 1938 with regard to the questions of untouchability. Gandhiji described this spiritual experience thus: "It related to my twenty one day's fast for the removal of untouchability. I had gone to sleep...At about 12 O' clock in the night something wakes me up suddenly and some voice...whispers.

'Thou must go on fast.'

'How many days, I ask'.

The voice says again, 'Twenty one days.'

'When does it begin?' I ask

It says, 'You begin tomorrow."[102]

Another occasion of such divine communication was in the year 1948, just a few days before he died. It was in connection with the Hindu-Muslim Riot. Gandhiji wanted to move the hearts of the Hindus, Muslims and the Sikhs. He wanted to end the riot and the horrible shedding of blood. He was determined rather to sacrifice his life than be a spectator to such dreadful scenes of hatred and violence. Gandhi said, "There are people who do not believe in the method of fast for the reclamation of the human mind...with God as my supreme and sole councellor, I felt that I must take the decision without any other adviser.... If there is clear indication, as I claim there is of the inner voice, it will not be gain said. I plead for all absence of argument and inevitable endorsement of the step...Death for me would be a glorious deliverance rather that I should be a helpless witness of the destruction of India, Hinduism, Sikhism and Islam."[103]

We can understand from the above that there is a clear indication of the inner voice or the voice of God, whatever we may call it, which directed and dictated the course of his action. Having heard this voice Gandhiji felt that it was needless to have any other adviser and was prepared even to die according to the dictates of the inner voice. Even the Dandi March to violate British Salt Law was prompted by intuition and he says, like a flash it came.'[104] Gandhiji again says "could I give further evidence that it was only the voice that I heard and that it was not the echo of my own heated imagination? The sceptic[18] free to say that it was all self delusion or hallucination. It may well have been so. I can offer no proof to the contrary. But I can say this, that not the unanimous verdict of the whole world against me could shake me from the belief that what I heard was the true voice of God... For me the Voice was more real than my existence."[105] Hence it would not be improper to call Mahatma Gandhi a mystic.

GANDHI AND RELIGIOUS PRACTICES

1. Idols and Temples

Idol worship is the most significant part of the Hindu religion. Mahatma Gandhi favours image worship for those person who are unable to concentrate his mind on God without a concrete symbol. The idols of deities are associated with the high religious principles like truth, purity, holiness, omniscience, omnipresence and so on and are of great help at the early stage of spiritual growth. If it is possible for a man to realise his oneness with God without the aid or medium of an image, he may very well do without it. But to ask a person to reach God without the help of an image at the primary stage is like forcing a lame man to walk without the help of a stick. Man is in need of the external performance of religion only at the initial stage.

The finite individual tries to ascend to the infinite through the image, the cross and other rituals. But gradually the individual transcends the limits of his own finite religion and rises to a higher plane of God realisation. Gandhi says: "Whether the temples should contain images or not is a matter of temperament and taste. I do not regard a Hindu or a Roman Catholic place of worship containing images as necessarily bad or superstitious, and a mosque as good or free from superstition merely because of their exclusion of images....and the worship of the images of child Krishna or Virgin Mary may become ennobling and free of all superstition. It depends upon the attitude of the heart of the worshipper."[106] Gandhiji defends Hinduism and repudiated the allegation that Hindus believe in many Gods and are idolators. Gandhi was of the opinion that we cannot do away with idol worship in some form or other, which he calls the house of God. A Christian worships the image of virgin Mary and swears by the *Bible*. All these are nothing but the expression of their faith in some form of image. Gandhiji believe that an image worship is inherent in man's nature and is a valuable aid to devotion. A human being who is finite and limited find it difficult to do away with some form of a concrete object in his search for the Supreme Being.

Mahatma Gandhi supported the idea of temple worship. But according to him people should do it with a spirit of reverence and not mechanically. Gandhi said: "Temples are to Hindus what churches are to Christians. In my opinion we are all idolators, that in Hinduism we have images of stone or metal inside temples makes to me no difference. Thousands of Hindus who visit temples in simple faith derive precisely the same spiritual benefit that Christians visiting Churches in simple faith do. Deprive the Hindu of his temple, and you deprive him of the thing he generally prizes most in life. That superstition and evil have grown round many Hindu temples is but too true. That, however, is an argument for temple reform, not for lowering their value for Harijans or any Hindu. It is my conviction that temples are an integral part of Hinduism."[107] Thus what Gandhiji wanted was not the abolition of image worship or temple worship but a true spirit of reverence and the reform of the existing superstition that stand in the way of true spiritual realisation.

2. Prayer and congregational prayer

Prayer is another aspect of religion. People aim at communion with God by means of prayer. In his autobiography *The Story of My Experiments with Truth'*, Gandhi wrote, how he was saved on many occasions by prayer and Ramanama in his hours of trial.[108] To the question 'What is prayer?' Gandhiji replied: "prayer means asking God for something in a reverent attitude. But the word is used in order to denote any devotional act....it is a yearning of the heart to be one with the Maker, an invocation for his blessing. It is in this case the attitude that matters not words uttered or muttered. And often the association of words that have been handed down from ancient times has an effect...the utterance of the word Rama will instaneously affect millions of Hindus then the word God."[109] Again he said: I believe that prayer is the very soul and essence of religion, and therefore prayer must be the very core of man's life, for a man can live without religion....Bradlaugh, whose atheism is well known insisted on proclaiming his inner most conviction. He had to suffer a lot for thus speaking the truth, but he delighted in it and said that truth is its own reward...that is why I have said that even a man who disowns religion cannot and does not live without religion."[110]

Gandhiji said, there is an eternal struggle raging in man's breast between the powers of darkness and light, and he who has not the sheet anchor of prayer to rely upon will be a victim to the powers of darkness. The man of prayer will be at peace with himself and the whole world. The man who goes about the affairs of the world without a prayerful heart will be miserable and will make the world also miserable. Apart therefore from its bearing on man's condition after death, prayer has incalculable value for man in this world of the living. Prayer is the only means of bringing about orderliness and peace and repose in our daily acts."[111] Prayers, according to Gandhi should be unselfish, prayer does not mean asking for something in return. Moreover it is a bhakta, who served God by serving his fellow men, Narasimha Mehta in his prayer 'Vaisnava jana to' emphasised this point of service to the fellow beings. It says "He is true Vaishnava who knows to melt at others woe.' Moreover prayer brings about determination to act in a righteous manner. We may worship God by any name, for in essence He is nameless. The names Ram, Rahim, Krishna or God does not matter as long as we are true to our devotion.

Gandhiji is not in favour of erecting huge temples or halls for offering prayers because the cost born on erecting them is immense. The amount spent for building temples, churches, mosques etc. may be utilised for serving the suffering beings. Though Gandhiji is not opposed to temple worship or image worship, he discourages the spending of huge amounts on building sacred shrines or buildings.

In the Satyagraha Ashram Gandhiji once gave a talk on prayer to students in which various questions were discussed. One of these was that of suggesting congregational prayer to be made compulsory in hostels. Gandhi expressed his view on congregational prayer thus: "A congregational prayer is a mighty thing. What we do not often do alone, we do together. Boys do not need conviction. If they merely attend in obedience to the call to prayer, without inward resistance, they feel the exhaltation...But all the same the unconscious effect can't be resisted...All who flock to churches, temples or mosques are not scoffers or hambugs. They are honest men and women. For the congregational prayer is like a daily bath, a necessity of their existence. These places of worship are not a mere idle superstition to be swept away at the first opportunity.'[112]

In Gandhi's prayer meetings verses from the Vedas, Upanishads, Gita, Bible, Koran etc. were recited. He did so because he wanted to draw out the best of every religion. Gandhi found illumination through the medium of prayer and could not possibly live without it.

Gandhiji in his Autobiograhy describes how God is help of the helpless and the strength of the weak (Nirbal ke bala Ram). During a Vegtetarian Conference at Portsmouth, Gandhiji was put up in one of the houses of the prostitutes. The hostess and others after dinner started narrating indescent jokes. Gandhi too for a moment forgot the moral ideals and weakness got the better of him. Just then, as Gandhi says "God through the good companion uttered the blessed warning 'whence this devil in you, my boy? Be off, quick: only vaguely I understood that God had saved me on that occasion. In all my trials—of a spiritual nature, as a lawyer, in conducting institutions, and in politics—I can say that God saved me. When every hope is gone 'When helpers fail and comforts flee, I find that help arrives somehow, from I know not where. Supplication, worship, prayer are no superstition, they are acts more real than the acts of eating, drinking, sitting or walking....

Such worship or prayer is no flight of eloquence. It is no lip homage. It springs from the heart when it is emptied of all but love...... Prayer needs no speech.....I have not the slightest doubt that prayer is unfailing means of cleansing the heart of passion."[113]

Fasts

Fasting is an important religious practice followed by Hindus. But it was Gandhiji who used it for the first time in social and political matters as a method of correction of social evils and political injustice.

Hinduism, specially the philosophy of Yoga has emphasised the control of the palate and fasting as a means to spiritual upliftment. Prayer and fasting are closely related. Fasting prepares a man physically and mentally for prayer. Gandhi says "Fasting is a great institution in Hinduism, as perhaps in no other religion, and, though it has been abused by people not entitled to fast, it has on the whole done the greatest good to Hinduism. I believe that there is no prayer without fasting and there is no real fast without prayer. My first was the prayer of the soul in agony."[114] Fasting in the literal sense means abstinence from food. But fasting may also mean control of the other senses and organs. It thereby prepares one for prayer and the spiritual quest. It is in fact the yearning of the soul to merge in the divine. It should be noted that Gandhi took to fast as the ultimate resort, when all efforts failed him. He said "The reader may rest assured that I took the final step after I had realised to the full my utter helplessness. And I cried out to God even like Draupadi, when she seemed to be abandoned by her five brave protectors. And her cry did not ascend to the throne of the Almighty in vain. That cry must not be from the lip. It has to be from the deepest recesses of one's heart. And, therefore such a cry is only possible when one is the anguish. Mine has expressed itself in a fast."[115]

Thus Gandhi believed that it was God who handed to him the mighty weapon of fasting as a means to awaken his rivals. Gandhi undertook the famous twenty one days fast to end the rivalry between the Hindus and the Muslims. He also undertook several other fasts on different occasions to gain his ideals in social and political matters.

Fasting has also been used as a form of Satyagraha for the removal of public wrong and also for self purification. The ultimate goal of fasting, however is the realisation of God by means of self purification. Thus Gandhi both in theory and practice, have given a new meaning and a wide dimension to the age old idea of fasting. Spiritual fasting is described as tapas and all tapas have the tremendous effect of exerting purifying influence.

Rituals

Gandhi like Vivekananda believed that the aim of religion

is to get rid of nature's control over us. Religion does not mean mere conformity to ritual and dogmas. Every human soul is potentially divine. The goal of religion therefore is to manifest this divinity of controlling the outside agencies. We can attain this either by bhakti yoga or karma yoga. Doctrines, dogmas, rituals, books, temples or forms are of secondary importance. Religious doctrine or ritual should ultimately conform to reason and rituals which does not stand this test of reason cannot be accepted. Though religious truths can not be demonstrated logically it must be at least be reasonable. Blind faith according to Gandhi is no better than death. Therefore, Gandhiji finds it difficult to accept any religious doctrine, even if it be of Hinduism, if it does not appeal to reason and is in conflict with morality. That he vigorously fought against the long standing custom of untouchability is a clear evidence of this truth.

THE CONCEPT OF FREEDOM

Few people in the world have worked for the freedom of man, not in the political sense, but in the sense of total freedom as Mahatma Gandhi. His concept of human freedom comprised of every aspect of human personality.

From his very childhood Gandhi felt choked by the oppression of the foreign rule. He fought for political freedom because he knew that without it all other freedom was meaningless. But truly speaking, political freedom was less important to Gandhi than the freedom of man in his moral and spiritual aspects. His sense of freedom therefore stood for all round emancipation—political, racial, economic social and spiritual or religious.

Gandhi said "Our will is free, we cannot command result; we can only strive for it."[116] Human nature is not fixed and so we should direct ourselves by the exercise of will, than by habits. Again Gandhi said in an article written in 1928: "The outward freedom that we shall attain will only be in exact proportion to the inward freedom to which we may have grown at a given moment. And if this is the correct view of freedom, our chief energy must be concentrated upon achieving reform from within."[117]

Taking political freedom first, Gandhi believed that political freedom is the birthright of individuals and nations. Just as every individual has the right to eat, drink and breathe, so also every county has the right to manage its own affairs no matter how badly. Freedom is the very breath of life and no man can realise his true status without it.

Just as Plato found an affinity between the order in the soul and the order in society, so also is the case with swaraj or political freedom. This is why Gandhi said that 'the swaraj of the people is the sum total of the swaraj of the individual."[118] According to Plato there are as many classes in society as there are functions of the soul, and the harmonious relations of these classes to each other correspond to those obtaining in a healthy soul. Those who have philosophical insight embody reason and ought to be the ruling class; the members of the warring class possess the spirited element; their task is defence; the agriculturists, artisans, and merchants represent the lower appetites, and have as their function the production of material goods. The ideal society forms a complete unity, one large family.[119] Political slavery according to Gandhi is a symbol of bondage which one experiences at one's individual level. But the attaining of political independence is but one step along the path of liberation for all. Here Gandhi seems to add new dimensions to the ancient Indian analysis of bondage. "The movement towards swaraj is a movement of self purification."[120] Again Gandhi says, "Government over self is the truest swaraj, it is synonymous with moksa or salvation."[121]

Gandhi pointed out with all emphasis that his ambition was much higher than simply gaining the political independence of India. Through the liberation of India he sought to deliver the so called weaker races of the earth from exploitation.

With the same zeal, Gandhi fought for racial and social freedom. The racial discrimination which prevailed then in South Africa strongly moved Gandhi's mind and he was determined to resist it through the means of satyagraha. Back in India he fought hard to restore the dignity of man by his long drawn war against untouchability.

Gandhi also tried his best to secure the economic freedom of man. According to him economic doctrines had no basis in morality. His opposition to machinery was largely due to his concern for the welfare of man. His insistence on swadeshi is only a step towards the betterment of the condition of the poor and the downtrodden. The other aspect of Gandhi's struggle, to restore human freedom lay in what he did for the Indian womanhood. Gandhiji helped the Indian women who were suppressed by age old customs and traditions to get back their freedom.

Now, coming to the individual Gandhiji, like the great existentialist thinkers be it Karl Jaspers, Martin Heiddegger or Jean Paul Sartre, attached the greatest importance to the individual self, its growth and development. Justice for the individual was the greatest concern of Gandhi. But with all emphasis on the status and dignity of the individual, Gandhiji never forgot the society of which the individual is an integral part. Gandhi therefore dedicated his life to remove the ills that stood in the way of a perfect society.

Gandhiji's life, therefore, was an unending struggle to liberate mankind from all threats of exploitation. Gandhi himself said that he would consider to have finished his work only when he succeeded in convincing the human family that every man or women, however weak in body is the guardian of his or her self-respect and liberty.

MOKSA OR SALVATION

Most of the religions especially Hinduism and its different philosophical schools believe that liberation of the soul or Moksa is the highest ideal or the summum bonum of life. According to Hinduism, the most important goal for each individual is to achieve freedom from the bondage of the wheel of birth and death by the realisation of God within himself. Gandhi in accordance with this belief accepted that the ultimate aim of human beings is the realisation of God.

Mahatma Gandhi gave his own interpretation of the concept of individual salvation though it is not much different from the Gita doctrine of Moksha. Gandhi distinguished between those who renounce this world to attain spiritual perfection in their quiet isolation and those who secure self-realisation by being in constant touch with the world, by fighting the evils of society in a spirit of detachment. Gandhi himself belonged to the second category. He wanted to see God face to face through the medium of love and service to humanity. Gandhi wrote, "What I want to achieve, what I have been striving and pinning to achieve these thirty years is self-realisation, to see God face to face, to attain moksa. I live and move and have my being in pursuit of this goal."[122]

In Gandhi's own words: "My national service is part of my training for freeing my soul from the bondage of flesh—thus considered, my service may be regarded as purely selfish...to attain my end, it is not necessary for me to seek the shelter of a cave. A cave dweller can build castles in the air, whereas a dweller in a palace like Janaka has no castles to build. The cave dweller who hovers round the world on the wings of thought has no peace. A Janaka, though living in the midst of pomp and circumstance may have the peace that pass the understanding. For me, the road to salvation lies through an incessant toil in the service of my country and through it of humanity."[123]

According to Gandhi moksa or salvation is possible through self-control, penance and steadfast devotion to truth. Salvation in turn comes from righteousness in thought and action.

To Gandhi, the kingdom of God is not something that can be attained in some unknown future, but it is a possibility lying dormant in every person. It is a condition of mind and soul, which radiates peace, love, truth and justice.

Many critics observed that Mahatma Gandhi had no clear concept of salvation. He has nowhere dealt with it exclusively except in his autobiography, where he states that his aim in life is to attain self-realisation. Some thinkers believe that liberation of the soul is not possible until the entire cosmos is perfect. So the liberation of one does not simply mean true liberation. Since this ideal state that is liberation of all is a far off dream, liberation or salvation remains unrealised. So it is a continuous spiritual striving.

Again there are other views regarding the initiative involved in the realisation of moksa. One view states that salvation is entirely dependent on God, and man can do nothing but wait on his pleasure. The other view says that salvation is dependent on man's own effort. Realisation of the kingdom of God is the meeting point between the effort of man and the grace of God. According to Gandhi life itself is an opportunity for salvation and therefore we should strive for it as long as the body lasts. Gandhi's idea of salvation is found to have been influenced by Hinduism, according to which the most important goal for each individual is to achieve freedom from the bondage of the wheel of birth and death by the realisation of God within himself.

COMMENTS AND CONCLUSION

Mahatma Gandhi though a very religious man was not interested in theology. Gandhiji deepened the meaning of religion by making it practical and more common. The sort of action he termed religious were constructive ones which involved service and sacrifice. There would be no individual salvation for Gandhi without action on behalf of the community.

Mahatma Gandhi is an idealist in his philosophy of life and religion, but he is a relativist and pragmatist in the way of enforcing it. Gandhi cannot be called a pragmatist in the true sense of the term because he did not identify the truth with the useful. But we can called him pragmatist in the sense of being practical. Absolute perfection, according to him should be achieved by means of relative goodness. This reconciles the opposition between idealism and pragmatism. His active participation in life and his mystic vision of reality made him a pragmatic idealist or a practical idealist. In trying to follow this ideal, it is true that he falls back on inconsistencies, but these inconsistencies can be excused on the ground that he himself admits to be a finite being struggling to attain perfection. The idea of non-violence though unrealisable in its perfection, is at least realizable to a great extent, and if practised in its true spirit, is bound to take the world in the way to peace.

Gandhi is accused of being ascetic in character in following strictly the principles of religion. This, however, cannot be accepted because Gandhi never supported the mortification of the body. He laid out instead rules for the maintenance of a strong and healthy body. Moreover Gandhi does not exclude the enjoyment of the minimum bodily comforts, though he was against any form of luxury. A life of rigidity and simplicity is a necessity for a person in the way to spiritual perfection.

Another great contribution of Gandhi in the field of religion was to make it common. Religion was not to be thought as an exclusive practice, the preserve of the twice born. It was to be available for all, irrespective of any qualification. As an advaitin, he saw no difference between man and man and claimed the right of the practice of religion for all.

The philosophy of yoga was taken from its religious context by Gandhi and equated with ordinary work. Gandhi's karma yoga was designed to appeal to the ordinary man. He wanted to set an example of his life which was one of simple karma yoga. The only Guru to depend on this yoga was God. This was indeed a new interpretation of the technique of yoga.

No doubt, Gandhi has not preached anything new. He has interpreted the ancient Hindu ideals but he did so in the light of new perspectives. Gandhi is a great reformer and revivalist of Hinduism. Gandhi drew out the best of Hinduism and other religions in order to suit the conditions of a modern society. In the next three chapters we shall see how Gandhi puts his religious principles into practice in the different field of politics, economics and society.

REFERENCES

1. *Harijan*, March 28, 1936.
2. *Harijan*, 22.9.1946.
3. *Harijan*, 1.7.1946.
4. *Young India*, 2.3.1939.
5. M.K. Gandhi, *Ethical Religion*, p. 49.
6. *Young India*, 5.3.1925
7. *Young India*, 31.12.1931.
8. Dr. S. Radhakrishnan, *Eastern Religions and Western Thought*, p. 21.
9. *Young India*, 31.12.1931.
10. *Harijan*, 4.4. 1946.
11. *Young India*, 1.10.1925.
12. S.M. Tiwari, *Four Questions on Gandhiji's Philosophy*, p. 208.
13. N.B Sen, *(ed.), Wit and Wisdom of Mahatma Gandhi*, p. 14.
14. *Young India*, 22.9.1927.
15. N.K. Bose, *Selections from Gandhi*. p. 254.
16. M.K. Gandhi, *All Men are Brothers*, p. 56.
17. M.K. Bose, *All Men are Brothers*, p. 258.
18. *The Collected Works of Mahatma Gandhi*, Vol. 20, pp. 235-236.
19. M.K. Gandhi, *An Autobiography*, p. 48.
20. M.K. Gandhi, *An Autobiography*, Vol. II, p. 210.
21. M.K. Gandhi, *In Search of the Supreme*, Vol. III, p. 210.
22. Mahadv Desai, *The Gita according to Gandhi*, pp. 127-128.

23. *Gita* Chapter II, SI, 62. 63.
24. M.K. Gandhi, *My Religion*, p. 9.
25. *Gita*, Chapter III, SI. 19.
26. *Gita*, Chapter V. SI. 10.
27. Dr. Devanesan, *The Making of the Mahatma*, p. 30.
28. K.K.L. Karna, *Mahatma Gandhi-Contribution to Hinduism*, p. 43.
29. M.K. Gandhi, *Christian Missions, their Place in India*, p. 123
30. *Gandhi's Challenge to Christianity*, Navajivan Publishing House, Ahmedabad, p. 33.
31. *Gandhi's Challenge to Christianity*, Navajivan Publishing House, Ahmedabad, p. 35.
32. M.K. Gandhi, *Christian Mission*, p. 50.
33. M.K. Gandhi, *From Yerauda Mandir*, p. 50.
34. *Harijan*, 23rd February, 1947, p. 36.
35. *Leo Tolstoy's Letter to Mahatma Gandhi* dated 7th Sept., 1910.
36. M.K. Gandhi, *The Black Flap of the Science of Satyagraha*, Bharatiya Vidya Bhavan, Bombay, 1962.
37. M.K. Gandhi, *An Autobiography*, p. 78.
38. N.B. Sen, *(ed.), Wit and Wisdom of Mahatma Gandhi*, p. 134.
39. *The Holy Quran*, 31.22.
40. Romain Rolland, *Mahatma Gandhi*, p. 6.
41. M.K. Gandhi, *In Search of the Supreme*, Vol. II, p. 312-313
42. M.K. Gandhi, *An Autobiography*, p. 133.
43. M.K. Gandhi, *In Search of the Supreme*, Vol. II, pp. 306-307.
44. *Young India*, 9.9.1926.
45. R.R. Kiwakar, *Gandhi's Life, Thought and Philosophy*, pp. 47-48.
46. *Harijan*, 14-5-38, p. 109.
47. Mahadev Desai, *The Gita According to Gandhi*, p. 124.
48. *Young India* 5.3.25.
49. *Kathopanishad* II. 3.12.

50. *Young India* 31.12.1931.
51. St. John 8:12.
52. *Young India* 31.12.31.
53. C.S. Shukla, *Gandhi's View of Life*, p. 59.
54. *Gita* Chapter IX, SI. 31.
55. *Harijan*, 7-7-.46.
56. *Gita* Chapter II Sl.47.
57. *Young India* 9-7-1925.
58. *Young India* 21-1-1921.
59. *Young India* 11-10-1928.
60. *Young India* 11.10.1928.
61. ——— 11-10-1928.
62. D. Miall Edwards, *The Philosophy of Relgion*, p.
63. *Selected Works of Mahatma Gandhi*, Vol. V, p. 382.
64. *Young India* 5-3-1925.
65. ———, 13-12-24.
66. C.S. Sukla, *Conversation of Gandhiji*, p. 37.
67. *Young India* 25-9-1924.
68. R.R. Diwakar, *Gandhi-The spiritual Seeker*, p. 19.
69. C.S. Shukla, *Conversations of Gandhiji*, p. 37.
70. *Harijan*, 2.2.1934.
71. *Young India* October, 11, 1928.
72. *Young India* September, 25, 1924.
73. *S. Radhakrishnan (ed.), Mahatma Gandhi, Essays and Reflections*, p. 155.
74. K.K.L. Karna, *Mahatma Gandhi-Contribution to Hinduism*, p. 57.
75. *Yajurveda*, Chapter, 36, 23.
76. *Atharvaveda*, 16:7, 5.
77. *Yajurveda*, 36, 23.
78. Mahadev Desai, *The Gita according to Gandhi*, pp. 127-128.
79. *Young India*, August 6, 1931.

80. S.L. Malhotra *Violence and Non violence in the Gita,* "the Studies of Gandhi ed. By V.T. Patil, p. 21.
81. R.K. Prabhu and U.R. Rao, *The Mind of Mahatma Gandhi,* p. 43.
82. M.K. Gandhi, *Autobiography,* p. 41.
83. *The Collected Works of Mahatma Gandhi,* Vol. XX, p. 164-165.
84. Mahadevam, *Truth and Non Violence,* A UNESCO Symposium on Gandhim, pp. 88-89.
85. *Young India,* Nov. 3, 27.
86. *Young India,* January 3, 1927.
87. E.B. Cowel and A.E. Gough, *Sarva Darsana Samgraha,* Jaina System translated, p. 48.
88. M.K. Gandhi, *In Search of the Supreme,* Vol.II., p. 102.
89. M.K. Gandhi, *In Search of the Supreme,* p. 102.
90. M.K. Gandhi, *In Search of the Supreme,* Vol. II, p. 103.
91. *Young India,* March 24, 1927.
92. *The Modern Review,* Calcutta, October 1953, an article, N.K. Bose reporting an interveiw with M.K. Gandhi.
93. *Gita* Chapter 16: Sl.1.
94. *Harijan,* Dec. 8, 1946.
95. M.K. Gandhi, In Search of the Supreme, Vol. II., p. 99.
96. M.K. Gandhi, From Yeravda Mandir, p. 21.
97. *Gita* Chapter III Sl. 35.
98. M.K. Gandhi, From Yeravda Mandir, p. 41.
99. D.M. Dutta, *The Philosophy of Mahatma Gandhi,* p. 96.
100. *Young India* April 30, 1925.
101. *Svetasvatara Upanishad* III. 8.
102. *Harijan* Dec. 10, 1938.
103. *Delhi Diary,* January 12, 1948.
104. *Harijan,* May 14, 1938.
105. *Harijan,* July 8, 1933.
106. *Young India,* Nov. 5, 1933.
107. *Harijan,* Feb. 11, 1933.

108. M.K. Gandhi, *An Autobiography,* pp. 53-54.
109. *Young India,* June 10, 1930.
110. *Young India,* January 23, 1930.
111. *Young India,* January 23, 1930.
112. *Young India,* Sep. 23, 1926.
113. M.K. Gandhi, *An Autobiography,* pp. 53-54.
114. *Harijan,* Feb. 23, 1926.
115. *Young India,* Sep. 21, 1924.
116. *Harijan,* May 6, 1939.
117. *Young India,* Jan. 1, 1928.
118. *Harijan,* March 25, 1939.
119. *A History of Philosophy* by Frank Thilly, pp. 91-91.
120. *Young India,* June 12, 1934.
121. *Harijan,* March 25, 1939.
122. M.K. Gandhi, *An Autobiography,* p. 12.
123. *Young India,* April 3, 1924.

3

IMPACT OF RELIGION ON GANDHI'S POLITICAL THOUGHT

INTRODUCTION

The introduction of religion into politics by Mahatma Gandhi is a matter of great significance. The prevailing tendency of the time was to separate religion from politics. Gandhiji's attempt to introduce religion into politics would appear to be a retrograde step. But a close scrutiny will show that this is not the case. By introducing religion into politics Gandhiji wanted to introduce morality into politics. For him religion and morality were closely interlinked.

Gandhi said "To see the universal and all pervading Spirit of Truth face to face one must be able to love the meanest of creation as oneself and a man who aspires after that cannot afford to keep out of any field of life. That is why my devotion to truth has drawn me into the field of politics; and I can say without the slightest hesitation and yet in all humility, that those who say that religion has nothing to do with politics do not know what religion means."[1] Years later, Gandhiji said: "The whole of my life is saturated with the religious spirit. I could not live for a single second without religion. Many of my political friends despair of me, because they say that even my politics are derived from my religion. And they are right. My politics and all other activities of mine are derived from my religion. I go further and say that every activity of a man of religion must be derived from his religion, because religion means being bound to God, that is to say, God rules your every breath. If you recognise that truth naturally God regulates every activity of yours."[2]

The above statements of Gandhi clearly points out to the fact that his political outlook was influenced by the spirit of religion. He clung to the moral and religious considerations even in the field of politics. He understood that as a religious man his place was not in the mountain or in a cave of isolation but in the political field, and the political struggle which he fought was to establish the rights of the weak and liberty of the suppressed.

Gandhi's love for humanity attracted him towards politics. He realised that if one is to seek God in man, he can only do so by removing the obstacles that stood in the way of human rights and happiness. As he puts it "I count no sacrifice too great for the sake of seeing God face to face. The whole of my activity whether it may be called social, political, humanitarian or ethical is directed towards that end. And as I know that God is found more often in the lowliest....Hence my passion for the service of the suppressed classes. And as I cannot render this service without entering politics, I find myself in them. I am but a struggling servant of India and therefore of humanity."[3]

The principles of Truth and non-violence (Ahimsa and Satya) forms the pivot of Gandhi's political activity and these are basically religious principles. There is no doubt, of course, that religious reformers before Gandhi have taught the power of truth and non violence. What then is the difference between them and Gandhi? The answer is simple. Religious men and saints before Gandhi have taught that truth and non-violence were religious virtues and could be practised only by a few men of religion But it was Mahatma Gandhi who brought down Truth and non-violence from the Himalayan heights of spiritualism to the life of the day to day common man. He showed to the world that there is nothing bad about politics so long as it is guided by moral and religious principles. He himself selected the path of politics as a means to realise his spiritual goal. It is true that great religious men like Ramkrishna Paramhamsa and his disciple Vivekananda appealed to the masses to engage themselves in humanitarian activities and keep themselves away from the dirty politics as far as possible. But still they could not completely do away with politics. Their activies some what took a political colour when they raised their voice for reformation, restoration and revival of India. Thus though politics as such is avoided, it still produces some kind of political effect. The social, religious and humanitarian activities which helps to bring about cooperation and solidarity amongst the people adds to the political strength. As Gandhiji explained: "There have been no religious movement in the world without its social, economic and political consequences."[4] From times unknown, history proves that success in the political field is mainly due the display of the power of force, deception, cunningness, violence, unfair means and the like. Great rulers and conquerors believe in the maxim of 'Might is Right.' But Gandhi was dreadfully against such a system. Even in politics, he remained true to his belief that the means are as important as the end. Hence success in politics, also should be achieved by just and truthful means. Thus Gandhiji revolutionised politics by introducing the maxims of ethics and religion.

Once Bal Gandhar Tilak in a letter to Mahatma Gandhi remarked that politics is a game of worldly people and not of 'sadhus' and instead of the maxim 'Akkohena Ekhoham jine' as preached by Buddha, he prefers to rely on the maxim of Srikrishna 'Ye yatha man prapadynate'.

['He is dealt in the same way as he worship me.']

In his reply to this letter Gandhiji remarked that to him there was no conflict between the two texts quoted by the Lokamanya. The Buddhist text lays down an eternal principle. The text from the *Bhagavadgita* shows how the principle of conquering hate by love, untruth by truth can and must be applied. And this is the law not for the unwordly but essentially for the worldly. The epitome of all religions is to promote purusartha, and pursusartha is nothing but a desperate attempt to became a sadhu i.e. to become a gentleman in every sense of the term.[5]

Gandhi found out by a series of experiments both in private and political life how the maxims of truth and non-violence could be employed in order to achieve a desired goal. Here we trace the birth of the principle of satyagraha. He tried this first in South Africa where he helped the suppressed people to assert their rights and later in India.

SATYAGRAHA IN THE LIGHT OF ANCIENT RELIGION

Now what was the method which led to the success of Gandhi in politics? It was nothing but 'Satyagraha,' 'Satya' means 'Truth' the equivalent of love and 'agraha' means Firmness' or 'force.' Satyagraha is therefore translated a soul force.

While in South Africa Gandhi invited suggestions for a proper Indian word for non-violence resistance. Many suggestions came to him but they were all negative. Gandhiji's best friend Maganlal Gandhi suggested to him the word 'Sadagraha' which literally means "holding fast to Good' but this too was not acceptable to Gandhi. So ultimately he modified it and called it "Satyagraha', which means 'holding fast to truth.' Gandhi said, 'Its (Satyagraha's) equivalent in the vernacular rendered into English means Truth force. I think Tolstoy called it Soul Force or Love Force, and so it is."[6] He wanted to give it a positive content. At the same time, according to him it should be sufficiently indicative of the human struggle for the establishment of truth, and he found all these meanings in the word 'Satyagraha' which has a positive character.

Satyagraha should not be confused with passive resistance. Passive resistance is the negative aspect of Satyagraha. It consists of non doing of something unjust. Satyagraha is positive action to establish Truth based on non-violent means. Satyagraha thus excludes the use of violence in any form. Satyagraha can assume various forms such as civil disobedience that is the disobedience of unjust laws, non-payment of unjustifiable taxes, rents etc. non-cooperation or withdrawal of all support from the unjust ruling power, closing down of business as a mark of protest, hunger strike and so on.

Now, what are the qualities that a satyagrahi should possess? Gandhiji has always warned us against the misuse of the device of satyagrah. Such a method could be adopted by person who are pure, selfless and courageous. The people who follow such a method should possess an indomitable will and a strong moral character. The right of civil disobediences or breaking of laws can be followed only by those who have scrupulously obeyed laws. Gandhi thus said "If we follow the rules of society in ninety nine cases, we can say to its that in the hundreth case it is wrong."[7] Gandhi explains how satyagrah is constitutional "He ever obeys the laws of the state to which he belongs, not out of fear of the sanctions, but because he considers them to be good for the welfare of society. But there are some occasions, generally rare when he considers certain laws to be so unjust as to render obedience to them to be a dishonour. He then openly breaks them and quietly suffers the penalty breach. And in order to register protest against the action of the law givers, it is open to him to withdraw his co-operation from the state by disobeying such other laws whose breach does not involve moral turpitude."[8]

In describing the moral character of a satyagrah Gandhiji was perhaps influenced by the Gita's ideal of 'sthitaprajna.' A satyagrahi is not moved by pleasures and pains, joys and sorrows, victory or defeat. He keeps only God in mind and is ready even to die for the cause of justice (sukhe dukhesame kritva labhalabho jayajayo).[9] The war that a satyagrahi fights is a religious war (dharmayuddha) and his weapons are all divine—truth, humility and sacrifice.

Thus, Gandhiji attached the greatest importance to the moral character of the individual. A Satyagrahi tries to obey the dictates of his conscience. A Satyagrahi should possibly try to satisfy all. But in trying to satisfy all, he may be able to satisfy none. Therefore, it is best for him to satisfy his own conscience and leave the world to form their own judgment favourable or otherwise. Here we have an echo of the Christian belief that the voice of conscience is the voice of God.

In the midst of different public activities Gandhiji found it important to develop his inner resources. Gandhiji believed that in trying to emancipate India, we should first try to emancipate our own self because in our emancipation lies the emancipation of India. Thus, we find that all of Gandhiji's activities were inspired by this fundamental conviction that political freedom was the expression of moral freedom and this could be won by a struggle not against an external but an internal enemy. To put it otherwise individual swaraj or control of the self precedes national swaraj or freedom. Soul force as a weapon of political struggle needs a pure and strong soul of each and every volunteer.

The principle of Satyagraha is also a deduction from the ancient religious ideas. Satyagraha seems to be a restatement of the old Hindu traditions of 'tapasya' or self suffering and 'dhurna.' Different schools of Hinduism believe that the ultimate end of the human life is self realisation or Moksha which can be attained by tapasya or self-suffering. The Risis of ancient times underwent self mortification by sitting in the same position for days together, without food and water and exposing their body to intense cold of the Himalayas. The object of all this is self-purification by detachment to one's body and also to draw the mercy of the Gods.

This attitude of self-sacrifice is also manifest in the practice of 'dhurna' which is a means for securing justice.

It is well known that in olden times a person or creditor who could not realise his dues, would sit at the door of the debtor and go on a long fast.

Gautama Buddha too believed in peaceful means of non-violence to end disputes and conflicts. Buddha says in his Dhammapada:

"Akkohena kkoham jine" which means nothing but 'conquer hate by love, untruth by truth, violence by suffering." Again Buddha says in *Dhammapada* (Chapter 1 verses 3-5) "he abused me, he beat me, he defeated me, he robbed me"- in those who harbour such thoughts hatred will never cease. 'he abused me, he beat me, he defeated me, he robbed me' -in those who do not harbour such thoughts hatred will cease. For hatred never ceases by hatred at any time; hatred ceases by love, this is the old rule.[10]

Jesus Christ also advocated the same rule of 'return hate by love. The *Bible* says "Resist no evil, whosoever shall smite thee on the right check turn to him the other also."[11] Gandhi has also admitted that he has also found 'instances of pure satyagraha in Islamic literature.'[12] He drew great inspiration from the personal character of the prophet and other ideal Muslim character such as Hazrat Ali, Hasan and Hussan Abu Bakr and many others.

But here a special point deserves mention. These ancient religious principles of tapasya, self suffering etc. (or the teaching to return love for hate) remained confined only to the spiritual plane. It was practiced by only few religious men. As Sir Nirmal Kumar Bose has observed "The Brahmanical tradition of tapasya or self-suffering for truth was, we are afraid associated with the pursuit of a spiritual life alone, in which spirituality was exclusively associated with other wordliness; while the daily life of the general run of mankind was left alone to be ruled by common rules which are in vogue everywhere...Ashoka, the great Buddhist emperor of India, abjured war, but his did not lead him to the logically necessary step of giving up the fruits of conquest which had already been secured by dint of arms. His non violence remained confined, more or less, to certain personal spheres of life. Not that this progress, or incorporation of the principle of Ahimsa or non injury was a small thing in itself, but the point is that in India though the different sects tried to develop the tradition of peace, they generally succeeded in watering only a limited number of the fields of life by its means. It was in the first decade of the present century that the above tradition found a new expression in the field of inter-communal relations in South Africa under the leadership of M.K. Gandhi. Tolstoy considered the non-violence resistance of the Indian community in South Africa to be an experiment of the highest significance of the whole world."[13]

Thus, Gandhii was the first man to employ a religious technique in other fields of life—social, economic and political.

Faith, as we all know plays a very important part in one's religious life. Faith in an Infinite power is the essential element in every religion. This element of faith also plays a significant part in the process of satyagraha. Satyagraha has a strong foundation in the belief in the existence of God, and a satyagrahi is ready to sacrifice even his life for the sake of truth which is another name for God, believing that some day he will be rewarded by God for its just cause. Moreover, satyagraha carries with it the belief in rebirth. Being aware of the fact that the soul survives the body, the person taking Satyagraha as the means is never impatient to see the triumph of truth in this present life. Gandhiji found out that even dreadful enemies could be won over by this method of love and non-violence. It is required to have complete trust and faith on others. Distrust creates greater distrust. Gandhiji advised that if our enemy deceives us for twenty times, we should be ready to trust him the twenty first time.

In the essay *Gandhian Contribution to the Theory of Politics* Dr. N.G.S. Kini, observed that the Gandhian frame of reference has at its centre the notion of an all pervading. Atman inherited from the Upanishadic Gita tradition which is indeterminate immediacy (Anirdeshyam, Aparoksham). Ahimsa as the central principle informing Gandhian action is derived from Atman which is commonly shared by the adversaries and combatants. Himsa results when this common factor is veiled. To remove this veil which is a source of contention, discord, ego centredness and exploitation, Gandhi used Atmasakti (satyagraha) and foster again the common factor (saman, Atman) which again unites the opponents in a fillial bond. This filial bond is the basis of all society and at the macro level when approached as co-operation, inherent in a system of interdependence, that is Dharma. When we have in view the interdependent aspect of the factors we have Dharma. It is the aspect of the selfsame Atma i.e. SAT. Since society is approached as co-operation inherent in a system of interdependence, non-operation with the exploiter is the proper remedy to restore Dharma when disturbed. In case of doubt, "inner voice" which again involves an intuitive procedure is the final court of appeal. This inner voice is the basis of Dharma.

In giving primary to inner voice as the principal source of discovering Dharma and justice, Gandhi was merely re-stating a well recognised principle in Manu and Yajnavalkya for discovery of Dharma in the case of doubt-atmanastuti (manu), Priyamatmanah (Yajnavalkya) but the implications which Gandhi drew from this principle to construct a natural Law. Philosophy on the principles of satyagraha were unique and not anticipated by Manu or by Yajnavalkya.[14]

Thus Gandhi derived his concept of sayagraha from the negative implication of Rita (the idea of system) and the methods of non-cooperation and civil disobedience from the negative implication of Dharma (the interdependent elements in the system). The genius of Gandhi consists in adapting and re-interpreting these traditional concepts to fight against British imperialism.

2. Satyagraha in Practice

Gandhiji had the opportunity to put the religious method

of Satyagraha into practice first in South Africa and then in India. South Africa was therefore the first laboratory where he experimented upon the instrument of satyagraha.

A strong sense of colour prejudice prevailed then in South Africa. The coloured people had no right to vote, they could not move about freely in roads and public parks, they could not travel in first class compartment, their marriages were not recognised, they could not purchase lands and so on. Gandhiji, himself was the object of humiliations several times. Once he was thrown out of the train for travelling in the first class compartment. Gandhiji patiently bore these humiliations several times but he was determined to fight for the rights of the Indians and the coloured people not by resorting to violence but by the peaceful method of satyagraha.

The condition of the Indian labourers whom the 'whites' considered as slaves or coolies, were still worse. They were the victims of all sorts of cruelty and misbehaviour. One of the racial persecution was the imposition of a three pound tax on Indians and their children excepting girls below 12 and boys below 16.

Gandhiji had helped the British Government in the Boer War with the hope that it would relax some of the restrictions. But it was all in vain. The *Transval Government Gazette* of August 22, 1906 published the draft of an act requiring all Indian men and women and children above the age of eight to submit to official registration and finger printing on payment of fines, imprisonment and deportation from the province. The mass meeting of three thousand Indians assembled at the Empire Theatre, Johannesburg solemnly resolved to submit themselves to imprisonment rather than submit to tyranneous laws laid down by the British. A Muslim gentleman Haji Habbib, rose to support the resolution. He appealed to the sense of honour and courage of his Indian brethren and asked them to pass the resolution with God as their witness. Gandhiji made it clear that such a resolution taken in God's name carried a great sanctity. It might lead them to untold sufferings like jail, hard labour, loss in trade, confiscation of property and the like. Hence he advised everyone to think well before submitting to the resolution.

There were three rounds of satyagraha in South Africa. The first had started in September 1906 which continued upto 30th January, 1908. During this time Gandhi visited England and tried to influence the leading Englishmen and Indians with all the grievances of the Indian community. They succeeded for some time but the Black Asiastic Act was passed and Indians refused to register under the Asiastic Law; Gandhiji and about a hundred and fifty Indians went to jail. Soon after Immigrants Restriction Act was passed and General Smuts told Gandhiji that he would be willing to repeal the Asiastic Act but under certain rigid restrictions. The situation became intolerable and Gandhiji advised the Indian community to burn the registration certificates publicly as a protest against the government.

Since injustice and oppression on the part of the Government went on increasing and since Indian Satyagrahis silently bore all the sufferings, their cause aroused sympathy all round. The situation was made worse when marriages not performed according to Christian rites were declared illegal. This reduced the status of Indian women to concubines of their husbands and disinherited even legitimate children. Kasturaba and a number of Indian ladies courted arrest and bore patiently the sufferings and humiliations of prison life. At last after subsequent negotiations the Indian Relief Bill was passed on June 1914. The taxes were abolished; Hindu, Muslim and Parsi marriages were declared legal, the immigration laws were relaxed and promise was made for the just administration of the existing laws. Thus Gandhiji's effort by means of satyagraha succeeded and proved itself to be a powerful weapon for future times. The last sloka of the *Bhagavadgita* says:

> *"Yatra yogeshwarah Krisno yatra partho dhanudherah*
>
> *Tatra Sri Vijayo bhuti."*[15]

["Where there is God to help and man to act, victory is certain."]

This applies very well to Satyagraha which Gandhi practised.

3. Emergence of Gandhi in Indian Politics

In 1869 when Gandhi was born India was a poor and exploited country. The people were choked with the domination of the foreigners. Indians were weak, submissive and superstitious and Indian society was badly divided. With the spread of English education social reforms initiated by some great personalities became popular and gradually some amount of political consciousness was infused in the mind of the common masses. Consequently the Indian National Congress was established in 1885. When Gandhiji returned back to India after his successful fight in South Africa to safeguard the cause of the Indians, he found that India was still very backward socially, politically and economically.

Gandhiji realised that the problem of India was many-sided. The people needed courage and self respect to free themselves of the inferiority complex and slavish mentality that had grown upon them after years of bondage. Gandhi saw that to overcome this situation the country had to undergo a thorough change in the field of education, social setup, economic and political condition. Thereafter Gandhiji strove hard to bring about a silent revolution with his unique method of truth and non-violence. This struggle did not remain confined merely to the influential section of the urban people but permeated even to the people of the most remote villages in every nook and corner of the country. There was a change in the pattern of education, social life became more free than ever before and the people became more self-reliant.

When Gandhi returned to India after his stay in England, he was very much unknown to the Indian people, though a few persons like Gopal Krishna Gokhale understood his potentiality as a person and political leader. As Gokhale remarked "He is without doubt made of a stuff of which heroes and martyrs are made. He has in him the marvellous power to turn ordinary men around him into heroes and martyrs. During the passive resistance struggle in the Transvaal—would you believe it, twenty seven hundred sentences of imprisonment were borne by our countrymen there under Mr. Gandhi's guidance to uphold the honour of the country...They were touched by Mr. Gandhi's spirit and that brought the transformation, thus illustrating the great power which the spirit of man can exercise over human minds and even over physical surrounding."[16]

On his way to India at the close of 1914, he was yet uncertain of his role in his homeland. "I have been," he noted, "so often prevented from reaching India that it seems hardly real that I am sitting on a ship bound for India. And having reached that what shall I do with myself? However, 'Lead kindly light, amid the encircling gloom, Lead Thou me on.' That thought is my solace."

During 1915, Gandhi was touring different parts of India in order to have knowledge of the condition of India including the life of its people. In December 1915 the Indian National Congress met in its annual session at Bombay which was joined by the All India Muslim League and the two organisations met at the same place with the spirit of brotherhood between the leaders of the two organisations. At a joint Hindu Mohammedan dinner, the organizers were wearing a brilliant badge which combined the crescent and the Lotus, thus, symbolizing the union of the two faiths in the service of their brotherhood. Gandhi attended this Congress where he expressed his averred faith in Hindu-Muslim brotherhood.

The Congress meanwhile attended to the demand for India's right for a better life and it was alarmed at Britain's constant attempt to delay the constitutional reforms towards the attainment of self government in this country, so as to give a more effective control to its people over it.

The Viceroy, Lord Hardings was very much alarmed at the move of the Congress and the League. Revolutionary activities abruptly came up at a number of places which greatly alarmed the government. The Ghaolr movement in the Punjab was a violent outburst while revolutionary spirit swept the people of Bengal. The Government on its part, resorted to severe measures of repression to cow down India. Government's grave suspicion of all bands of nationalists made the matter worse. Gandhi made it clear that if the government imposed a total distrust on the people the people had no other alternative but to go underground. Gandhi however avoided the two extreme of a despotic government and a terrorist youth and followed the middle path of a more rational politics. Gandhi realised that an open advocacy of their cause was better than terrorism and anarchism. Gandhi said "let us frankly and openly say whatever we want to say to our rulers and face the consequences if what we have to say does not please them."[18]

The successor of Lord Hardinge was Lord Chemlsford, a viceroy who assumed his charge at a very crucial period. Soon after the Home Rule Movement started under the leadership of Mrs. Annie Besant and Bal Gangadhar Tilak. Seeing that the government still was indifferent to the people's demand in spite of India's constant help in manpower and money in the war, the National Congress in its Lucknow Session in 1916 passed a resolution on self government.

The Government steps to put down the rebellion became more stern. Indians were subjugated under the Defence of India Act, the Criminal Law Amendment Act, The Regulations of 1818 and 1827 and the Press Act. The revolutionaries were given the most drastic punishment by mass imprisonment. Gandhi was very much pained to see such an attitude of the Government towards a nation in co-operation. Gandhii informed the Government that if they paid no heed to the honour and self-respect of the ruled, there would be a resistance from the ruled against tyranny and injustice which he termed as passive resistance.

On 20th August 1917, Montagu made his famous declaration in the British House of Commons that, "The Policy of His Majesty's government, with which the Government of India are in complete accord, is that of increasing association of Indians in every branch of administration, and the gradual development of self government institutions with a view to the progressive realisation of responsible Government in India as an integral part of the British Empire.'[19]

Though the Montagu declaration was not satisfactory to many, Gandhi decided to cooperate with it in the hope of some reforms and by it he expected a better future but unfortunately things took a very different turn.

During such a period of hope the British Government appointed Sir Sydney Rowlatt to investigate if India would be quiet after the war and if not to suggest means by which any threat to government could be dealt with effectively. Rowlatt was there to destroy all cooperation and good will between the ruler and the ruled and to keep the people calm in the iron grip of fear. Thus ended all cooperation between the Indians and the British. Rowlatt inflicted all sorts of punishments by the enactment of new Laws and there emerged the famous Rowlatt Bills which wanted anarchical offences to be tried by a strong court with no right of appeal. Persons believed to be connected with the revolution could be imprisoned as the government pleased.

After the war ended, the Indians suspected greater restrictions on Indian freedom. At Delhi in December 1918 the Congress demanded that the Defence of India Act which was essentially connected with the war should be repealed. On the other hand the Government was ready to implement the Rowlatt Bills. The Indian members of the Legislative Council warned the Viceroy that the Rowlatt Bills might lead to mass agitation. Mahatma Gandhi declared that so long as the Rowlatt Bills were there the people would not pay any taxes. Gandhi realised that the times needed such drastic steps. In February 1919 Gandhi announced that he would lead a passive resistance or Satyagraha movement if the Rowlatt Bills were passed. The method which Gandhiji adopted was that of non-violence which called for Civil Disobedience to all the Laws of the land in a peaceful manner. Such a method Gandhiji believed followed from his moral sense of duty. Obedience to something unjust or wrong is immoral and hence morality demands its disobedience. Gandhi wrote to prove to the Government that its authority is finally dependent upon the will of the people and not upon force of arms especially when that will is expressed in terms of Satyagraha. To yield to a clear moral force cannot but enhance the prestige and dignity of the yielded."[20] Thus within months Gandhi's famous Non Co-operation Movement struck the blow on the mighty British empire with the help of the lofty ideas of morality and highest values.

The Satyagraha practised in South Africa was renewed in the case of Champaran where Gandhiji fought for the rights of the poor labourers. This was repeated in Kheda and Ahmedabad. During the viceroyalty of Lord Irwin Gandhiji fought against the Salt Law with the noble weapons of satyagraha. The Salt Law hurt the poor classes because they were taxed on an essential commodity. Gandhiji adopted satyagraha to defy it. The struggle continued for a long time until the tax was abolished. Pandit Nehru gave notice to the authorities at Allahabad, that on a particular evening, in violation of the Salt Act, he would make salt at his residence. On the appointed day police raided the premises and arrested Pandit Nehru. This immediately led to a general disturbance. Gandhiji with a number of followers from different groups began his historic March to Dandi on 12th of March 1930. Undoubtedly, of course victory was on the side of the satyagrahis.

It is interesting to note that at the time of this 1930 movement Gandhi had formulated a set of rules for the satyagrahis. "The satyagrahi must harbour no anger, must suffer the anger of his opponents, putting up with assaults but refusing to retaliate,but he must not submit out of fear of punishment, or the like, to any order given in anger...He must protect his opponents from insults or attacks, even at the risk of his life...as a prisoner he must behave in an exemplary manner."[21] The satyagrahis object is to convert and not to coerce the wrong doer. We should hate the wrong and not the wrong doer. This is why when there was eruption of violence at the movement of Chauri-Choura, Gandhi at once suspended the movement.

Radhakrishnan wrote about satyagraha thus:

"Gandhiji embodies the pride of India. And in his satyagraha is reflected the eternal patience of her wisdom. Gandhiji admits that submission to injustice is worse than suffering it. He tells us that we can resist through an act of non-violence which is an active force. If blood be shed, let it be our blood. Cultivate the quite courage of dying without killing...Gandhiji today is not a free man. You may crucify the body of such a man, but the light in him which is from the divine flame of truth and love, cannot be put out."[22] Indeed Mahatma Gandhi has shown to the world that the force of arms is powerless when matched against the force of love or soul force.

Being seriously concerned with the moral content of a political system Gandhiji tried his level best to set the house in order. He realised that if India was to really succeed it was necessary for the people to have a life of moral dignity. India was not only a slave politically but also morally. After a close attention Gandhiji found that the roots of moral slavery were the rise of machinery and the rise of professional classes who unconsciusly helped to strengthen the British rule in India and set up a society according to the western pattern. In his book *'Hind Swaraj'* Gandhiji severely criticised the modernisation of India in various fields of life. This westernisation and modernisation. Gandhiji believed would sap India's religious and moral spirit. He thought that if India could free herself from the evils of the western world, political freedom would be much easier. But he did not want anybody to be bitter against the Englishmen. At each step he reminded the people that the war that Indians were fighting were not against the British but it was against the British rule. Gandhiji declared that if we shun the Englishmen as our enemy, Home Rule would be delayed but if we treated them justly, India would receive their support. Thus finding out the proper means and method of the struggle, Gandhiji strove hard to establish Swaraj.

4. Satyagraha in Post Independent India

In post-independence India Mahatma Gandhi's ideas were sincerely followed by a band of sarvodaya workers under the leadership of Acharya Vinoba Bhave and later on by Jayaprakash Narayan. During this period there have been many movements for the redress of local or regional grievances and these movements have from time to time succeeded who used the techniques shown by Mahatma Gandhi.

Outside India we can refer to Khan Abdul Gaffar Khan, the Frontier Gandhi who is a firm believer in non-violent civil resistance as an instrument of change. The non-violent movement led by him for independent Pakhtoonistan may be realised some day.

Dr. Martin Luther is another name to have been influenced by the spirit of Satyagraha. This Negro leader of America fought for the emancipation of the negroes by the same method. He dreamt of a America which is free from the evils of racial discrimination. His premature death by the bullet of an assassin was a great below to his movement which had achieved considerable success.

Rajendra Prasad in his Introduction to Pyarelal's book, *Mahatma Gandhi—The Last Phase* speaks about the mighty power of satyagraha as follows.

"The theory of Satyagraha is nothing new. It was elaborated

and enunciated long ago by Patanjali. Gandhiji's credit lies in the fact that he demostrated its potentialities for solving individual and social problems, not only by living it by himself but by evolving a technique for his followers and by teaching them its use. The method and procedure had to be changed from time to time to suit varied environmental, circumstances causes and problems, that needed to be tackled, and above all according to the varied human material involved in each case. But the fundamental principles remained throughout. Gandhiji never attempted to write a synthetic treatise to elaborate it but provided innumerable demonstration of it in its application to day to day problems, that arose and called for solution.... Satyagraha is a living principle. It cannot be summed up in inflexible formulas. It has to be cultivated following a discipline, a way of life...[23]

The above remark of Dr. Rajendra Prasad clearly points out the practical aspect of satyagraha and how it can be applied in day to day problems in any field of life—social, economic or political. Satyagraha may prove itself to be the most powerful weapon to resist violence and secure social, economic or political emancipation.

SWARAJ IN THE LIGHT OF RELIGION

The word 'Swaraj' is derived from early Indian texts such as the Upanishads and the meaning of it is 'One who rules himself.' So the word 'Swaraj' itself has as reference to the ancient Hindu religion. In the *Taittiriya Upanishad* the perfect soul is described as "pranarama mana anandam santi samriddham swarajyam"[24]

Pranarama (equanimity of the sense)

Mana Anandam (blissful state of the mind)

Santisamriddham (glorious with peace)

So Swaraj according to the Upanishads is the rule of the self.

In Gandhi's Government the self rule is at the root. It goes to the extent of saying that "The Swaraj of the people is the sum total of the swaraj of the individual."[25] Thus though the achievement of political freedom was the immediate goal of Gandhi's movement in India, it was only a means to a higher end, namely spiritual freedom. Gandhi attached the greatest importance to the spiritual well being of an individual. If this was attained by every individual being, political swaraj was inevitable, Gandhi said: "On the principle that the greater includes the less, national independence or material freedom is included in the spiritual."[26] Gandhi thus made it clear that self government or swaraj entirely depends upon our internal strength. Thus he showed that political swaraj of a large number of people is no more than the self rule of the individual and therefore it was to be sought by the same means as that of the individual freedom—the means is nothing but the spiritual ideas of love, truth, and non-violence.

It is impossible on our part to think of political freedom without spiritual freedom of the individual. Gandhi therefore said "I do not believe that the spiritual law works on a field of its own. On the contrary it expresses itself only through the ordinary activities of life. It thus affects the economic, the social and the political fields."[27] Gandhiji's first concern in the political life is neither the empire, nor the state, nor the government, nor the ruler but the individual, its freedom and growth underlying the idea of Moksha or self-realisation of religion.

Gandhiji had treated Swaraj as a synonym of 'Rama Raj.' But he did not take Rama Raj from the Hindu standpoint. Gandhi said "By Rama Raj I do not mean Hindu raj, I mean by Rama raj, divine raj, the kingdom of God."[28] This reference to the kingdom of God undoubtedly points out that in shaping his political structure he had the religious ideals at the background.

Explaining the concept of Rama Raj, Gandhiji further said "Rama symbolised justice and equity, Rama symbolised truth and charity."[29] Thus it is clear that by Rama raj Gandhi meant some lofty principles of religion which should guide every individual and the different political, economic and social systems existing under it. If Gandhi thought of swaraj in the political sense of the term which was to free India from the foreign yoke, his ultimate concern was the lofty moral or religious principles like justice, equity, truth etc. which would be the governing principles of that political system. Swaraj in the economic sense means to liberate the economy of India from imperial domination and exploitation. The reason behind his hatred against western economy and western civilisation was its immorality and irreligious nature. Gandhi said, "This civilisation takes note neither of morality nor of religion....This civilization is irreligious and it had taken such hold on the people of Europe that those who are in it appear to be half mad. They keep up their energy by intoxication."[30] And if Gandhi had any attraction for the Indian culture and Indian heritage, it was not because it was his own but because of its religious nature and its moral beackground. He wrote in *Hind Swaraj*, "The tendency of the Indian civilization is to elevate the moral being, that of the western civilisation is to propagate immorality."[31]

Other important aspects of the meaning of the term swaraj are self restraint and fulfilment of one's duty. Accordingly Gandhi wrote, "Real swaraj consists in self restraintment. He alone is capable of this who leads a moral life; does not cheat anyone, does not forsake truth and does his duty to his parents, his wife his children and his neighbours. Such a man will enjoy swaraj wherever he may happen to live. A nation that has many such men always enjoys Swaraj."[32]

Thus self-restraint and the performance of one's duty occupy a significant place in the interpretation of the meaning and sense of Swaraj. In Young India Gandhi wrote—"The root meaning of swaraj is self rule, "Swaraj' may therefore be rendered as disciplined rule from within...the word swaraj is a sacred word, a Vedic word, meaning self rule and self restraint and not freedom from all restraint which independence often means."[33] Gandhi also pointed out to the fact that swaraj must aim at such a civilization which makes human being aware of their duties.

Gandhiji also considered swaraj to mean 'Dharma Raj. Buy Dharma raj he meant a kingdom of God based on high religious principles. It is a government where each individual performs his 'swadharma' or one's own duty. This seems to be an echo of the *Gita* doctrine of swadharma or performance of one's duty without attachment.

According to Gandhi Swaraj can be obtained only by practising the ideal of Swadeshi. Addressing a public meeting on the anniversary of Lokamanya Tilak at Poona, Gandhi said 'Not an inch of cloth must be imported from foreign lands....They (the people) must be prepared to wear Khadi and spin cotton. They must encourage the weavers to take up Swadeshi yarn for weaving into cloth. Swadeshi was a religion. Swaraj was an impossibility without rigorous obedience to this religion...Swadeshi was the simplest possible method to obtain Swaraj. It would cothe the naked and feed the hungry."[34]

Again Gandhi said "Non-cooperation has two aspects discarding old and creating new, destruction and re-construction. We cannot advance even one step without adopting Swadeshi. Through it alone can all our powers be developed. In Swadeshi alone is present both purposeful destruction and purposeful creation.

"... Without swadeshi swaraj is much of an impossibility as a flower in the sky. For success in swadeshi, we shall have to discard the use of foreign cloth altogether and shall have to produce more cloth in the country. So far we have been afraid to destroy. As we have now discovered the Ratnacintamani (The fabulous gem which fulfilled one's desire) of the spinning wheel, we have got hold of the supreme tool for creation...it has been said on the basis of experience, that renunciation cannot be kept up in the absence of aversion to objects of desire. We should feel the same aversion or dislike towards foreign cloth as for anything which is filthy."[35]

About the middle of July 1921, Gandhiji put into circulation a pledge to use only hand woven swadeshi clothes. It was about this time that the 'bonfire' of foreign cloth became the 'burning' topic of the day. Gandhi appealed to all people to take a pledge on August 1, 1921, abjuring the use of foreign cloth. The people took the Swadeshi vow. The first bonfire of foreign cloth was held at a public meeting at Parel. It was reminiscent of the meeting in Johannesburg in August 1908, at which the Indians had made a bonfire of the registration certificates. Gandhi expressed the significance of burning as such: "I look upon the ceremony of burning as a sacrament. The outward fire is the symbol of the inner fire that should burn up all our weaknesses." And in a letter to Andrews he explained "What I am trying to do just now is to perform a surgical operation with a hand that must not shake....The people are silently and unconsciously transferring the hatred of sinner to sin itself."[36] Thus Gandhi emphasised the point that Swadeshi was the first necessary principle for the attainment of Swaraj. Both these principles thus go hand in hand.

2. Non Cooperation—the means to attain Swaraj

How was swaraj to be established? Gandhi's reading of history convinced him that the British people did not yield to justice pure and simple. It was too abstract for their common sense. They would respond when the Indian people had shown sufficient strength of purpose and undergone a measure of self-sacrifice, or when justice was allied with force whether it was brute force or soul force, they did not mind.

But Gandhiji was sure, that the force he should employ was non violence, non-cooperation. He deprecated methods of subterfuge, secrecy and violence. At the Gujarat Political Conference on June 1, 1921, he moved the resolution which advocated non-cooperation. For him morality was higher than politics, Gandhi wanted that "the people must continually purify themselves even in front of their opponents, and at the risk of their action being mistaken for weakness. In the process of putting themselves in the right, they must not count the cost. That is the implication of following truth for truth's sake."[37]

In Gandhi's view the primary aim of the movement was self-purification, to revive the Kshatriya spirit. 'Even our prayer should be not for swaraj, but for strength to win it.' Again he said 'We are not even trying to change the British' we are trying to reform ourselves.'[38]

Criticism

The poet Rabindranath Tagore severely criticised Gandhi's programme of non-violent non-cooperation and therefore it needs special mention. It was a challenge that Gandhi met firmly and categorically. Tagore felt that he cannot find anything in non-cooperation and he came to the conclusion that non-cooperation is not dignified enough for the India of his vision; that it is the doctrine of negation and despair. He fears that it is a doctrine of separation, exclusiveness, narrowness and negation.

To the above challenge Mahatma Gandhi replied thus: "In all humility I shall endevour to answer the poets doubts....I would like to assure him and India that non-cooperation in conception is not any of the things he fears, and he need have no cause to be ashamed of his country for having adopted non co-operation. Nor need the poet fear that non co-operation is intended to erect a Chinese wall between India and the west. On the contrary non-cooperation is intended to pave the way to real, honourable and voluntary cooperation, based on mutual respect and trust....He (Tagore) has a horror of everthing negative. His whole soul seems to rebel against the negative commandments of religion. Passion for rejection is a stronger power in the beginning then acceptance of an ideal. It is necessary to reject untruth as it is to accept truth. Non-cooperation with evil is as much a duty as cooperation with good.... And if India is ever to attain the Swaraj of the poet's dream, she will do so only by non-violent non-cooperation."[39]

Coming to the success of the non-cooperation movement, Mr. Gandhi said it had succeeded far beyond the expectations of the people. It had driven out of the minds of the people all fear of the authorities, of suffering, of sacrifice and work for the sake of the country. People were willing to do anything for their country.[40] Gandhiji thus proved the tremendous success of the technique of non-violet, non-cooperation for the establishment of Swaraj.

THE STATE AND THE INDIVIDUAL

Gandhiji did not elaborate his views about the nature of his ideal state. However, his writings give us an account of his conception of an ideal state.

Gandhiji attached more importance to the individual than to the state. He believed that the realisation of the spiritual perfection of an individual was the ultimate end of all human endevour. The object of the state therefore was to help the all round growth of the individual and ensuring his peace and progress by enforcing such laws that are conducive to his welfare and to see to the prevention of exploitation. Gandhiji was well aware of the fact that like a foreign government even a national government might become an obstacle to the freedom and growth of the individual. If therefore the state becomes too powerful, it might stand in the way of the free development of the individual. Gandhiji said: "The individual is the one supreme consideration...I look upon an increase of the power of the state with the greatest fear, because although while apparently doing good by minimum exploitation, it does the greatest harm of mankind by destroying individuality which lies at the root of all progress."[41]

In his idea of state Gandhi was very much influenced by the maxim of Thoreau that *the government is the best which governs the least*. Gandhi thus wrote: "Political power means capacity to regulate national life through national representatives. If national life become so perfect as to become self-regulated, no representation becomes necessary. There is then a state of enlightened anarchy. In such a state everyone is his own ruler. He rules himself in such a manner that he is his own master. In an ideal state, therefore, there is no political power because there is no state. But the ideal is never fully realised in life. Hence the classical statement of Thoreau that that government is best which governs the least."[42]

Gandhi's view of the state is also influenced by his concept of an ideal society. In his ideal society, social life is self-regulated, there is no exploitation or inequality. Thus, the state which justifies its existence for an ideal society, obviously become unnecessary.

To Gandhiji the state was not an end in itself but one of the means of enabling people to better their condition in every department of life. The state is only one of the means to secure the greatest good of all (Sarvodaya).

A man owes loyalty to the state as to other associations. But this loyalty is regulated by the conscience of the individual. Here Gandhi brings about the religious element of conscience in matters of state regulation. If one feels that the state behaves unjustly nd the laws enforced by the state are not conductive to human welfare then Gandhi permits disobedience to the state but it should always be the moral duty of the individual to withdraw their cooperation by non-violent Satyagraha which Gandhi adopted for paralyzing the British rule in India.

Gandhi's idea of an ideal state which stands to establish a harmonious and peaceful society is therefore not simply the concentration of power in the hands of a few people but it is means for the promotion of morality and happiness. The realisation of such a state it is believed will naturally save India from the crisis of the present society where the state once in power takes all liberty in its own hands.

THE GOVERNMENT

The foundation on which the kind of Government prescribed by Mahatma Gandhi rests is decentralization. Gandhi was not in favour of centralization of power in the hands of a few at the centre. He believed that an ordinary man in the village should not feel that pressure of an all powerful state above in his day to day life. He must be able to have his say in the affairs of his immediate environment. When a man grows under the heavy hand of central power at every step his share of democracy becomes nominal. The power concentrated at the top tends to be tyrrancial and this is contrary to Ahimsa, the religious principle of Gandhiji. This is why Gandhiji recommended decentralization as formulated in his scheme of 'Panchayat Raj' which forms the pivot of the government recommended by Gandhiji.

Gandhiji did not say anything definitely as to what kind of Government India should have. Nevertheless he gave us an idea of an ideal democratic republic. His Government like other institutions is founded on the principles of Ahimsa and it should be one which truly represented the will of the people. The nature of a democratic government should be determined by the people's choice; so he did not prescribe the exact form of government. The Government was to be run by such representatives of the people who have made productive contribution to the nation and they should have first hand knowledge about the problems of the people. The system of election was adult franchise, male and female, above the age of twenty one or even eighteen. Side by side with adult franchise he pledged for universal adult education. He did not favour majority rule as he believed that the interest of the minority would be neglected in such a rule. He wanted India to have swaraj or self rule in which the government was to be run by the consent of the people. It is no doubt that in a popular democratic government the majority view has to be the basis of practical application. But the majority should always try their best to pay attention to the interest of the minorities and they in turn should be able to fight for their legitimate demands. Thus to safeguard the interest of the minorities Gandhi took resort to the system of Panchayat Raj or village republics. Here Gandhi has put into practice his religious ideas of justice and equality in respect of all human beings, the creation of one God.

As to the nature of the village republic, Gandhiji wanted every village to be self-sufficient with regard to its basic necessities like food, clothing, water supply. "My idea of village swaraj is", Gandhiji wrote, "that it is a complete republic independent of its neighbours for its vital wants and yet inter-dependent for many others in which dependence is necessary. Thus every villages first concern will be to grow its own food and cotton for its cloth...The government of the village will be conducted by the Panchayat of five persons, annually elected, by the adult villagers, male and females possessing minimum prescribed qualification. They will have all the authority and jurisdiction required. Since there will be no system of punishment in the accepted sense, this Panchayat will be its legislature, judiciary and executive combined to operate for its year of office. Here there is perfect democracy based on individual freedom. The individual is the architect of its own government. The law of non-violence rules him and his government. He and his villagers are able to defy the might of the world. For the law governing every village is that he will suffer death in the defence of his and his village honour."[43]

Religious Significance of Ramarajya

The above is the picture of Gandhiji's Ramarajya as he calls it. The religious influence is also underlying in it when Gandhiji calls the individual to be the architect of his own government and the law of non violence is given the priority. Gandhiji has shown here the importance of sacrifice for the sake of justice when he says that the honour and dignity of the individual and the village should be preserved even at the cost of one's life.

Moreover the use of the word Ramarajya was significant. Rama was not merely a king but a God. Ramarajya could mean the kingdom of God. Ramarajya is significant in another sense also. Ram's rule was an enlightened one where peace and happiness prevailed and where true democracy existed, though in the form of a monarchy. As all are children of God it is only natural that everyone should receive a fair deal. Gandhiji knew that the welfare of all which was the ideal of Ramrajya depended on the moral strength of the members of Ramrajya. This is why he insisted that moral and religious values should guide all our actions. His Ramrajya was a moral kingdom where truth, love and respect for every living being were of supreme importance.

Gandhi gives us his idea of Ramrajya in the following way when a friend, interpreting the term 'Ramrajya' literally, asks if it will ever be possible to establish Ramrajya till we have men like Dasharatha and Rama. Gandhi say "We only mean by Ramrajya 'Swaraj' or the rule of dharma or people's rule. Such rule can be established only when the people themselves come to have regard for dharma and learn to be brave. It is the effort of the congress, of all non co-operators, to see that the people become so. If the people are to be emancipated only by some kind, they will become his slaves, though in himself he may be a man of virtue....We are not even trying to change the British, we are trying to reform ourselves."[44] Gandhi makes it clear that Ramrajya can be established, only when the people forming the 'Rajya' reform themselves by the virtues of religion.

Gandhi's ideas of village republics can be traced back to ancient India's political setup. In *Manusmrti* and Santi Parva of the *Mahabharata*, the reference to 'Gramsanghas' is found which is nothing but the village republic. Kautilya in his *Arthasastra* also refers to them. Description of *'Janapada'* which is a kind of federation of numerous village republics, is found in Valimiki *Ramayana* too. *Rigveda*, *Jatakas*, Vishnu and *Manusmritis*, *Dharmasutra* and others are testimony to the fact that in ancient India a village republic was the basic unit of administration and autonomous to a great extent. In these systems the individual gets the prominence. He has his say in all the affairs of the village. In this way the individual, is the smallest unit of the state and he finds the best opportunity for his growth. This emphasis on the individual freedom and growth is a religious emphasis. This attracted Gandhiji more towards the village panchayats which should be the lowest parliament so to say in the Gandhian system of government.

According to Gandhi in this political structure consisting of innumerable villages "there will be an ever widening, never ascending circles. Life will not be a pyramid with the apex sustained by the bottom. But it will be an oceanic circle whose centre will be the individual, always ready to perish for the village, the latter ready to perish for the circle of villages, till at last the whole becomes one life composed of individuals...sharing the majesty of the Oceanic circle of which they are integral units. Therefore the over most circumference will not wield power to crush the inner circle but will give strength to all within and derive its own strength from it."[45]

The economy must be conductive to the pattern of an Oceanic circle, not a pyramidal pattern. The inner and outer circles are coeval. They imperceptibly merge into each other, they strengthen each other in ever widening circles.

The above setup reminds us of the ancient Hindu archetype of Mandala. The reference to the theory of Mandala is found in Kautilya's *Arthasastra*. They theory of Mandala presupposes the existence of at least a dozen states which are of moderate size. At most the state visualised in it can be supposed to be as large as a modern state in present day India. Then we have a Janapada. A Janapada in its origin, appears to have been a territory, on which a particular people or tribe was settled, the Pancala Janapada, the Kosala janapada and so on. There is a well known reference to the sixteen Mahajanapadas in Buddhist literature which was in existence at the time of the rise of Buddhism. When it is remembered that all these sixteen janapadas were situated in the north and northeast it is to be assumed to be much smaller than that suggested by the theory of mandala.

RIGHT AND DUTY

Gandhiji in accordance with the teaching of Hindu philosophy urged the people to think first of their duties and the rights will naturally follow. The *Bhagavadgita* which is one of the most important texts of Hinduism devotes a large section to the performance of one's duties on this life. According to the Gita 'Duty for duties sake' should be the true end of life. Duties should be done without any consideration of pleasure of pain, profits or loss, victory or defeat. (sukhe dukhe same kritva labhalabho jayajayo)[46] Gandhiji believed strongly in this gospel of the Gita. As he said "The true source of rights will not be far to seek. If leaving duties unperformed we run after rights, they will escape us like a will-of-the wisp. The more we pursue them the further will they fly."[47] In the *Gita* again (Chap III sl. 13) it is said "The righteous men wove at the residue of the sacrifice are freed from all sin, but the wicked who cook for themselves eat sin"[48] Thus it requires one to eat (enjoy the right of eating) only after one has performed sacrifice or in other words performed one's duty. Gandhiji was much influenced by the Gita in his insistence on one's duty. He has urged every individual in the society to perform the duties entrusted to him or her with faith in God. Gandhi believed that God would naturally reward such a person with abundant rights who has performed his duties earnestly.

Concept of Duty according to Hinduism

In his concept of 'Duty' also Gandhi owes a great deal to the Hindu religion. The Hindu view of duty has been stated as follows by Dr. Bhagavan Das:

"In its exact ethical sense duty means an action which is due, which ought of be done, which is owed; it is an obligation to be discharged. Nature is ever restoring disturbed equilibrium, and the universal law of Karma of action and re-action, is the full statement of this fact. She is balancing her accounts. Duties are the debts a man owes to his fellows, paid to discharge the obligations under which he lives for benefits received."[49]

Duty is the expression of the concept of Dharma, the force which sustain the universe. Hindu thought has classified duty into five categories namely sacrifice to Brahman, sacrifice to Gods, sacrifice to ancestors, sacrifice to animal creation and sacrifice to fellow beings. By fulfilling these different duties a man realises his unity with this world of creatures. But it should be noted that though the Hindu religion has called for the fulfillment of one's duty in different levels, Gandhiji was more concerned with the fulfilment of duty only in the last sense that is sacrifice or in other words service to fellow beings. Mahatma Gandhi did not give much emphasis to sacrifice either to Brahman or to Gods or to ancestors. He believed that duty towards the fellow beings is itself a duty towards God, for God manifested Himself through His creation. Gandhiji, no doubt expressed a considerable sympathy for the animal creation by calling for prohibition of cow slaughter and so on.

Mahatma Gandhi's insistence on self-discipline as a qualification for Satyagraha on the social and political level is an expression of his conception of duty. This may be compared to the insistence of duty in the ancient Indian way of life as expressed in the Varna and Ashrama dharma. Gandhiji emphasised that varnashrama which was a healthy division of work was purely a question of duty. The last chapter of the *Gita* (verses 40-48) speaks about the duty prescribed for each of the four types of people (Caturvarnya) and exhorts that perfection can be attained only by the performance of one's duty.[50] The reason is that one's duty is prescribed according to one' nature, svadharma being determined by Svabhava. Gandhiji is a strong believer in this *Gita* ideal of the conception of duty.

Regarding the source of knowledge of duty, Gandhi refers to the individual conscience as the inner voice and the other relating to the individual's obligations to society in terms defined by social traditions, customs and institutions. The appeal to the Inner Voice, the higher law or the Voice of God, becomes the deciding factor in situations of moral crisis and acts as a lighthouse in the dark stormy ocean of ignorance. This appeal to the Inner Voice as the source of the knowledge of duty unmistakably points out to Gandhi's insistence on the principles of religion in dealing with important matters.

GANDHIJI ON WORLD PEACE

Gandhiji consistently with his basic teachings of Ahimsa was deadly against war. He was of the opinion that the various problems of life could be solved by the simple method of non-violence. It is well known that India had been a peace loving country from times immemorial. The ancient Vedic seers cried out 'Dau santih, antariksham santih' or let there be peace everywhere. Buddha taught that a man should overcome anger by love, evil by good and a lie by truth. Not only Hinduism, even in the *Bible*, Jesus Christ has declared 'Do good to them that hate you, and pray for them that despitefully use you and persecute you. The *Quran* teaches us that if we are good and kind to our fellow men God will be gracious to us on the day of judgment. Gandhiji fully appreciated this insistence on peace by different religions. Mahatma Gandhi was convinced of the fact that mankind and its civilization could be saved from destruction only through the means of non-violence.

With his faith in the method of non-violence, Gandhi prescribed to the world the non violent technique of satyagraha as an effective substitute for the violent armed warfare. Gandhi believed that before this peaceful method of non violent 'the bayonet runs to rust and the gunpower turns to dust. According to him the very presence of Godliness in human beings establishes the possibility of permanent peace. "Not to believe in the possibility of permanent peace, is to doubt the divinity or godliness of human nature."[51] This statement is an affirmation of his fundamental metaphysical belief that, permanent peace becomes possible when man realises himself and recognises his essential unity with Truth or God. When a person achieves this state of realisation he develops the spirit of renunciation of imperialism, territorial gains or that of power and destructive weapons used for violence. War is a state of mind which reflects greed and the spirit of exploitation. The way of liberation from the tragedy of war is through a bold and unconditional acceptance of the non-violent method with all its glorious implications."[52] Gandhi's belief in the identity of self with the Truth finds expression in his idea of the essential unity of mankind who should live in a united world of peace and non-violence.

Gandhi was himself a witness to the two disastrous world wars during the last century. He therefore maintained that the major unsolved problem of international relations is war and so long as this problem is not solved the ideal of world peace cannot be achieved.

It has been the tendency of the modern world to create international institutions or law courts to settle disputes arising between different nations but such law courts or institutions would be unnecessary if we adopt the Gandhian method of non-violence. Gandhiji's idea of passive resistance may prove to be a stronger and most effective method towards an early solution of a problem than any artificial device.

E. Stanley Jones has observed, "Almost simulataneously two great forces emerged in the world—atom force and atma force, one physical and the other spiritual. The atom force has been used in its advent for physical ends—destructive physical ends. . . . And how destructive . . . But humanity is afraid—afraid that there is no alternative. We must use physical force and now physical force means atomic force or be enslaved. But at this juncture and in this dilemma a new possibility emerges—emerges in a little man in a loin cloth—Mahatma Gandhi with his atma power, the power of non-violent, non-cooperation. So two forces are before us to choose between: the atom and the atma-one means universal destruction and the other means universal deliverance."[53]

Now, how can the principle of Satyagraha he applied in the international field. When two nations like America and Russia fight each other is it possible to remain non-violent? According to Gandhiji non-violence is useful weapon even in such cases, but it requires a well trained resolute band of workers who can even face death to achieve its goal.

A CRITICAL SURVEY OF GANDHI'S POLITICAL IDEAS

Gandhi's ideal state was the state in which men are naturally good and hence need no external government. As Gandhi said in 1931: "Political power means capacity to regulate national life through national representatives. If national life becomes self regulated, no representation becomes necessary. In such a state everyone is his own ruler. He rules himself in such a manner that he is never a hindrance to his neighbour. In the ideal state therefore there is no political power for there is no state."[54] Again Gandhi said, "let the people purify themselves. Let them cease to indirectly participate in the evils of the state and it will disappear by itself."[55] Thus in Gandhi's ideal state the people would be so good and pure that the state would become unnecessary.

But the question here is: Would such a society of Gandhi's dreams ever come about? Can we conceive of a state of affairs when all evil will be eliminated. Good and evil are the two sides of the same coin. As such where there is good there must also be evil. In such a society in which there would be no evil of any kind, which would be inhabited by men with the character of a saint is perhaps a Gandhi's dream difficult enough to be actualised. Realising this Gandhi later on modified his early stand by emphasising that while the totally non-violent or stateless society was the ultimate ideal, the immediate realisable society was one which governed the least. This clearly shows that ultimately he could not rule out the possibility or the existence of some form of state control.

Gandhiji cites many reasons as to why he opposed the existence of a state. Gandhi rejects the state because it gives no place to conscience.[56] The government is based on majority rule but in matters of conscience, Gandhi believed,that the law of the majority had no place. Moreover, Gandhi was against majority rule because he believed that wisdom is not born of mere numbers. He wrote thus "Swaraj will be an absurdity if individuals have to surrender their judgment to a majority."[57] In *Hind Swaraj*, Gandhi condemned the parliament as a sterile woman and a prostitute— 'sterile woman' because parliament could conceive of no good policy on its own according and 'a prostitute since it had no real master'.[58] Gandhiji also was against parties, elections and legislations passed by parliaments because of its arbitrary nature, Gandhi was of opinion that political parties divided people, elections were a source of deception and untruthfulness and legislation passed by parliament could not be effective unless there was a previous conversion of hearts. To quote Gandhiji, "Unless we become manly and fearless, no number of rights showered upon us can secure us our liberties".[59]

But how far was Gandhiji justified in his rejection of the state, political parties, elections and legislations? The difficulty arises because Gandhi regards the state as an artificial institution. In fact modern living is inconceivable apart from the control of the state. The state arises out of the moral necessity of human beings. In primitive societies men were egoistic and selfish. Each individual cared only for himself as a result of which there was chaos and confusion. The survival of the fittest was therefore the law of the primitive societies. But gradually with the spread of civilization, men realised that some form of control in the shape of government or state was necessary to reconcile the will of an individual with that of others for the interest of a common good. The state or government needs to restrain such individual who work against the social will. So the existence of the state is a moral necessity. The increase in the powers and function of the state need not also be viewed with suspicion so far as it is concerned with the welfare of the masses and provided that these 'functions' have been entrusted to the government after rational consideration.

Moreover Gandhi's opposition to legislation, parties and elections are also subject to criticism. Legislation are not always arbitrary imposition on individuals. It it true that men should act according to the dictates of his conscience in case of his personal decisions but this cannot hold good in case of decisions affecting a large number of people. In such circumstances only legislation is the answer for the solution of the numerous problems arising in the society. We cannot assume that every person in the society is just and moral. Legislation is a must to eradicate the evils of society and to create the conditions for men to live a moral life. For instance in the absence of landlaws, men would have the freedom to acquire anybody's land by force without having the right of ownership. The absence of marriage laws would give a person the liberty to marry anyone at any time according to his whims and fancies. One could imagine the situation arising out of such lawlessness. Should or could we allow anyone to kill somebody on the ground of his conscience or will? The fact to be considered here is that the government or the state should not be allowed to become despotic or to behave in the way it likes. There should be a proper exercise of the democratic rights of the people and they should have a say in the exercise of its functions. But this does not mean that we should do away with the state or the legislations altogether on the ground that it goes against the freedom of the individual or morality.

In place of political parties, Gandhi wants that decisions should be taken unanimously. But is it ever possible to have a unanimous decision on any matter in a country having so many crores of people? Such an idea of unanimous decision may be possible in a small village having a few people but it is the most impractical thing in a vast country like that of India.

Moreover Gandhiji's idea of village panchayats or of decentralized state with the village as the key unit though beautiful theoretically presents some difficulties. Gandhi wanted that each village unit would be self-sufficient as far as possible and would be governed by a unanimously elected panchayat which would take all its decisions unanimously. It is very difficult in fact to select the five panchayats unanimously in village which are full of conflicts in matters of caste, creed and minor considerations. Instead of promoting brotherhood, the village panchayats would tend to create more bitterness, division and hatred amongst the villagers. Thus the Gandhian "Gram Rajya' far from bestowing freedom would rather minimise freedom of the individual which was the primary concern of Gandhiji's ethics and religion. But all these criticisms of the Gandhian conception of politics should not suggest that his views are without any relevance today. Decentralization and local governments are undoubtedly the most important elements of democracy. These small units make people feel that they have a major share in the functioning of the government. A healthy local community can also act as a fit laboratory for putting into test on a small scale certain new projects. His views have a special appeal in the present society when we badly feel the evils of centralization of powers.

CONCLUSION

On the occasion of the Second Round Table Conference, when Gandhi went to Europe and was staying with Pierre Ceresole, the Originator of the International Voluntary Service for Peace in Switzerland he was asked by Pierre, "Tell us what qualities you think a leader for this age would need?" Gandhi replied "Realisation of God every minute of the twenty four hours."[60] The above at once points out that the leader of a political system, in a sense the whole of the political system must be based on religion and lofty principles. This reminds us of the qualities prescribed for the king in our ancient writings. Kautilya in his *Arthasastra* gives us a list of qualities that a king who was the leader of that age should possess: "Aquisition of learning is not enough for a ruler. He must be able to exercise control over his sense (Indriyajaya), and keep such passion as lust, anger, avarice, pride and so on in check."[61] It is also considered that he should avoid addiction to vices. Seven vyasanas or vices, three arising from temper and four originating in lust are mentioned and their relative seriousness discussed at length. It is declared that a vyasana prevents him from realising his own highest good.[62] (Vyas yati enam sreyasah). This highest good which is mentioned in Kautilya's *Arthasastra* is nothing but the self realisation of religion. Mahatma Gandhi's ultimate endeavour was also self realisation. The Rajkot incident of 1939 serves to emphasise how Gandhi was extremely careful to see that his religion was satisfied even at the expense of his politics. The ruler of Rajkot opposed the popular demand for reform, and Gandhi decided to fast. The Viceroy intervened and adjudicated in favour of Gandhi and the reformers. Gandhi realising that he had been guilty of forcing the ruler to reform by the power of his reputation and not by soul force, reversed the viceroys' decision although the reformers were very much discontented. He was determined to purify the corrupt sphere of political life and each political mistake that he committed took him nearer to God. We have seen therefore, all the political ideas of Gandhiji whether it be of satyagraha, swaraj, state, government or his attitude towards war are all influenced deeply by the lofty principles of religion. When carefully observed each of the principles seems to have some kind of reference to the ancient religious tradition or to religious principles. For example his teaching that we should cling to truth at all costs, we should never injure our enemy, that we should hate the wrong and not the wrong doer, that one should 'Do or Die', that we should have the moral courage to stand for justice at all costs, even if its means death, that we should have an immense faith in God are all political principles with a religious overtone.

Mahatma Gandhi's philosophical anarchism has two basic elements (a) his profound faith in the moral freedom of man as a member of the society (b) his deep seated belief in the doctrine of non-violence or universal love.

Again Gandhi's ideal of non-violent state involves a contradiction in terms because the state necessitates some amount of violence. Some amount of physical force is indispensable for the proper functioning of the state. Therefore Gandhiji tries to make a compromise between the stateless society of the anarchist and the state of violence and force by saying that, that society is perfect which governed the least. Thus the are two aspects of the Gandhian polity the ideal and the practical. On the one hand he gives us an ideal which may serve as the guide and a source of light in the dark world of political confusion. On the other hand he accepts a modified ideal of practical politics as the ultimate ideal. That golden age Mahatma Gandhi believed would come some day. He compares his ideal to Euclid's point or line. Euclid's line is one without breath, no one has so far been able to draw Euclid's line. But Geometry has made a considerable progress only by keeping this ideal line in mind. What is true here is true of every ideal. Mahatma Gandhi's opposition to the state is the result of certain ethical and religious considerations. 'As a philosopher of history and culture, Gandhi is a believer in spiritual idealitional determinism which follows from his belief in the reign of God in the cosmos. "To Gandhi duty to one's conscience and obedience to God are far greater than the dictates of the state. This in its turn calls for individual moral freedom to enable oneself to surrender completely to the service of the society which is God's creation. Moreover Gandhi felt that any action that is done under pressure or compulsion of the state cannot be truly called moral. Thus Gandhiji's rejection of the state or legislation or majority rule can be deduced ultimately from his conception of morality and religion.

REFERENCES

1. Gandhi, M.K., *The Story of my Experiments with Truth*, p. 383.
2. *Harijan*, March 2, 1934.
3. *Young India*, Sep. 11, 1924.
4. C. Sukla, *Conversations of Gandhi*, p. 53.
5. M.K. Gandhi, In search of the Supreme, Vol. II, pp. 309-10.
6. N.K. Bose, *Selections from Gandhi*, p. 218.
7. *Navajivan*, Nov. 14, 1921.
8. Written Statement before the Huter Committee October 1919.
9. *Bhagavadgita* chapter II, Sl. 38.
10. *Dhammapada*, chapter I Verces 3-5.
11. *The New Testament*, St. Luke 6.29.
12. *Collected Works of Mahatma Gandhi*, Vol. XIV, p. 351.
13. N.K. Bose, *Studies in Gandhism*, pp. 82-83.
14. V.T. Patil, *(ed.)*, *Studies on Gandhi*, pp. 5-6.
15. *Bhavadgita*, chapter 18 sl. 78.
16. *The Colelcted Works of Mahatma Gandhi* Vol. XII, Gandhi's letter December 1914.
17. *Collected Works of Mahatma Gandhi*, Vol. XII, Gandhi's speech, February 6, 1916.
18. *Collected Works of Mahatma Gandhi* Vol. XV, Gandhi on Satyagraha, March 20, 1919.
19. *Parliamentary Paper, House of Commons*, Statement of E.S. Montagu, August 20, 1916.
20. *Collected Works of Mahatma Gandhi* Vol. XV, Gandhi on Satyagraha, March 20, 1919.
21. D.G. Tendulkar, *Mahatma Gandhi*, Vol. III, p. 17.
22. Jonses, E. Stanley, *Mahatma Gandhi*, an interpretation quoted in p. 124.
23. Pyarelal, *Mahatma Gandhi, The Last Phase.*
24. *Taittiriya Upanishad*, chapter 1.6.2.

25. *The Selected Works of Mahatma Gandhi,* Vol. VI, p. 442.
26. *Young India,* 20th March 1930.
27. *Young India,* Sept. 3, 1925.
28. *Young India,* Sept. 19, 1925.
29. *Young India,* May 28, 1931.
30. M.K. Gandhi, *Hind Swaraj,* p. 37.
31. M.K. Gandhi, *Hind Swaraj,* p. 63.
32. M.K. Gandhi, *India opinion,* July 18, 1908.
33. *Young India,* March 19, 1931.
34. *The Collected Works of Mahatma Gandhi,* Vol. 20, pp 401-402.
35. *The Collected Works of Mahatma Gandhi,* Vol. 20, p. 413-414.
36. *The Collected works of Mahatma Gandhi,* Vol. 20, p. 499.
37. *The Collected Work of Mahatma Gandhi,* Vol. 20, p. 249.
38. *The Collected Works of Mahatma Gandhi,* Vol. 20, p. 122.
39. *The Collected Works of Mahatma Gandhi,* Vol. 20, pp.162-164.
40. *The Collected Works of Mahatma Gandhi,* Vol. 20, p. 240.
41. *The Modern Review,* 1933, p. 413.
42. *Young India,* July, 2, 1931.
43. N.K. Bose, *Selections from Gandhi,* pp. 73-74.
44. *The Collected Works of Mahatma Gandhi,* Vol.1. 20, p. 122.
45. *Harijan,* July 22, 1946.
46. *Bhagavadgita,* Chapter II, sl. 38.
47. *Young India,* January 8, 1925.
48. *Bhagavadgita,* Chapter III, Sl. 13.
49. *Sanatana Dharma,* An Advanced textbook by Madras Theosophical House, p. 311.
50. *Ghagavadgita,* chapter 18, Sl. 40-48.
51. M.K. Gandhi, *All men are brothers,* p. 123.

53. Dr. Radhakrishna, (ed.), Mahatma Gandhi-100 years, the essay R. Stanley Jones pp. 176-177.
54. *Young India,* July 2, 32.
55. *Young India,* Feb. 23, 21.
56. *Young India,* Dec. 15, 21
57. *Young India,* Dec. 8, 21.
58. *Harijan* January, 5, 1942.
59. *Young India,* March 13, 20.
60. Gandhi, World Citizen by Muriel lester, 1945, p. 47.
61. *Kautilya Arthasastra,* 1.6.
62. R.P. Kangle, *The Kautilya Arthasastra* part III translated, 8.1.4.
63. *Harijan,* Sep. 15, 46.
64. B.B. Majumdar, *(ed.), The Gandhian Concept of State,* p. 63.

4

IMPACT OF RELIGION ON GANDHI'S ECONOMIC THOUGHT

INTRODUCTION

Gandhiji was not an economist, nor did he claim to be well acquainted with modern theories of economics. However, his approach to the economic problems and their solutions have been quite unique. In fact his economic thoughts were largely shaped by his own practical experience. Religion which formed the pivot of Gandhi's life also influenced his economic ideas. The *Gita*, the *Bible*, the writings of Tolstoy, Ruskin, Marx and so on moulded his economic thoughts. Like other fields of human activities, he felt that economics too could not be divorced from morality and religion Thus he viewed economic problems also from the stand point of religion.

The real force behind Gandhiji's economic reorganization can be traced back to India's spiritual tradition. God lives in every living being and one's spirit is strengthened if one loves equally all living beings. Love for all mankind finds expression in truth and non-violence and this truth and non-violence obviously forms the basis of Gandhian economics.

The love for his fellow beings as children of the same Father prompted Gandhiji to dedicate his life to uplift the economic conditions of the poor and downtrodden, whom he considered to be 'daridranarayana'. As Louis Fischer observes "Gandhiji's paramount compulsion was to help the underemployed and since he and his God were partners, he enlisted the Almighty in his task. "To a people famishing and idle the only acceptable form in which God can dare appear is work and promise of food as wages: If we do not waste our wealth and energy, the climate and natural resources of our country are such that we can become the happiest people in the World."[1] Poverty leads to moral degradation. Gandhi therefore strove to uplift India's economy. He dreamt of an India which is happy economically as well as spiritually.

But it should be remembered that spiritual happiness is impossible without the minimum economic self sufficiency. Gandhiji was well aware of the fact that man is a spiritual being who seeks his spiritual end but material fulfilment in cooperation with others is important. It is impossible for a starving man to concentrate himself on religion or spiritual matters. Gandhiji himself said, "It is impossible to soothe the suffering and hungry humanity with a song from Kabir. The only poem the hungry millions ask for is invigorating food."[2]

Vivekananda expressed a similar view in the Parliament of world Religions in Chicago. In his concern for the hunger stricken peasant of India he expressed Gandhi's feelings. "It is an insult to the starving people to offer them religion; it is an insult to the starving men to teach him metaphysics."[3] Vivekananda saw that God and not religion was the crying need of India. But to Gandhi the two terms were closely related.

In his book *Only one Way Left Dr. G.F.* MacCleod has presented the way for religion entering life in a more practical way. The world's greatest problem according to him was how to share bread. Gandhiji saw the meaning of this in India where there were uneven distribution of wealth and income. Both Gandhi and Dr. MacCleod saw that it was a mistaken notion of religion to confine it to the non-material realm. It is right to pray God for help but the prayer should not be merely verbal. Thus for example if we pray for the preservation of good health of the community, we must take necessary steps to provide nutritious food, cleanliness and proper sanitation. The community must co-operate with God and make its religion practical. The providing of the basic necessities of human life to the poor and hungry millions was hence the first concern of Gandhiji's economic thinking.

In his approach to economic development Gandhiji believed that for the upliftment of the starving dumb millions, economic well being must go hand in hand with spiritual well being. "I want all those for the soul.... It is the evolution of the soul, to which the intellect and all other faculties have to be devoted."[4] With regard to the question "Does economic progress clash with real progress? Gandhi clarified that economic progress should not be at the cost of real progress. Material progress should be achieved by preserving the essentials of humanity and religion.

Both Gandhi and the socialists believe in constructing a social order in which human personality will be able to find its fullest expression. But while the other socialists use the expression in the physical or material sense, Gandhiji used it is the metaphysical or religious sense. As Gandhi wrote, "Man's ultimate aim is the realisation of God, and all his activities, social, political and religious have to be guided by the ultimate aim of the vision of God."[5]

Gandhi believed in the age old Hindu tradition that dharma (religion), artha (economy), kama (desire) are only the means to the supreme goal of moksha (salvation). Thus artha is essential no doubt but it cannot be an end in itself. The hoarding of immense wealth is not the end of human life. This also has influenced Gandhi's concept of minimisation of human wants.' Artha helps in sustaining the individual in his path towards spiritualism or moksha, which alone is the summum bonum the ultimate goal of all human endeavour.

Gandhiji's economic ideas also owes a great deal to the ancient Hindu and Jaina teaching of 'Aparigraha' or non possession. Aparigraha usually means abstisence from all attachment and it is considered to be one of the most important of the five great views towards emancipation. As attachment to the world of objects means bondage to the world and the force of this causes rebirth. Liberation is impossible without the withdrawal of attachment. Gandhiji too believed that the desire for worldly things, more than what is required is a hindrance in the way of realisation of perfection and spirituality. Renunciation of earthly possession is always a prize favoured by the ancient religions. And Mahatma Gandhi who was deeply religious could not escape this tremendous influence. His economic ideas were largely shaped by such influence.

The spirit of renunciation and sacrifice which is manifested in the economic policy of Mahatma Gandhi is explicit in the very first verse of the *Isopanishad*. it is stated "By the Lord pervaded let this all be, whatever moving things there is in the moving world." This is the foundation of Upanishadic ethics and religion. We are therefore required to base our life and conduct on this basic truth. Such a life will be one of renunciation leading to the highest enjoyment of Ananda in its infinite manifestations. In it there is no room for greed, delusion or conflict.

"Isavasya midam sarvam yat kincha jagatyam jagat.

Tena tyaktena bhunjitah ma grahdhah kasyacit dhanam"

(Isa. 1)

["with that renounced thou may enjoy, Covet not the wealth of any one at all."]

The reference to wealth here is significant because usually man hankers after wealth in an unlimited way. The *Katha Upanishad* states "A man is never to be satisfied by wealth."[6] The *Brihadaranyaka* is more emphatic on this point when it says "Of immortality however there is no hope through wealth." (yathaivo upakarano jivitam tatharvate jivita yadamritasya tu nasasti vity iti.) These thoughts of the ancient Hindu tradition are implicit in the economic thoughts of Mahatma Gandhi.

Gandhi was also greatly influenced by Ruskin's book *'Unto This Last'* and he had devoted a full chapter in his autobiography under the heading "The Magic spell of the book". In Gandhiji's own word, "The book was impossible to lay aside, once I had begun it. It was impossible to lay aside, once I had begun it. It gripped me..... I could not get any sleep that night."[8] He summed up the principles of *'Unto This Last'* in three principles: (1) That the good of the individual is contained in the good of all (2) That a lawyer's work has the same value as the barber's in as much as all have the same right of earning their livelihood from their work and (3) That the life of the tiller of the soil and the handicraftsman is the life worth living.[9]

Donald Bishop once asked Gandhi: "What is the purpose of social and economic system,"? Gandhi answered "its purpose is to create an environment in which people can live in harmony and can develop their talents and energies for well being of their own and of all."[10]

Gandhi with a strong fellow feeling for his country could vividly see the "living pictures of despair. You could count every rib. You can see every artery. There was no muscle, no flesh....Their is an eternal compulsory fast."[11] Again he said, "Hanuman tore open his heart and showed that there was nothing there but Ramanama. I have none of the power of Hanuman to tear open my heart, but if any of you feel inclined to do it, I assure you, you will find nothing here but Rama whom I see face to face in the starving millions of India."[12] But Gandhi did not believe in helping them out of this poverty by giving them relief. "They cannot be given it. They must earn it and they can only earn it by the sweat of their brow."[13] This forms the basis of Gandhiji's theory of Bread labour.

BREAD LABOUR

Gandhiji wanted that the poor people whom he considered 'daridranarayan' should stand on their own feet. So he was guided by the theory of bread labour which means that everyone should contribute towards earning his or her bread. According to Gandhiji one has no right to consume anything without sharing the labour required to produce it. Gandhiji has tried to get support for this theory from the *Gita*. In the third chapter of the *Gita* which is Karmayoga, Lord Krishna describes the cosmic cycle of Karma which should be followed by each and every individual. Again it is stated in the *Gita* that those who eat without any sacrifice eats stolen food and they are thieves".[14] Even the *Manusmrit* says: "He eats but sin who cooks for himself; a meal of what remains after sacrifice has been offered is ordained to be the food of the good."[15] The *Bible* also says: "Eat thy bread by the sweat of thy brow."[16] All these signify that to eat without performing some sacrifice is selfishness. In other words one has no right to eat without any labour in any form. Gandhi himself admits that he has taken the idea of bread labour from the *Gita*. As Gandhi said "God created man to work for his food and said that those who ate without work were thieves."[17]

The ideal of Varnashrama dharma teaches that one should earn his own livelihood by performing the tasks and duties that are allocated to one by his caste or varna. Every form of labour is essential in a society. In the Rudradhayaya of the vedas people belonging to different classes were entrusted with various works of the society. They were identified with the Supreme God Rudra. It goes on saluting men of different professions thus:[18]

"Carmarabhyo namah, rathakarabhyo namoh, mrgajibhyo namoh, asvapatibhyo namoh," and so on.

Karmara (blacksmith), rathakara (the maker of carriages),

Mrigyajhbhyo (hunters), asvapatibhyo (persons who bred horses) are all saluted as Rudra (God.). This shows that everyone should earn his bread by these different means. It also supplies the need of the society.

According to Gandhi even scavenging was respectable

as an occupation. The only thing is that everyone ought to perform sufficient body labour to entitle him to means of livelihood. The rich who multiply their wants without offering manual labour, exploit the poor, using them as a means for the gratification of their wants. Bread labour does not however include intellectual labour in the strict sense. The needs of the body, if possible, must be supplied by the body. Bread labour should be voluntary and if people are convinced of its value and necessity then there would be enough for all. "Compulsory obedience to the law of bread labour breeds poverty, disease and discontenment. It is a state of slavery. Willing obedience to it must bring contentment and health And it is health which is real wealth, not pieces of silver or gold."[19]

So Gandhiji takes personal effort (sarira srama) as the primary need for the economic growth of the individual as well as of the nation. Moreover bread labour and the idea of 'sarva srama samanatva' can help to a great extent in doing away with the superior-inferior relationship.

MINIMISATION OF WANTS

Gandhiji advocated strongly the principle of minimisation of wants. According to him we should remain satisfied with the basic necessities of life and should not hanker after abundance of wealth. Conquering greed is an essential prerequisite of such a principle. For this view Gandhiji no doubt is indebted to the long standing spirit of renunciation of the ancient Indian tradition. Gandhiji was greatly inspired by Buddha who although being a prince adopted voluntary poverty. Jesus Christ the son of a shephered lived in a humble way throughout his life. The simplicity of these great men attracted the mind of the Mahatma. Gandhi was determined to adopt the maxim of simple living and high thinking in his personal life and showed it to the rest of the world. The man in the loin cloth was convinced of the teaching of the Upanishads that our mind is like a restless bird, the more it gets the more it wants. Gandhiji said "

I do not want anything more for workers and peasants than enough to eat and clothe themselves and live in ordinary comfort as self respecting human beings."[20]

Minimisation of human wants paves the way for economic equality. Gandhi said "In India we have got... people having to be satisfied with one meal a day... you and I have no right to anything, than we really have, until these people are clothed and fed better. You and I..... must adjust our wants and even undergo voluntary starvation in order that they may be nursed, fed and clothed."[21]

According to Gandhi "possession implies provision for the future. A seeker after truth, a follower of the Law of Love cannot hold anything for tomorrow. He never created more than what is strictly needed for the moment. If, therefore we repose faith His Providence, we should rest assured that He will give us everyday our daily bread meaning everything that we require."[22]

Thus the religious spirit in Gandhiji desists him from possessing more than what one requires. It is a well known fact that the saints and seers of ancient times possessed nothing and had to even beg for their livelihood.

EQUALITY

The principle of equality is a virtue prized by almost all the great religions of the world. In South Africa Gandhiji was very much pained to see the existing inequality and the tyranny against the weaker section of people. On returning to India Gandhi was determined to gain both social and economic equality for the masses. Gandhiji considered economic equality as the basis of socialism. Gandhi said: "Working for economic equality means abolishing the eternal conflicts between labour and capital. It means the leveling down of the few rich in whose hands is concentrated the bulk of the nation's wealth on the one hand and the levelling up of the semi-starved naked millions on the other."[23]

Gandhiji insisted that every person should have a right to the basic necessities of life that is food and clothing.

One can afford to have luxuries only after the necessities of each and everyone have been fully satisfied. Gandhiji wanted everyone to have equal wages whether he is engaged in physical or intellectual labour as far as practicable. A teacher, a lawyer, a doctor, a labour, a cultivator, all should get equal wages as far as possible.[24]

But it should be noted that economic equality of Gandhiji's conception did not mean that everyone would have the same amount. It simply means that everyone should have enough for his or her needs. An elephant needs a thousand times more food than an ant. Everyone should have enough according to his needs. Gandhiji said in *Harijan*. "It does mean, however, that everyone will have a proper house to live, sufficient and balanced food to eat, and sufficient khadi with which to cover himself."

Equality should be attained by means of religion or morality

This concept of equality is preached by the communists and Marxists but the difference between these and the Gandhian concept of equality lies in the means of attaining it. According to Gandhiji, if the means of attaining this equality is bad, the very beauty of this ideal will be shattered. Thus Gandhiji brings down morality and religion when he emphasises on just and good means in attaining equality. Thus with the idea of non-violence and truth Gandhi prescribes a non violent way of attaining equality. Gandhi wrote: "This socialism is as pure as crystal. It therefore requires crystal like means to achieve it. Impure means result in an impure end. Hence the prince and the peasant will not be equalised by cutting off the prince's head. One cannot reach truth by untruthfulness. Truthful conduct alone can reach truth."[26] Again Gandhiji said "Truth and Ahima must incarnate is socialism.... It (satyagraha) is the highest means, the greatest force. Socialism must not be reached by any other means."[27]

Equality as preached by the Bible

In his ideas of equality Gandhi was very much influenced by Ruskin and his book *'Unto this Last.'* Ruskin in turn was influenced by the teachings of the Bible. On the basis of the study of the Bible, Ruskin preached three cardinal truths. The first truth which he preached was the universality of objects. This is similar to the Hindu concept. 'All land belongs to Gopal." The second principle sought to establish the freedom of the individual and the third stood for the maintenance of the dignity of the poor. The Bible gives us a parable which conveys abundantly the idea of sarvodaya and equality of wages.

Once Jesus went to Galibe and entered the region of Judaea, a large number of crowd followed him. Jesus tried to explain to them the concept of Heaven and Eternal life. In order to explain it, Jesus uses the parable of the vineyard. One day Jesus went out of his house to hire some labourers for his vineyard. In his first encounter the householder agreed to pay a Denarlus (worth about 20 cents in those days) each a day to the workless wayfareres and so he sent them to work into his vineyard. After three hours he went out again and saw some more labourers standing in the market place and he asked them too, to work in his vineyard and that whatever was right he would pay them. So the second batch of workers went into his vineyard. The householder again went out about the sixth hour and ninth hour and he did the same. Finally about the eleventh hour when the householder went out he found some others yet standing unhired all day. The householder asked them too, to go and work in his vineyard. When the day was over, the owner of the vineyard gave instructions to his trusted steward. "Call the labourers and pay them their wages, beginning with the last upto the first." So all of them beginning with the last and each received a Denarus without any discriminations.[28]

This brought protest from those who were working for the whole day in the vineyard. The owners reply was that they got what they asked for and hence they had no reason to feel unhappy. More or less the need of all were more or less equal.

VILLAGE SELF-SUFFICIENCY

Village self-sufficiency means that all the requirements of a village like food, clothing and other necessities of life should be grown or manufactured in the village. Gandhiji believed that "Everyone must have a balanced diet, a descent house to live in, facilities for the education of one's children and adequate medical relief."[29] To satisty these basic needs one need not depend on any external agency. The ideal of bread labour is a key to self-reliance. The development of cottage and small scale industries is meant to give each and every individual work and thus make them self supporting. The large scale industries cannot give employment to all the villagers The idea of village self sufficiency was to protect the masses from exploitation which large scale industrialisation brings about. This again has its religious significance. When everyone is regarded as the creation of the same almighty God, the question of exploitation by the privileged class of the weaker class should not arise. Everyone has an equal right to the basic necessities of life which should be produced locally as far as practicable. Herein lies the importance of the spirit of Swadeshi.

Gandhi wrote: "My idea of village swaraj is, that it is a complete republic, independent of its-neighbours for its vital wants and yet inter dependent on many others on which dependence is necessary. Thus every village's first concern will be to grow its own food and cotton for its cloth. It should have a reserve for its cattle, recreation and play ground for adults and children.... The village will maintain a village theatre, school and public hall. It will have it own water works."[30]

However, Gandhiji maintained that village self sufficiency has its limits. It may not be possible for a village to supply all essential things required by the people. Gandhiji did not rule out the manufacture of certain goods by the industries which cannot be manufactured locally by the cottage industries. For that he recommended cooperative system of production. Thus Gandhi's self-sufficiency does not mean that villages will not export or import. But as far as possible every one will make the best use of his capacity to fulfil his own demands.

Gandhiji tried his best to preserve the beauty and health of the Indian villages. Hence his stress on the maintenance of the Indian villages. He believed that 'small is beautiful.' Gandhi himself said that if the villages in India go, nothing of India would remain. Gandhiji was also aware of the fact that religion and spirituality owe their origin and depends for its strength solely on the villages. Religion and religious life is closely associated on the natural living of man and natural living is inconveivable apart from the villages.

DECENTRALIZATION

Gandhi believed that in a decentralised economy participation of the people is the most important consideration. To achieve a decentralised order one requires a careful clarification of individual rights, initiative and participation. It encourages division of labour and equal distribution. It also affects the general health of the masses due to the pollution of the atmosphere.

Gandhiji therefore visualised a decentralised economic policy where there would be no exploitation in the economic field. The development of cottage and small scale industries occupy the most important positon in a decentralised economy. People should pay more heed to cultivation and small industries. In the economic field therefore Gandhi was in favour of 'production by masses' in place of 'mass production. Thus the doctrine of decentralization naturally implies that production should be brought about by the masses and the benefits of distribution should be such that it reaches the last person.

Gandhi advocated the view that the land should belong to the tiller. Land and all property should be his who will work it. He explained his view in these words: "All land belongs to Gopal....Gopal literally means shephered, it also means God. In modern language it means the state, that is the people."[31] Here Gandhi emphasises the age old religious viewpoint that everything in this universe is created by God, the Supreme Being and He alone is the master of all.

It must be mentioned, however, that Gandhiji did not oppose centralization in some aspects. He realised that some key industries, means of communication and such other may be undertaken in a centralised way. As Gandhiji said: he could visualise electricity, ship building, iron works, machine making and like existing side by side with village handicrafts. But the order of dependence will be reversed. Hitherto the industrialization has been so planned as to destroy the village and their crafts. He does not believe that centralization would be conducive to the common welfare of mankind.

Merits of Decentralization

Decentralization which was the most important principle of Gandhian economy has its own importance. Firstly decentralization will produce larger national wealth with smaller capital. Secondly decentralization will create greater opportunity for productive expenditure by reducing the necessity for defence expenditure. Simple homes from which there is nothing to take way requires no policing. Rurally organised India will also run less risk of foreign invasion than urbanised India. Moreover the decentralised sector through villages and cottage industries is labour intensive and hold potentialities for solving the unemployment problem. These industries could use raw materials and labour available locally, and adopt simple techniques of employment giving opportunities to a large section of the people.

These are the merits of decentralization in the economic field. But what about the religious significance of the economy of decentralisation? It is believed that decentralisation implies a greater importance to the rural sector which is the abode of peace, health and character. A centralised economy lead to the concentration of population in the cities leading to many problems of urbanization. The problem of housing, slums, pollution, overcrowding, violence, immorality, disregard for spiritual values are all the results of a centralised economy. It is natural for Gandhi therefore to shun such an economy which has no respect for religion an spirituality.

Moreover a centralised economy leads to inequality, arbitrary competition, production of luxury goods and harmsful articles which take us way from the path of morality. Violence, anarchy, injustice and exploitation are more pronounced in urban life than in rural life. A decentralised economy offers greater scope for equity and equanimity.

MACHINERY

Gandhiji wanted that man should not be subservient to technology, rather technology should remain under the control of man. He objected to the use of machinery as an instrument of greed and which deprived the mass of the opportunity of labour but it would be wrong to think that Gandhii was totally opposed to the use of machines. Gandhiji had stated: "Machinery has its place. But its must not be allowed to displace necessary human labour."[32] Gandhi said "I am against its indiscriminate multiplication. I refuse to be dazzled by the seeming triumph of machinery. But simple tools and instruments and such machinery as saves individual labour and lightens the burden of millions of cottages, I would welcome."[35] Such machines as sewing machines were allowed in every village.

Gandhiji pointed out that machinery helped a section of people to live by exploiting the poor masses. Thus the motive of using machinery on large scale is greed which Gandhi tried to attack with all his might. Mechanisation may help a country where population is scanty. But it is an evil in India with a vast population. Therefore Gandhiji insisted on a proper balancing of man power, small machinery and large machinery judged on the criteria of religious and moral values. Gandhiji was of the opinion that heavy industries deprived people of the pleasure of creation which Gandhiji used to call 'rasa'. People working in cottage and small scale industries derive a spiritual pleasure by creating something beautiful and useful which the big machines deprive them of.

As Louis Fischer observes: "On a higher philosophical level, Gandhi simply realised earlier than most, the dangers and horrors of a civilization in which machinery may enslave man instead of performing its essential function of liberating him...the faster machines moves, the faster man lives and the bigger the nervous tension he suffers due to the machine. Culture, leisure, indeed living, becomes so interlinked with machines that man himself may be innerly impoverished....To Gandhi mechanisation or any other forms of progress was not an end in itself; he judged material advances by their moral and spiritual effect on human beings. The individual was his central concern."[34] Thus, Gandhiji took care to see that in the race for mechanization man does not lose their religious values.

THE SPINNING WHEEL OR CHARKHA IN THE LIGHT OR RELIGION

While rejecting large scale machinery Gandhiji wanted the most elementary type of machinery which he could put in the homes of the millions. Such a useful means he found in the spinning wheel or charkha. 'An idle mind is a devil's workshop'- so goes the saying. Gandhi was convinced that the spinning wheel could provide the millions of villages with productive occupation during the idle hours. Thus Gandhiji tries his best to keep the people engaged in their leisure which in turn would give them easy means of livelihood based on bread labour.

The spinning wheel can be interpreted in terms of religion. In fact Mahatma Gandhi got the first glimpse of the spinning wheel or the charkha in the *Bhagavadgita's* third chapter, in the slokas of the jagat chakra. The meaning of these sokas are: "From food springs all life, from rain is born food, from sacrifice comes rain and sacrifice is the result of action. Know that action springs from Brahman and Brahman from the imperishable, hence the all pervading Brahman is ever firm founded on sacrifice. He who does not follow the wheel thus set in motion here, below, he, living in sin, ating his senses, lives, O Partha, in vain."[35]

Towards the beginning of the non-cooperation movement, Gandhiji wrote in an article in *Young India*, (Oct. 20" 1921) that he had derived his idea of the spinning wheel first from the *Gita*. "The reader will be interested to know that my belief is derived largely from the *Bhagavatgita*. In these verses is contained for me the whole truth of the spinning wheel as an indispensable sacrament for the India of today. If we take care of today, God will take care of tomorrow."[36]

The slokas of the jagat chakra points out that everything in this Universe is born due to the sarifice of another. Thus for example, from sacrifice we get clouds, from clouds form rain, rain in turn produces food and food nourishes human beings.

"Evam pravartitam chakram nanu vartayatihayah

Aghayu indriyaramo mogham parthasa Jivati.'[37]

Therefore it is one's duty to tune himself with this ever moving cycle of the world.

But when we say that we must move in accordance with this every moving cycle, what do we mean? The ancient seers and sages said that such actions meant 'yajna' or sacrifice. In ancient times 'yajna' or sacrifice was the only thing done for the sake of others. In the Purusasukta hymn of the *Rigveda* creation has been described as a gret form of sacrifice. According to it God has sacrificed himself for the sake of creation. Every item in the jagat chakra of the Gita is a symbol of sacrifice. Only by means of such sacrifice and action for the sake of others can we realise our identity or oneness with the universe.

Gandhiji did not accept the teachings of the Gita or any other religious teaching as it was. He was concerned only with the basic teachings and he modified it to suit his views and the needs of his time. So he have the concept of 'yajna' as found in the Gita his own intrpretation and meant physical labour by it. As Gandhiji said "Work here undoubtedly refers to physical labour, and work by way of sacrifice can only be work to be done by all for the common benefit. Such work-such sacrifice can only be spinning. I do not wish to suggest that the author of the Divine Song had the spinning wheel in mind. He merely laid down a fundamental principle of conduct. And reading it and applying it to India, I can only think of spinning as the fittest and most acceptable sacrifical body labour. I cannot imagine better worship of God than that in His name. I should labour for the poor even as they do."[38]

So spinning was the best available form of physical labour to establish communion with the poor masses. The rich men need not spin, he can use the cloth produced by the poor. But even the rich should spin, not as a hobby, but to realise his oneness with he poor. In doing so he will also add to the production in the country in whatever meagre form it might be. There can be no better method of self purification than spinning and this self-purification is the most important means of spiritual upliftment. It also purifies the heart of the spinner through concentration and selfless work. This is why the term 'sutra yajna' was coined by Gandhiji. There are many types of yajna's cited in the Gita which lead to the destruction of sin which in other words means 'citta suddhi'. Gandhiji recognised spinning as a means to this end and that is why he regarded spinning as 'sutra yajna'. Verrier Elwin speaks highly about the importance of the spinning wheel. He says "A person who wants to subdue his passions has need to be calm. All commotion within him ought to cease, and so quiet and gentle is the motion of the spinning wheel, that it has been known to still he passions of those who have turned it is the fullness of faith."[39]

The Buddhist dharma chakra which was adopted by Asoka as the national symbol for his empire and which has been adopted by our Government as the central figure in the national flag can be explained in the light of this chakra of the *Gita*. This acted as a source of inspiration for Mahatma Gandhi.

From the economic standpoint the utility of the spinning wheel can be felt more in the villages where thouands of people move about under-fed and ill clad. Few people in the villages get a square meal a day, they have no proper clothes to cover themselves, no proper houses to give them shelter. This is the common sight in most of the Indian villages. For us who lives in cities midst plenty it is difficult to realise their true pathetic condition. There are many such people who after their day's labour collect a bundle of firewood to be sent to the towns and that day fortunately they get something to satisfy their hunger, though that may be the only single meal.

Spinning wheel can help us in such tragic times. The income from producing the thread can add to one more meal a day, give them at least a cloth to cover themselves. On the other hand the rich can also contribute to the country's production through spinning.

Thus the spinning wheel or the charkha while being a part of the economic programme of Gandhiji has also a religious significance in it.

PRODUCTION, DISTRIBUTION AND CONSUMPTION

Gandhiji was in favour of production by each and every one and not mass production. He wanted the production pattern should be such that its benefits could reach the millions of poor people. He wanted cottage and small industries to exist side by side with agriculture so that it would provide employment to the vast majority of people.

Gandhi's method of distribution was based on justice and equality.

This was the result of his sense of brotherhood and oneness with all beings created by God. He wanted that very individual should have a house to live in, balanced food and enough clothing with which to cover himself. These benefits should reach the last man of India. Gandhi asserted that the possession of huge wealth by individuals should be held as a crime against humanity. The ideal of Gandhiji is equal distribution but as it is very difficult to realise such a state one should work for equitable distribution.

With regard to consumption Gandhiji advocated the principle of voluntary poverty. One should remain satisfied with the basic necessities of life. Gandhiji therefore preached the ideal of trusteeship which considers the state to be the trustee of the enormous wealth or surplus wealth. According to Gandhi therefore civilization consisted not in the multiplication of wants but in the deliberate and voluntary restriction of wants.

MIXED ECONOMY

The economic programme of Mahatma Gandhi brings out several sectors of production. At the basic level is the small scale industry mostly owned by the workers themselves and they are concerned with the manufacture of goods locally needed. It is self-employment sector. This constitutes the major part of the economy. Next to it is the village co-operative sector engaged in the supply of goods which cannot be sufficiently supplied by the self employment sector. This can be regulated by the Panchayat of the village selected by the adult population of the village. The third sector relates to the goods which are produced as a result of the joint effort of several villages. The urban areas may have certain industries relating to machinery, electricity and so on owned either by state or the cooperative societies. The state ownership is mostly confined to the heavy industries.

The primary motive of Gandhiji in introducing such a mixed economy was his idea of social welfare. He realised that for the benefit of the people, whose service he regards as the highest religion, confinement to only the private or the small scale sector will be inadequate. Certain things that are required cannot be produced by the village industries, hence he introduced that large scale sector also.

COOPERATION

Gandhiji had faith in cooperation as a means to uplift the condition of our economy. Apart from the individual effort, agriculture and village industries could be conducted by the method of cooperation. As Gandhiji said "the world today is moving towards the ideal of collective or co-operative efforts in every department of life. Much in this line has been and is being accomplished. It has come into our country also, but in such distorted form that our poor have not been able to reap its benefits..... I believe that we shall not derive the benefits of agriculture until we take to cooperative farming....As what applies to land applies equally to cattle."[40]

Cooperation is also encouraged from the religious spirit of man. For the sake of peace and prosperity, it is essential for us to work in cooperation amongst one another.

GANDHIAN SOCIALISM

Gandhiji with his deep faith in religion had a different view of socialism. His approach and the means to achieve socialism differs from that of Karl Marx, Lenin or Mao Tse Tung. The greatest beauty of Gandhi's concept of socialism is in the fact that he gave a very simple and a practical idea of socialism. With regard to the question "What is socialism?' Gandhi answered: "socialism is a beautiful word, and so far as I am aware, in socialism the members of the society are equal, none high, none low."[41]

Gandhiji gave in this context the analogy of the limbs of the body. All the parts of the body whether the head or the limbs are equally important. So are the members of the society. Equality of the members of the society in all spheres of life is the essence of socialism. Gandhiji considered economic equality as the main key to socialism. "working for economic equality means abolishing the eternal conflict between the labour and capital. It means the levelling down of the few rich in whose hands is concentrated the bulk of the nation's wealth on the one hand and the levelling up of the semi-starved, naked millions on the others."[42]

Socialism as Inspired by Religion

The religious influence in Gandhi, has moulded his idea of socialism in a different perspective. Other socialists like Marx were also concerned with equality but they never bothered about the means. But according to Gandhiji socialism should be achieved by non-violent peaceful means. The end cannot be good if the means are bad. A tree sprouting out of a seed of a poisonous tree cannot bear fruit with juices of nectar. Herein Gandhiji tries to introduce religious principle like truth and non-violence which increases its beauty. According to Gandhiji truth and Ahimsa must incarnate in socialism. Socialism was not related to material progress alone but he was more concerned with spiritual development.

Gandhi was against the western type of socialism because it suppressed freedom of the individual. Freedom according to Gandhiji is necessary in the pursuit of truth. Gandhi's philosophy was based upon the long standing religious belief on the freedom of the human soul. Like Kant, Gandhi believed that freedom was the chief postulate of morality and religion. Thus Gandhiji expressed that to deprive a man of his natural liberty is worse than starving his body. It is the starvation of the soul which no amount of bodily comfort can restore. Gandhiji said: "I want freedom for full expression of my personality. Under socialism, there is no individual freedom. You own nothing, not even your body."[43] By socialism here Gandhi meant western type of socialism. Again he said: "Where there is no freedom of thought and action, there can be no religion. In the absence of religion, a people cannot but perish."[44]

Socialism Gandhi believed should be evolved out of the traditions and culture of the country. Gandhiji did not propogate the abolition of the rich or capitalist class but advised the principle of trusteeship. So there was no question of force or violence against the capitalist. The approach was a completely peaceful and non-violent one. Therefore it was in perfect tune with the spiritual virtues.

Did Gandhi Support Capitalism?

When we say that Gandhi was not against capitalism, do we mean that he support capitalism? Gandhi's idea of socialism therefore needs to be clarified here. Gandhi has been often described as a 'socialist with a difference'. As Gandhiji described his idea of Socialism in a conversation with Louis Fischer at Panchagani in the last week of July 1946. "While I have the greatest admiration for the self denial and spirit of sacrifice of our socialist friends," said Gandhiji, "I have never concealed the sharp difference between their method and mine. They frankly believe in violence and all that is in its bosom. I believe in non violence through and through."[45]

In Gandhi's vision of an ideal state, all ownership of the means of production would be socialised, but the transition to it from capitalist ownership, which was contemporary to him, would be a strictly non-violent process. For Gandhiji the idea was to reform capitalist ownership, and make it fit with his ethical ideal and the principle of trusteeship to take for his personal consumption only as much as he needs and to turn the rest of his riches to meet the needs of society.

In 1936 K.G. Mashruwala contributed series of articles under the caption "Gandhism to Socialism" which were edited and corrected by Gandhiji himself. There he explained Gandhi's idea of socialism as follows:

"He (Gandhi) would like to dispossess every person of all kinds of belongings. If he tolerates the institution of private property, it is not because he likes it, or holds it to be necessary for the the progress of humanity, but because he has yet to discover a truthful and non-violent method of abolishing that institution. I think, that all socialists believe that possessions are absolutely essential to make mankind happy. Gandhiji does not accept that position in theory. But as a practical proposition, he feels, that mankind is not going to give up possessions, within a time which can be estimated. The only thing therefore to be considered is in what capacity persons having actual control over and possession of property should be deemed to have it, or in what spirit they should be suffered to possess it, Gandhiji says that... "Where persons possess property, they must be deemed to hold it in trust for society and not for themselves."[46]

Now the question arises: Who was the rightful owner of the property purported to be held in trust? What was the nature of this property which fell under this category? And what was the nature and extent of property, which be allowed by Gandhiji to be treated as private.

K.G. Mashruwala tries to explain it as such. The theory of trusteeship make no distinction between private and non private property. All property is held in trust, no matter who possess it, and its nature or quantity is. Indeed, the theory of trusteeship applies not only to tangible and transferable property, but also to places of power and position and to intangible and non-transferable property such as the muscular energy of a labourer....Who is then the owner? Gandhiji, would say God. To God alone belongs the universe and all that is in it, animate or inanimate, tangible or intangible. To take an instance, neither the shareholders, directors, managing agents, technicians, and the labourers, jointly or separately, nor even the state is the absolute owner of an industry. Every one of them must use those powers honestly and diligently and take no more of it for personal consumption than what is just and proper under the conditions in which humanity lives..... Everyone who has contributed to the success of the industry to the best of his capacity may take a wage (if he needs) but the wage should be in accordance with his needs and not in accordance with the value of his contribution. The monetary wage would be no guide for evaluating a man's capacity or worth.

The idea of ownership being thus disposed of, the next question is who are beneficiaries of the property? The answer is, the entire creation is the beneficiary. For instance, it is not only those actually engaged in working in an industry that are entitled to its fruits: but everything is to be shared with every one else, not forgetting even non human life.

The question as to the nature and extent of property Gandhiji would allow to be used as private is now easily answered. That which is due to a worker and needed by him he may use in a discrete manner for proper purposes. If, however, for any reason, he does not need it, he should give it over to one who needs it or return to the common fund of his unit."[47]

Thus it is evident that even in his idea of socialism Mahatma Gandhi takes resort to religious ideals.

Gandhi differes from the other socialists in one more important respect which is that he is ready to accept the rich. The persons endowed with aptitude and qualities are free to peroduce more goods in the society and earn money. They may take active part in trade and commerce of the country and increase personal and national income. What Gandhiji wants of the rich people is that they should keep away from exploiting others in the process and should not enjoy or appropriate more than what they actually need. This Gandhiji used to call the theory of Trusteeship. The money must be used for the good of the society and not for personal consumption. He is only a trustee of the extra income after meeting the requirements for his personal and family expenses. Gandhiji had no faith on coercive methods and legislations. What he valued most was the change of heart in the individuals that would make the society an ideal one. Even in matters of big industries and companies Gandhiji exhorted for the adoption of this method of trusteeship.

The principle of trusteeship is therefore not renunciation of holding but renunciation while holding property. Gandhi also made distinction between possession and possessiveness. In his view the evil lies not in possession as such but in possessiveness. If any rich man went to Gandhi to renounce his wealth and business activities, Gandhi would advise him that he wanted neither the renouncement of his wealth nor his business activities, but what he wanted was their application for the service of the poor and the oppressed. He wanted the rich class to become trustees of the nation and to run their business for the welfare of he people. Thus the rich man will have possession of his wealth of which he will use what he reasonably requires for his personal needs and will remain as a trustee for the rest which will be used for the welfare of the society. In this the honesty of the trustee is assumed. As soon as a man takes himself as a servant of the society, earns for is sake, spends for its benefit, then purity enters into his earnings and there is ahimsa in his activities. So Gandhi here *tries to introduce purity which is are ligious virtue in the economic filed of earning.*

Gandhi said "I must know that all the wealth does not belong to me what belongs to me is the right to an honourable livelihood, no better than that enjoyed by millions of others. The rest of my wealth belongs and must be used for the welfare of the community.... I want them to outgrow their greed and sense of possession and to come down in spite of their wealth to the level of those who earn their bread by labour.[48] According to Gandhi the trusteeship theory is a means to end exploitation and he suggests the weapon of non violent satyagraha for ushering trusteeship.

Religious influence in his idea of trusteeship

It is important to note that Gandhi's theory of trusteeship canbe traced back to the 'Vratas' of Jaina religion-asteya and aparigraha (non-stealing and non possession). Non-stealing and non-possession again are elaboration of ahimsa. When I take something which I do not need I am guilty of depriving others which is another form of himsa or violence.

Even according to the Hindu scriptures amassing of huge wealth is regarded as adharma (evil). It is an evil to desire for more than what he actually needs. Thus in the *Bhagavata Purana* a man who wants more than what he needs is dubbted as a thief and goes further to say that he deserves punishment.

"yavat bhriyeta jatharah tavat

Svattam hi dehinah adhikam

Yo hi manyeta sa steno dandam arhati."[49]

Manu also prescribed soma Yajna (an elaborate sacrificial performance) requiring a huge amount of money for a person who amasses three years income so that wealth accumulated by person is distributed among the various persons of the community, supplying the commodities of a yajna Gandhiji had/applied this fundamental principle of Asteya of Hindu religion into the economic field and consequently his ideas of trusteeship has been influenced by it.

GANDHI'S ECONOMIC DEALS IN PRACTICE

As is always said that Mahatma Gandhi did not preach his idea only in words. But he tried to put each and every principle into daily practice. He did not simply advocate that spinning is an important aid to self purification but he himself took to spinning in his daily life. He did not only preach the gospel of simplicity, but his very life itself was a glaring example of utmost simplicity. He ate very simple food and dressed himself in a loin cloth.

Gandhiji also undertook certain important steps for economic upliftment of the masses. When Gandhiji went for his daily walk with the others, everyone was asked to collect small pieces of stones as much as he or she could carry and deposit them all the in backyard of Gandhiji's house. This was done to build a small road to connect Gandhiji's house with the main road which was a few hundred yards away. When Gandhiji was questioned about it, he replied that he wanted to add some useful work to his walk and everyone who felt it need should be involved in building it. Gandhiji wanted every citizen to contribute according to his ability for economic and social welfare.

Another important aspect is that Gandhiji fought hard to remove injustice in the economic field since corruption in one sphere was bound to affect other spheres of life. Here the case of Champaran may be mentioned.

The lives of the peasants of Champaran was very pathetic. They mainly depended for their livelihood on the cultivation. They made great profits at the cost of the peasants and their lives were made miserable. There were several attempts of revolt but all efforts were nipped in the bud. When the cultivation of indigo became uprofitable due to the development of chemical substitutes, the planters tried to shift the heavy losses to the poor peasants. They were beated and placed in temporary prisons, houses were looted, cattle were seized, many illegal devices were imposed and marriages were taxed.

When all efforts failed the people turned to Gandhi to find a solution to the problem. Gandhi wanted to inquire into the condition of the peasants of Champran and to study the situation so that he could understand it in order to remedy the ills, Gandhi went to Champaran and began to interview the peasant as well as the planters. But after a few days, he was ordered to leave the district of Champaran, failing which he was told would be arrested.

On the day of the trial, the Government prosecutor pressed the Magistrate to postpone the case, but Gandhi would not allow. The Magistrate then tried another approach. "If you leave the district now and promise not to return, the case against you will be withdrawn." To this Gandhi replied: "That cannot be. Not to speak of this time alone I shall make Champaran my house even after my return from jail."[50]

Thus after a long struggle with the Government, a unanimous report favouring the peasants was submitted. The Government had to yield at last. It was essentially a compromise. portion of the illegal taxation was to be refunded and the tinkathia system was to be abolished by law. This oppressive system which had been in existence for about a century was abolished and the planters rule came to an end.

This is only one instance from the life of Mahatma Gandhi to show how he implemented his thoughts into action.

A CRITICAL SURVEY OF GANDHI'S IDEAS ON ECONOMICS

Gandhian economy is build on the principle of "Simple living, High Thinking." Therefore the Gandhian theories of consumption, production and distribution are all derived from this basic principle.

(a) *Gandhian Theory of Consumption or limited wants*:

In *Hind Swaraj*, Gandhi wrote, Civilization in the real sense of the term, consists not in the multiplication of wants but in the deliberate and voluntary reduction of wants. This alone promotes real happiness and contentment and increases capacity of service. The mind is a restless bird. The more it gets the more it wants and still remains unsatisfied."[51] In a letter to Jawaharlal Nehru, Gandhi wrote, "We can realise truth and non-violence in the simplicity of village life. The essence of what I have said is that man should rest content with what are his real needs and become self sufficient."[52] Gandhi was of the opinion that every human being must satisfy his wants like food, clothing and shelter. Gandhi opposes the aquisition of wealth more than the minimum required. Gandhi believed that greed destroys human values like honesty, high thinking etc. Temptation to have more than what is necessary has led to increased production leading in turn to capitalism, exploitation and state control. A simple economy of limited wants does not invite aggression.

But the question is: how many people would accept Gandhiji's ideal of *Simple living and high thinking*? Limited wants means limited production but it becomes rather difficult to stick to such a principle in the competitive world of today when all the other nations are increasing their production and raising their standard of living. Moreover there are main objections to Gandhi's belief that high thinking is possible only in case of simple living. Bertrand russell said on one occasion, Nothing improves the moral level of the community as much as increase of wealth ....the harshness of the general outlook from the Rhine to the Pacific at the present day is very largely due to the fact that, so many people are poorer than their parents were."[53]

(b) *Gandhi's theory of Production*: Gandhi was opposed to large scale production for he believed that it leads to exploitation. Large scale production and industrialisation are the result of man's greed, according to Gandhi. The machine by taking the place of labourers creates unemployment and by its mechanical performance drives out all creative instincts and initiative. These evils are inherent in industrialisation according to Gandhi, and no amount of socialization can eradicate them. Gandhi once wrote in *Harijan* "Pandit Nehru wants industrialisation because he thinks that if it is socialised, it would be free from the evils of capitalism. My own view is that evils are inherent in industrialisation and no amount of socialization can eradicate them."[54] Moreover, according to Gandhi, industrialisation led to exploitation of the village by the urban areas because the cities with greater earning prospects deprive the talented villagers of earning their income.

Now, it can be argued that Gandhi's idea of production is not acceptable to many because it will inevitably reduce the national economy to a poor level in the competitive world of today. Besides Gandhi's view that drudgery and exploitation are inhernt in industrialisation is also questionable. In fact it may be otherwise that is drudgery may result in the absence of machines due to an increase in the number of working hours. The machines by reducing the time of work can save some time for leisure. Moreover exploitation may be there in a rural or simple economy as much as in urban, developed economy. Exploitation is a part of one's character and mentality and has nothing much to do with machines. It depends upon the character of the individuals forming the society. For example farmers in India are exploited by the middlemen who pay a negligible amount of money to them and sell the same product at a very high price in the market. This in fact has nothing to do with machines.

(c) *Gandhi's theory of distribution and trusteeship*: Gandhi while advocating his views on distribution seemed to change in view on many occasions. For example, in the beginning Gandhiji advocated the theory of absolute equality following Ruskin where he claimed that no profession is superior or inferior to the other and hence all workers whether lawyers, scavengers or doctors should be paid an equal amount of wages.

Later on Gandhi accepted a concept of equality more of less like that of Marxism from each according to his ability to each according to his need. Gandhi insisted that everybody should have a "living wage" which would ensure the worker a balanced diet, a descent home and sufficient khadi with which to cover himself. Differences of wages should be in the basis of differences in needs. Thus Gandhi wrote, ... Just as it would be preposterous if an ant demanded as much food as an elephant; in the like fashion if a man demanded as much as another with a wife and four children that would be a violation of economic equality."[55]

Again Gandhi at one time said everyone's work should include physical labour and Gandhi insisted that everyone should do agricultural work. Then Gandhi said that everyone must contribute according to his ability and each person for earning his livelihood should follow the hereditary and traditional calling of his forefathers.[56] Moreover it is surprising that Gandhi with a strong belief in equality should make such a remark: "A Shudra has as much right to knowledge as Brahmana but he falls from his estate if he tries to gain his livelihood through teaching."[57] How could Gandhi neglect one's aptitudes and inferests? Can we allow a stupid brahmana to teach or preachsimply by account of his birth? Or should a Brahmana with great capability for manual labour be deprived of earning his livelihood by the means of his own interest?

Coming to the Gandhian theory of trusteeship, its application to the modern society is rather questionable. According to Gandhi, "earn your crores by all means but understand that your wealth is not yours, it belongs to the people. Take what you require for your legitimate needs and use the remainder for society."[58] It is difficult to ensure that a trustee will keep only as much as he needs. Here the honesty of a trustee will have to be assumed. The labourers always assume that a trustee always works for their benefit. Today it is very difficult to have complete confidence in the morality of individuals and hence the trusteeship principle is more a dream then reality.

But the above criticisms should not make us blind to the fact that certain feature of Gandhiji's economic theory has far reaching significance specially in the case of Indian economy.

CONCLUSION

Gandhi insisted that the vast masses of people be rehabilitated and India's socio-economic structure be built on the agricultural economy. We have tried to imitate Western civilization by giving priority to the industrial sector over the agricultural. In a vast country like India the primary necessity is food and cloth for the people and raw materials for the industries which agriculture alone can provide and this should be the foundation of Indian economy.

The objection of Mahatma Gandhi against machinery found its sophisticated echo even in contemporary America, in the voice of Galbraith in is book *New Industrial State.* the highly industrialised community of the United State of America has been the marvel of many people today. People believe that such a highly industrialised nation is sure to promote the dignity and freedom of the individual. But Galbraith in his *New Industrial State* has shown that the reverse is the case. Imperceptibly the industrial economy has been transforming itself into a dragon that was swallowing bit by bit all the noble features of human life. The dragon is represented by the large Corporation. It is not only the freedom of the individual in the large corporation that is threatened but that of even a millionaire owner of the corporation himself. The group personality has emerged, integrating the individual into a group. In terms of freedom of the individual, consumer's choice, pattern of consumption, function of the market and the like, Galbraith concedes, that there is no difference between an industrial society of capitalist America and that of a totalitarian Socialist State and calls this resemblance the principle of covergence.[59]

Many criticisms have been levelled against the Gandhian economic system. Economists have dubbed his theory as outdated and impractical and people laugh at it. As V.M. Dandekar in his article 'Gandhian economic system' in the book *Gandhi in Today's India* writes: "it is a path leading to an alternative goal of human life and existence; a human society which is unmoved and immovable, unchanged and unchangeable using the same kind of plough as existed a thousand years ago, living in the same kind of cottages as there were in times immemorial.... a society which limits and minimizes its material needs and one in which everyone earns his daily bread by a full day's physical labour seeking happiness as a mental condition of life."[60]

Gandhi has already given an answer to such criticism in his own words in a lecture delivered at the meeting of the Muir Central College Economic Society at Allahabad "By economic progress, we mean advancement without limit, and by real progress we mean moral progress which again is the same thing as the progress of the permanent element in us. I hold that economic progress in the sense I have put it is antagonistic to real progress. Hence the ancient ideal has been the limitation of activities promoting wealth...That you cannot serve God and Mammon is an economic truth of highest value. We have to make our Choice."[61]

If we enter the race of material progress by following the economic ideals prescribed by Gandhi we may not be very successful because Gandhiji's economy is one of self sufficiency and simplicity. But we must bear in mind that Gandhi's economics is not an end in itself but only a means to ultimate self-realization.

Gandhiji as has been said was influenced by the ideals of religion in shaping his economic principles. Schumacher suggests that religious view of man often effect his economic judgements. The fourth noble truth of Buddhism is the eight fold path. This is the path one has to follow in order to rid himself of the cravings (tanha) that binds one to the samsaric world of suffering (dukkha). One of the requirements of the eightfold path is right livelihood which as Schumacher points out involves economics. In Buddhist thought therefore economics and religious values are inter-related and there can be no conflict between the two. That is to say a Buddhist way of life demands Buddhist economies. According to Schumacher the Buddhist philosophy teaches a man to develop his talents which help him to remove his self-centredness which perpetuates his cravings that binds him to the world of impermanence (annica).[62] Buddhist economy therefore lays more importance on the development of character than on the development of economy.

Even Hinduism attaches the highest importance to simple living and high thinking. The early Hindu society was regulated by the principle of Varnashrama dharma. There were four different stages, four different castes and four different ends of human life dharma, artha, kama, moksha. These set up kept away many of the problems of the modern society namely food, class conflict, competition, exploitation, illiteracy and so on. There were other rules of conduct like yama and niyama which taught one the art of self restraint through control of the palate, control over the senses and the restriction of human wants. These helped to solve the problem of food shortage, over-population, hoarding etc. Thus, Gandhiji realised the greatness of these ancient teaching and therefore formulated his ideas of economics from these basic principles of religion.

REFERENCES

1. Louis Fischer, *Gandhi: His life and Message for the World,* p. 84.
2. *The Collected Works of Mahatma Gandhi,* Vol. 21, p. 209.
3. *Chicago Addresses of Swami Vivekananda,* p. 36.
4. *Young India,* 13.10. 1921.
5. M.K. Gandhi, Pathway to God, Compiled by M.S. Deshpande, p. 30.
6. *Katha Upanishad,* Chapter, 1, 27.
7. *Brahadaranyaka Upanishad,* Chapter, IV 4.3.
8. M.K. Gandhi, *An Autobiography,* p. 224.
9. *Ibid.*
10. L.K. Bhratiya, *Journal of Gandhian Studies,* October 1979 the article, p. 20.
11. *Young India,* 37, 1024.

12. *Young India,* March 24, 1927.
13. *Young India,* oct. 13, 1921.
14. *Gita* Chapter II, Sl. 13.
15. *Manusmriti,* 3.118.
16. *In Search of the Supreme,* Vol. II, p. 113.
17. *The Collected Works of Mahatma Gandhi,* Vol. 21, p. 271.
18. *Yajurveda,* (Kanva Chap. 17) 8-1.
19. Bread and Freedom: The Gandhian Way, *Journal of Gandhian Studies,* April, 1981.
20. M.K. Gandhi, *My Theory of Trusteeship,* edited by A.T. Hingorani, p. 6.
21. *Ibid.*
22. K.K. Gandhi, *From Yeravada Mandir,* p. 34.
23. M.S. Deshpande, *Light of India Message of Mahatma,* p. 83.
24. M.K. Gandhi, *Ruskin Unto This Last* (A Paraphrase), p. 5.
25. *Harijan,* August 18, 1940.
26. *Harijan,* July 13, 1942.
27. *Harijan,* July 20, 1942.
28. *The Holy Bible,* St Mattew chapter 20, p. 1004.
29. *The Collected Works of Mahatma Gandhi,* Vol. 30, p. 79.
30. N.K. Bose, *Selections from Gandhi,* pp. 73-74.
31. *Harijan,* January 2, 1937.
32. *Young India,* Nov. 20, 1925.
33. *Young India,* June 17, 1926.
34. Louis Fischer, *Gandhi: His Life and Message for the World,* pp. 87-88.
35. *Gita,* Chapter III, Slokas 14-16.
36. *Young India,* october 20, 1921.
37. *Gita,* chapter III, Sl. 16.
38. *Young India* Oct. 20, 1921.
39. Verrier, Elwin *Religious and Cultural aspects of Khadi,* p. 18.
40. *Harrijan,* Feb. 15, 1042.
41. *Harijan,* July 13, 1947.

42. M.S. Deshpande, *Light of India Message of Mahatma*, p. 83.
43. *Harijan*, August 4, 1946.
44. M.S. Deshpande, *Gandhi Marg*, vol. 15, No. 3, p/ 214.
45. *Harijan*, August 4, 1946.
46. K.G. Mashruwala, *Gandhi and Marx*, p. 78.
47. *Ibid*, pp. 79-82.
48. *Harijan*, June 3, 1939.
49. *Srimad Bhagavat*, 7. 14.8.
50. D.G. Tendulkar, *Life of Mohandas Karamchand Gandhi*, Vol. I pp. 243-261.
51. *Hind Swaraj*, By M.K. Gandhi p. 61.
52. Dhebar, *Lectures on Gandhian Philosophy*, pp. 40-41.
53. Bertrand Russell, *Power, A New Social Analysis*, London Unwin Boosk, 1960, pp. 279-280.
54. *Harijan* Feb. 29, 40.
55. *Harijan*, August 31, 1936.
56. *Young India*, Oct. 20, 1927.
57. M.K. Gandhi, *Marnashrama Dharma*, p. 15.
58. *Harijan*, Feb. 1, 1942.
59. Dr. Rajaratnam, *The Relevance of Gandhi to our Times* the article on 'The Industrial State and Gandhi, pp. 60-61.
60. B.C.Das & G.P.Mishra, (ed.), *Gandhi in To-day's India*, p. 91.
61. B.C. Das and G.P. Mishra, (ed.), *Gandhi in Today's India*, p. 92.

5

IMPACT OF RELIGION ON GANDHI'S SOCIAL THOUGHT

INTRODUCTION

Man is a gregarious animal and so the life of an individual is inconceivable apart from a society. The primary aim of human existence according to Mahatma Gandhi is self-realization, and a society to Gandhi should be such as to promote the qualities of human personality to realise its final goal. Society, to Gandhiji is a place where God can be found face to face. The best way to realise God, therefore is to find him amidst his creation. Gandhi asserted: "If I could persuade myself that I should find Him (God) in a Himalayan cave I would proceed there immediately. But I know that I cannot find him apart from humanity."[1] The *Bhagavadgita* has defined the bhakta in different slokas. "to prapnuvanti mameva sarvabhuta hite ratah."[2]

"Engrossed in the welfare of all beings these come indeed to Me"—said Lord Krishna.

Gandhiji has also suggested a definition of bhakta as one who serve is fellow men. This is why Narasimha Mehta sang "Vaishanava jana to tena kahiyo pira parayi" —or 'he is a true Vaisnava who knows to melt at another's woe'. Gandhiji accepted this as one of his most important prayers.

Now the question is: What kind of society did Gandhi want to build up in India. Gandhiji subscribed to the belief that all human beings were one single family: and any action or institution which stood against this principle was therefore immoral. Exploitation or inequality of any form was a rejection of this principle. A truly religious man who aimed at perfection should therefore resist injustice wherever it existed and re-establish the unity and brotherhood of all men. Meanwhile I have to attain both the ends of perfecting themselves and perfecting society. The method adopted to establish unity in the way of purification of society like other fields of life is based on the two basic principles of Truth and non-violence. It is because of this that his religions played a very great part in whatever reformation he suggested for the society of India. We say India, because he was primarily concerned with the Indian society but this will apply anywhere in the world. Now before we deal with the problems of society, it will be better for us to have an idea about the historical background of Indian society.

HISTORICAL BACKGROUND OF INDIAN SOCIETY

The present Indian social setup in closely related with the past traditions and movements in the society. "The citizen's life touches the present most directly but the present is a continuation of the past, and therefore he should know something about the growth of institution".[3]

The present society it is believed is the result of mutual contract based on the individual's own interest, an exchange of obligations in return for certain privileges. The theory of social contract has been regarded as the most acceptable theory. Kautilya in his *Arthasastra* gives us an elaborate view of the origin of society thus:— "People suffering from anarchy as illustrated by the proverbial tendency of large fish swallowing the small one, first elected Manu, the Vaivasvata to be their king, alloted one sixth of the grains grown and one tenth of merchandise as sovereign dues. In return the kings took up the responsibility of maintaining the safety and the security of the subjects."[4]

The Sastra does not lay down rules in social matters as it does in political matters, yet it was bound to take notice of the facts of social life as it found them. And though much theory is mixed up in the references to social organization, one may still regard the social life as throwing light on the conditions that actually prevailed in those times. It is stated in Kautilya's *Arthasastra* that the ruler was required to protect the social order founded on the system of varnas and asramas. After conquering the earth the ruler is advised to enjoy it by maintaining the social order in conformity with the varnasrama system.[5] This kind of social order is regarded as having behind it the sanction of the Vedas.[6] This does not however mean that a religious society or state was prescribed in the sastra. No organised theological or religious sect was there to intervene in the affairs of the society to safeguard religious interest or to enforce religious sanctions. the theory of the four varnas though true of ancient Indian society, also refer to some mixed communities which gives us suggestions of inter dining and inter marriage. There were numerous communities in society whose place in the scheme of four varnas could not be easily determined. According to the *Arthasastra* (with which the *Manusmriti* agrees but not Yajnavalkya), the son of a Brahmin from a Kstriya woman, and that of a kstriya from vaisya women belong to their father's caste. A vaisya's son from a sudra woman in however, a sudra. This also points out to the fact that in ancient India the caste system was not as rigid as it was practised in later times. Besides there were the existence of different castes, each following a separate fixed profession. We therefore feel justified in looking upon Rajaka 'washerman', sutuvaya 'tailor', suvarnakara 'Goldsmith', Caramakara 'leather worker, Karmara 'Smith' and others as names of castes which had their origin in the differentiation of profession.[7]

Associated with the theory of varna we also have reference to the ashrams in the ancient Hindu texts. The law concerning marriage and the relation between husband and wife are discussed by the ancient Vedas, Manu and Kautilya. The different writings of the ancient India point out to a liberalistic attitude towards women, it deals with the question of harassment of the wife by her husband and under certain circumstances it also allows for separation. Similarly widows appear to enjoy a much freer life. On the *Arthasastra* there is reference to 'chandavasini vidhava', a widow living according to her will, that is indepdendently.[8]

The picture of religious life is given by the Dharmasastra. But Dharmasastra, it must be remembered had its origin in the Vedic school and was primarily concerned with the mode of life appropriate to the Aryans, that is the mode of life appropriate to the upper Varnas specially the brahmins. The masses of people mostly non Aryan were debarred from Vedic practices and it is believed that the others remained contended with the worship of images of Gods in temples with flowers, incense, gifts etc. thus the Dharmasastra mainly restricts itself to a description of the Vedic Way of life while the *Arthasastra* takes full notice of the varied religious life of all classes of people.

A significant point to be remembered while discussing the condition of the early Indian society is that it was not as rigoristic in its outlook as it is thought to be. For example the rigidity in respect of caste, status of women and so on is mostly an invention of later times. There were certain evils no doubt that were handed down to the later generations and which still prevail to some extent even in modern India. It must be noted that these ancient social tradition and practices influenced Mahatma Gandhi's attitude towards the social problems to a great extent.

GANDHI'S CONCEPT OF SOCIETY

The advent of Mahatma Gandhi on the social scene marks a turning point to the history of social development. As has been said, Gandhiji wanted to establish a new society, a society completely free from exploitation and oppression. Gandhi worked hard to set up a sarvodaya samaj and a 'soshan bihin' samaj (society free from exploitation). According to Gandhi every individual whether rich or poor, high or low should get equal opportunity for his development. The utilitarian ideal of the greatest good of the gréatest number did not satisfy Gandhi. Gandhiji wanted the upliftment prosperity of all. The late President Dr. Rajendra Prasad has explained the aims and objects of a sarvodaya samaj thus: "The Sarvodaya samaj has been established to strive towards a society based on truth and non violence, in which there will be to no distinction of caste or creed, no opportunity for exploitation, and full scope for development both for individuals as well as groups."[9] The basis of such a sarvodaya samaj is love. Its ultimate goal is the good and welfare of the entire human race. According to Gandhiji it is not enough simply to gain independence and capture political power, but side by side with the political struggle it was necessary to have an ideal form of society which would fulfill the aspirations of each and every member of the nation. The society which Gandhiji wanted to build up was an organic whole where the difference between individual and group vanishes. Here it would be appropriate to discuss the relation between the individual and the society according to Gandhi's view.

RELATION BETWEEN THE INDIVIDUAL AND SOCIETY

According to Gandhiji, the freedom of the individual and the opportunity to develop his potentialities whether material, mental or spiritual must be the first concern of the society. This is clear when he says that 'the swaraj of the people is the sum total of the swaraj of the individual'. This means that it is the individuals who go to make the society and the welfare of the latter depends upon the welfare of the former. If individual swaraj is attained then peace and prosperity will naturally follow. The Dvadasha vrata—the twelvefold vow which he prescribed for his followers are only spiritual sadhana of a man with a social welfare at the background.

This however does not mean that the individual is free to behave as he likes because a man who strives for individual swaraj cannot place himself above society. The individual must put himself in tune with the larger interest of the society. Thus according to Gandhi though we should have individual freedom, we must not forget that man is essentially a social being. He should learn to adjust his individualism to the requirements of social progress. Unrestrained individualism is the law of the beast of the jungle. The individual must strive for swaraj and in doing so he must remain dutiful member of the society and a responsible member of the state. The varnasrama system of ancient India, according to Gandhi, tried to maintain the relation between the individual and the society in an ideal way.

VARNASRAMA DHARMA

Varna and asrama were the two basic principles regulating Hindu society in ancient times and as such deserves special mention. The law of varnasrama can be traced back to our most ancient scripture, the Vedas. The law of varna stated that a man shall follow the profession of his ancestors for earning his livelihood. Varna therefore is in a way the law of heredity.

So far as the law of asrama is concerned, Hinduism laid down four asramas of life—the brahmachari, Grihasta, Vanaprastha and sannyasa, through which a Hindu should fulfil the purpose of his life. Formerly the law of varna was a means to earn one's livelihood. Thus the function of a brahmana was to teach the science of brahma or spiritual truth. This in turn secured him his livelihood. A Kshtriya was to perform the function of protecting the people, a Vaisya was required to perform wealth producing occupations for the welfare of the people and a Shudra was to perform other physical labour in the same spirit of service. Fulfilment of the law of Varna therefore, was extended to promote peace and contentment, put an end to starvation and end all clashes and conflict. But the tragedy is that it has been misinterpreted in later times which gave rise to many problems. Mahatma Gandhi tried his best to give a new light to the age old tradition of Varnasrama. Gandhiji use varnasrama as means to promote human welfare. To put it in Gandhi's own words: "Varnasrama, as I interpret it sastisfies the religious, social and economic needs of a community. It satisfies the religious needs, because a whole community accepting the law is free to devote ample time to spiritual perfection. Observance of the law deviates social evils and entirely prevents the killing economic competition....It ensures the fairest possible distribution of wealth. But when people in disregard of the law mistake duties for privileges and try for self advancement, it leads to confusion of varna and ultimate disruption of society. In this law there is no question of compelling any person to follow the parental occupation againsts his or her aptitude....today, the nations are living in ignorance and breach of that law and they are suffering for it."[10]

Thus if varna reveals the law of one's being, and the duty one has to perform, the question of superiority or inferiority does not arise. But Gandhiji was pained to see it distorted which have made us the laughing stock of the world.

In ancient times varna was determined by birth but could be retained only by following its obligations. One born of Brahmana parents will be called a Brahmana but if he fails to reveal the attributes of a Brahmana when he grows up, he can not be called a brahmana. Lord Buddha has expressed a similar view in his *Dhammapada*.[11]

"Na jada hi na gotrena na jachaa hoti brahmano Yamiha sacham cha dharmo cha so suchi cha brahmano" "Neither matted hair, nor noble birth, nor caste make a brahmana. The man of truth and law is the Brahmana." The Varnasram system is believed to be of divine origin and hence it is a mistake to allow itself to degenerate into a principle of conflict. The law of Varna carries within it the spirit of duty and service to which one is born. Gandhiji said "I do hold that it is the only ideal state that is easy enough to approach and that is not only for the Hindu but for the whole of humanity."[12]

Under such an order all property was to be held by their respective holders in trust of the community. The king would hold his balance in trust of his people and would collect taxes only to be used for the benefit of the people. The Sudra, in the mind of Gandhiji, is the Lord of all, because he is the greatest servant. He performs bodily labour in the spirit of duty and service and has nothing to call his own." In an age where competition is held to be the law of life, and possession in the largest measure of world's goods, the summum bonum, and when everyone counts one self free to follow any calling one likes, this attempt to hold up varna as the law of life may well be regarded as an idle dream, and an attempt to revive it as childish folly be that as it may, it is my firm conviction that it is true socialism. In the language of the Gita, it is the equality of the spirit without which no other equality is possible. The performance of it, how slight, is well for him who performs it and the rest of mankind."[13]

The laws of Manu, an ancient law book of the Hindu way of life, regards the four asramas as the best means of attaining co-operation for the common good. It gives place of pride, however to the householder, whose order supports the other three. "As all living creatures subsist by receiving support from the air, even so (the members of) all orders subject by receiving support from the householder.[14] It is the one order that allows full scope for realising the three main aims of life *Artha* (wealth) *Kama* (love), and *dharma* (duty or righteousness). The Vanaprastha stage involves withdrawal from the normal requirements of family life to a solitary place for study and meditation. When Gandhi, with the consent of his wife, took the brahmacharya vow, he regarded himself as having advanced to the Vanaprastha stage of life. The reason Gandhi gives for choosing to become a Vanaprastha is that he wanted to devote himself to the service of the community.[15] But this does not mean that by taking such a vow, he was keeping himself away from society. This is the reason why he was against being called an ascetic. Dr. Radhakrishnan says that "We feel that our society is in a condition of unstable equilibrium. There is much wood that is dead and diseased and that has to be cleared away. Leaders of Hindu thought and practice are convinced that the times require not a surrender of the basic principle of Hinduism but a restatement of them with special reference to the needs of a more complex and mobile social order."[16]

Gandhiji too believed that the law of varna restores life to self realisation. He says "Historically speaking, caste may be regarded a man's experiment or social adjustment in the laboratory of Indian society. If we can prove it to be a success it can be offered to the world as a best remedy against heartless competition and social disintegration born of avarice and greed."[17] But sad to say that the varnasrama dharma far from its advantages become responsible for the rigidity of the caste system and gradually gave rise to untouchability which had been the greatest curse of the Hindu society.

CRITICAL SURVEY OF VARNASRAMA DHARMA

Gandhi's ideas on Varnasrama are summed up in a booklet with the title 'Varnasrama dharma' published by the Navajivan Trust. Gandhi begins by claiming that Varnasrama is a discovery of the Hindus and that it has universal application. According to Gandhiji "Varna is intimately, if not indissolubly, connected with birth and the observance of the law of Varna means believing on the part of us all of the heredity and traditional calling of our forefathers in a spirit of duty."[18] By not living upto his varna a man, says Gandhi,will be doing violence to himself and becomes a degraded being, a patita."[19] Gandhi was once asked—"If the Sudra has all the qualities of a brahmin, can we not call him a Brahmin?" Gandhi's reply was "Not in this birth. It is a good thing for him not to arrogate a varna to which he is not born. It is a sign of true humility."[20] These statements of Gandhi is considered by some to be conservative and narrow. It must however be admitted that Gandhi did not of course go round peaching varna dharma as abolition of untouchability. Thus when Gandhiji was charged of being too orthodox by supporting varna dharma, Gandhi replied "I have gone nowhere to defend varna dharma, though for the removal of untouchability I went to Vaikom. I am the author of a Congress resolution for the propagation of khadi, Hindu-Muslim unity, removal of untouchability, the three pillars of swaraj. But I have never placed establishment of varna dharma as the fourth pillar."[21]

UNTOUCHABILITY

The caste system has been a blot on Hinduism and it has robbed the Hindu religion of its vitality and brilliance. Untouchability has been mainly a creation of the people than any scripture or divine being. Mahatma Gandhi's greatest effort therefore was to drive out this unsocial elements which had been a great source of suffering and humiliation. Though it is difficult to say precisely about the origin of th caste system it is generally believed that the Aryans who 'invaded' India distinguished themselves from the original inhabitants of India as the 'twice born'. Three classes of twice born were recognized. The Brahmins performed the sacred functions. They had the right to study the Vedas. The khstriyas maintained the political order and the military functions; and the vaisyas supported the economic order. It is maintained that "The superior linguistic, cultural and social cohesion of the Aryans vis-a-vis the various non Aryan tribes and people, assured Aryan domination—political, social and cultural over the greater part of India even more than their military victories."[22] The once born were the non-Aryans and were classified as Sudras. They were not allowed either to hear or to read the Vedas and they were entrusted to perform the lower kind of physical labour.

Outside these four different caste, were the outcastes who performed menial tasks such as scavenging. Any contact of them with the higher castes was forbidden, since they were considered to be untouchables. They lived separately and were totally kept outside the influence of society. Thus, the different castes which were originally distinguished in accordance with the functions later came to be distinguished in relation to birth (jati). The reference to the different classes is found in the hymn to Purusa in the Rigveda:

"When they divided Purusa, into how many parts did they arrange him? What was his mouth? What are his two arms? What are his thighs and feet called? The brahmin was his mouth, his two arms were made the rajanya (warrior), his two thighs the vaisyas (trader and agriculturist), from his feet the Sudra (servile class) was born.[23]

The reference to the four different castes is also found in the fourth chapter of the *Bhagavadgita*.

> *"Chaturvarnam mayam srastam guna karma vibhagacha"*[24]
> "the four fold order was created by me according to the divisions of quality and work."

A similar functional distinction is also found in the ideal state of Plato where social divisions are related to different states of the soul. A predominance of wisdom in the soul produces philosopher kings, a predominane of courage produces soldiers, and where vigour is found we have workers. These three fold division within the state corresponds to distinctions within the soul which were created by God and mythically expressed as gold, silver and bronze... but God as he was fashioning you, put gold in those who are capable of ruling, ... Silver in the auxiliaries and iron and copper in the farmers and other craftsmen.'[25]

Martin Luther also expressed a similar view when he maintained that the three classes namely, the teaching class, the defending class and the working class were all ordained by God. It is the duty of every man to perform his duty according to the class to which he belongs. The growth of the caste system is found to some extent in the Laws of Manu. The offsprings of the mixed marriages were looked down upon and especially the offspring of the result of union between a Brahmin woman and a Sudra man was called a "Chandala' and he was the most despised one who was excluded from all consideration of the dharma or law.

Gandhiji it should be noted defended the order of the caste system so far as it is related to the functional aspect, in the sense of the social functions which were related to one's status in the society but he was deadly againt the caste system when it stood for the practice of untouchability. According to Mahatma Gandhi all functions in a society were to be treated with equal respect and no form of labour were either superior or inferior in status. A man should try to develop the skills and proficiency of his forefathers no doubt, but a person's aptitude or interest should also be taken into account. Gandhi also maintained that a man's acceptance of his hereditary profession would necessarily put in check the development of ambition which would help one in its turn to release surplus energy for spiritual pursuit.[26]

As Gandhi said "Birth and observance of forms cannot determine one's superiority or inferiority. Character is the only determining factor,... no scripture which labels a human being as inferior or untouchables because of his or her birth, can command our allegiance, it is a denial of God and Truth.[27] Gandhiji himself was the victim of colour prejudice and racial discrimination in South Africa. He became an object of humiliation several times, simply because he was a 'black'. This created a strong impression on the mind of young Gandhi. He realised that all men are created equal, hence the question of superiority or inferiority cannot arise in a kingdom created by God. Hence Gandhi regarded untouchability as a denial of the principle of equality and therefore a sin against God. In the words of Gandhiji "Untouchability as it is practised in Hinduism today is in my opinion, a sin againt God and man, and is therefore, like a poison slowly eating into the very vitals of Hinduism. In my opinion, it has no sanction whatsoever in the Hindu shastras taken as a whole. Untouchability of a healthy kind is undoubtedly to be found in the shastras and it is universal in all religions. It is a rule of sanitation. But untouchability as we are observing today in India is a hideous thing....It has stunted the growth of nearly 40 million human beings. They are denied even the ordinary amenities of life. The sooner therefore it is ended, the better for Hinduism, the better for India and perhaps better for mankind in general."[28]

When Gandhiji was young he was taught by a Brahmin the text, "Jale vishnu Sthale vishnu' (there is the Lord present in water and there is the Lord present in earth) which ever remained in his heart. He was also taught the 'Rama Raksha' which never pointed to the contact with untouchables as a sin. Even the *Ramayana* does not bear any testimony to the existence of this custom. Gandhiji thought and often wondered,"how can the *Ramayana*, in which one who is regarded as an untouchable today, take Rama across the Ganges in his boat, countenance the idea of any human being as 'untouchable'?[29]

The people who are so called untouchables has immense potentialities latent in them. Some are more cultured and educated than the so called men of high castes. We can cite here the example of B.R. Ambedkar, who was himself an outcaste, and also a well-known lawyer. Gandhiji recognizes Ambedkar's intellectual distinction and eminence and shows how silly it was for orthodox Brahmins to count him untouchable simply because he was born a Mahar, or an untouchable.[30] Gandhiji tried to remove the practice of untouchable in every possible way both by precept and example. Gandhi felt so strongly about it that he expressed the desire that should he not attain moksha or liberation from the realm of samsara, he should be born as an untouchable, so that he might identify himself with their sufferings and sorrows. Gandhiji himself did that work of scavenging. He also persuaded his wife to follow his example. At Durban, the Gandhi house had no running water, each room had a chamber pot. Gandhi refused to employ an "Untouchable' or sweepter, who in India does all the unclean jobs. Gandhi, Kasturba and sometimes the older boys carried out the pots. But there was once a boarder in their house, who was an untouchable and who became a Christian later on. To the orthodox Kasturba, he was still an untouchable and she refused to clean his pot. For this refusal Gandhi had a quarrel with his wife and later forced her to do it cheerfully. In Gandhi's ashram later on an eighteen year old Brahmana boy was doing scavenger's work. The boy was born and bred in orthodoxy. He was a regular reader of the Gita and faithfully performed his sandhya. But he felt that his accomplishments were incomplete until he had become also a sweeper and if he wanted the ashram was sweeper to do his work well, he felt that he must set example himself.

When Gandhi was only twelve, a scavenger named Uka, an untouchable used to attend his house for cleaning latrine. Gandhiji often asked his mother why he was forbidden to touch Uka and if he accidentally did so, he was made to undergo all the rituals to purify himself. Gandhiji often protested against this issue of considering physical contact with Uka, standing for all untouchables as sinful. When we perform functions involving unclean jobs or infectious diseases, we remain untouchables so long as we do not clean ourselves. Gandhi cites the example of a nurse. In the process of nursing a patient with infectious diseases or a person bleeding profusely; the nurse so long as she dresses his wounds may remain an untouchable. But after she has cleaned and changed she no longer remains an untouchable. This is to show that one is not an untouchable by birth.[31]

Gandhiji's conviction that untouchability is a serious evil is supported even by the *Bhagavadgita*, the greatest book of inspiration to the Mahatma. During the Congress week a conference on untouchability was held at Belgaum in which Mr. Gandhi said "I regard the untouchables as an integral part of the Hindu community. I am pained when I see a single Bhangi driven out of the fold of Hinduism. But I do not believe that all class distinctions can be obliterated. I believe in the doctrine of equality as taught by Lord Krishna in the *Gita*. The *Gita* teaches us that the members of all the four castes should be treated on an equal basis. It does not prescribe the same dharma for the brahmana as for the bhangi. But it insists that the latter shall be entitled to the same measure of consideration and esteem as the former with all his superior learning. It is therefore our duty to see that the untouchables do not feel that they are despised or looked down upon. Let them not be offered left overs from our plates for their subsistence. How can I offer differential treatment to any person be he brahmana or bhangi, who worships the same God and keeps his body and soul pure and clean? ..... Just as we revere our mother for the sanitary service that she renders us when we are infants, and the greater her service the greater is the reverence for her, similarly the bhangis are entitled to our highest reverence for the sanitary service they render to society.[32]

Gandhiji relied on the *Gita* for strength in doing away with untouchability. "Today the *Gita* is not only my Bible or my *Quran* it is more than that - it is my mother....often in the course of my struggle against untouchability I am confronted with conflicting opinions....some of them tell me that untouchability as it is practised today has no sanction in Hinduism and they bless my efforts to eradicate it, but there are some others who maintain that untouchability has been an essential part of Hinduism. Which authority should I follow under the circumstances? I feel absolutely at sea. I then approach the mother and say, "Mother....Help me out of perplexity. And the mother, with a smile, say in reply: 'The assurance held out by me in the ninth chapter is not meant for brahmans only, but for the sinner and the outcastes, the down trodden and the disinherit too.[33]

"man hi Partha vyapasritya yepi syuh papyonayah Striyo vaisyastatha shudrast epi yanti Param gatim"[34] For finding refuse in Me, even those who though are born of the womb of sin, women, vaishyas, and shudras too, reach the supreme goal.

But the question arises here: By what method can untouchability be removed? Here again Gandhiji brings in his twofold maxims of truth and non-violence. Gandhiji had adapted an untouchable child as his own. Here he could not convert his wife because she could not bring herself to love the child as much as Gandhiji did. But Gandhiji believed that if he could ever convert his wife on this point the only way was by means of love and understanding. Untouchability like any other evils could not be removed by force. Thus Gandhiji believed that the orthodox Hindus could be converted only by patient argument. He wanted the untouchables to have the right of worship in any temple. Their children must get admission to any school without any discrimination being made and the untouchables should even be eligible to the highest office in this land. While Gandhiji was in Yeravada jail he undertook a first on behalf of the untouchables. It was a protest against the Hindu maltreatment of the untouchables and for the good of the Harijans. Gandhi regarded fasting as a weaker form of satyagraha and here, he believed, he could identify himself with the sufferings of the untouchables by self-imposed suffering. The fast had the powerful effect of creating a spirit of reform throughout India and also an improvement in the conditions of the Harijans. Though it couldn't abolish untouchability, it was useful in the sense that it made the practice of untouchability less socially acceptable.

Gandhi relates the question of untouchability to his basic ideas of Truth, Ahimsa and Sarvodaya when he states; "The observance of the vow of untouchabiity is not fulfilled merely by making friends with 'untouchables', but by loving all life as one's own self. Removal of untouchability means love for, and service of, the whole world, and it thus merges into Ahimsa.[35]

Gandhi was well aware of the fact that changes in the life of the Harijans could be brought about only by a change in the attitude and outlook of the people in the society. So simply making friends with the untouchables was not enough. This is why he insists on the purity of the Hindu way of life by enforcing the ethical and religious principles of Truth and Ahimsa and thus bringing about a complete change of attitudes. Closely related to the problem of untouchability is the problem of racial discrimination and colour prejudice of which Gandhiji was himself a victim in South Africa. Once when Gandhi boarded a train from Durban to Pretoria, a first class seat was booked for him. A passenger, noticing that Gandhi was a 'black' asked him to leave the first class compartment. He came back again with two officials, one of them asked Gandhi to go to the van compartment. When Gandhi refused, he was forcibly thrown out along with the luggage with the help of a police constable. Gandhiji felt very much humiliated and realised the fact that this treatment to which he was subjected was only a symptom of the deep disease of colour prejudice.[36] Gandhiji's first step in this direction was to call a meeting of the Indian in Pretoria and to present them a picture of the conditions of the coloured people in the Transvaal. He suggested the formation of an association on a permanent basis to defend the rights of the Indians and to put the case before the authorities from time to time. Gandhiji studied the railway regulations of the Transvaal,wrote to the railway authorities and told that even under their own rules the Indians were entitled to travel in any class for which they bought a ticket. The authorities replied that henceforth first and second class travel would be open to Indians provided they were properly dressed. Thus Gandhi's long struggle against untouchability and colour prejudice could achieve some result.

Henry Brailsford has paid a glowing tribute to this

achievement of removal of untouchability: "The campaign of this mystic, who cleaned latrines on one day and opened temples the next, is one of the strongest chapters in history and one of the noblest. Has any saint in human history done more to lighten the mistery of the oppressed and restore their self-respect? He had broken a cruel institution that dated from an ancient time, based on superstition...India honours Gandhiji today chiefly because he led the fight for independence. Humanity owes him an even heavier debt because he opened the road of the untouchables to freedom."[37]

HARIJANS AND TEMPLE ENTRY

Another notable achievement of Mahatma Gandhi in the social field was that he could secure for the harijans the right of free entry into the Hindu temple. Formerly the harijans or untouchables were denied this right.

According to Gandhiji the essence of Hinduism is latent in one single verse of the *Isopanishad.* "isavasga midam sarvam, Yatkincha jagatyamjagat."

It means 'All that I see in this great universe is pervaded by God.' God is thus present in everything, not to speak of human beings As such, how can the Harijans or the untouchables be denied the right to temple entry which are houses of God?

Gandhiji adopted the word 'Harijan' for 'untouchables. 'Harijan' means 'a man of God'. All the religions of the world describe God as the friend of the friendless, help of the helpless and protector of the weak. And in India, perhaps there is no one more helpless and more needy than these group of people classified as untouchables. Gandhiji fought for the equal rights for the harijans in all spheres of life. Since God is the creator of all beings it is unjustified that a section of the people be denied his blessings on the ground that they are 'untouchables. Therefore the harijans must be free to visit all temples that are open to the Hindus. According to Gandhiji it is the devotee's devotion that makes a temple a living shrine. As Gandhiji said "If you discover that you will not be allowed into a temple along with your Harijan companions, then you will shun that temple as you shun a scorpion or fire, you will then believe with me that such a temple is not inhabited by God. I will take by way of illustration the greatest temple known all over the world that is Kashi Visvanath in Banaras. The Lord who is supposed to reside there, is known as the Lord of the universe. Yet in the very name of Viswanath the savarna Hindus have the impudence to say to the Harijans—"You shall not come to this temple."[38]

Gandhiji implemented the technique of satyagraha on behalf of the untouchables who were forbidden to use the roads in the vicinity of the Vykom Temple in Travancore. The aim of this satyagraha was to open the road and the temple to the untouchables. He thus tried to eliminate the discrimination against the untouchables and Harijans. Thus Gandhiji put his idea of Sarvodaya into practice by showing his concern for the welfare of all men and Harijans in particular who were the most exploited class.

INTER-DINING AND INTER-MARRIAGE

Inter-dining and inter-marriage are important social problems specially in a Hindu society and therefore deserve special mention. Both inter-dinning and inter-marriage according to Gandhi are matters of choice not matters of regulation. They are in fact the result of social habits. Gandhiji does not regard inter-dining and inter-marriage as essential to the removal of untouchability. The Vedas and the Mahabharata are full of illustrations both of inter-dining and inter marriage. In ancient times, it is believed that there was no water tight compartment between varnas so far as marital and social relations were concerned. According to Gandhiji, we have done a great harm to Hinduism by making 'Varna' a matter of mere restrictions about food, drink and marriage. Gandhiji favoured inter-dining and inter-marriage because it helped to foster the sense of unity amongst various classes. He greatly encouraged couples of inter caste marriage with his blessings. But he also finds justification in marriage amongst one's own community. Gandhiji said in an article of "Hinduism" thus: "Hinduism reached the highest limit of self-restraint. It is undoutedly a religion of the renunciation of flesh so that the spirit may be set free ..... By restricting the choice of a bride to a particular group, he exercises rare self-restraint...prohibition against inter-dining and inter-marriage is essential for the rapid evolution of the soul."[39]

Some writers pointed out to Gandhiji's inconsistencies in his own writing here beceause in another article Gandhi writes:

"Restrictions in inter-caste dining and inter-caste marriage is no part of Hindu religion. It is a social custom which crept into Hinduism when perhaps it was in its decline....Dining and marriage restriction stunt Hindu society.[40] The point to be noted here is that in Gandhi's opinion a super imposed restriction on inter dining and inter-marriage would stunt the growth of a society but it does not mean that they are essential or indispensable for the promotion of the spirit of brotherhood. What is essential is that one should not despise people belong to any different caste and one should have an equal respect for persons belonging in to different caste. Now the question before us is: Can inter-caste marriage and inter dining be regarded as the effective means of removing untouchability? Gandhi's answer to this question is both affirmative and negative—he says, "My answer is, no and yes. 'No" because it is no part of the programme of the Harijan Sevak Sangh. Generally, marrying and dining are matters of individual concern. No one has a right to ask another to choose a girl for wife or to dine with anybody against his will. But my answer is at the same time 'Yes', because if a person refuses to take food touched by another person on the ground of untouchability or inferiority, he is observing untouchability."[41] But Gandhiji believed that dining and inter-marriage must be left to the choice of the individual as to whom and where he or she will marry or dine.

Gandhiji's one son Devdas fell in love with a Brahmana girl. As a reformer of Hinduism he did not object to the marriage but only wanted that it should stand the test of love. When Indira Gandhi was engaged to Feroz Gandhi, a Parsi, Gandhiji welcomed the union. But Gandhiji was opposed to either party changing religion for the sake of marriage. To-day our Government is trying to encourage inter-caste marriage by giving awards to such couples. But still the percentage of inter-caste marriage is quite low. What is required is a change of attitudes and beliefs. Unless there is a change in the outlook of the people, inter-caste marriage and inter-dining cannot be popularized.

THE PHILOSOPHY OF COW PROTECTION

Mahatma Gandhi's belief in Advaita finds its expression in his attitude towards the animal kingdom. His belief in the essential unity of all existence is the result of his faith in the ethical and religious principles specially of Hinduism. It is this belief in the essential unity of life that underlies his feeling of oneness with the animal kingdom and consequently his support of cow protection.

The word 'Cow protection' has a much wider significance for Gandhi, for he uses it to mean protection of all that lives. As Gandhiji said "cow protection to me is infinitely more than mere protection of the cow...cow protection means protection of the weak, the helpless, the dumb and the deaf. Man becomes then not the lord and master of all creation but he is its servant."[42] A true follower of Ahimsa cannot allow the killing of animals. Therefore Gandhi insisted that a Hindu who protects the cow should protect every animal. For him the cow epitomises the sub human world, it is a plea for justice on behalf of the animal world.

In the Hindu religion there is a famous sloka which salutes the cow as follows:

"Namo brahmanya devaya go brahmana hitayaca

jagadhitaya krisnaya govindaya namo namoh." Gandhi believed that it is not justified to kill animals for the sake of food and Gandhi quotes Goldsmith in support of his view. "No flocks that range the valley free, To slaughter I condemn, Taught by the power that pities me I learn to pity them.[43]

Non-violence towards animals and other living creatures is an important aspect of Hinduism and specially of the Jaina religion. Protection of the cow is a step for putting this lofty ideal into practice. Gandhiji believed that the animals should also be put on the same level as human beings so far as the right to live is concerned. To put in Gandhi's own words:- "For me the cow is a personification of innocence and cow protection means the protection of the weak and the helpless."[44] Again he said "The cow is a poem of pity. One reads pity in the gentle animal. She is the mother to millions of Indians. Protection of the cow means protection of the whole dumb creation of God."[45] Not only Hinduism, even Christianity and Islam do not favour the killing of animals and cow slaughter. This is evident from the following saying of the commandments:-

1. He that killeth an ox (male and female) is as if he slew a man. He that sacrificeth a lamb, as if he cut off a god's neck.[46]
2. It is good neither to eat flesh, nor to drink wine.[47]

Denouncing violence the prophet of Islam says "Fear God in respect of these dumb animals, ride them when they are fit to be ridden and get off when they are tired."[48] Again the Prophet said that the most excellent jehad is that of the conquest of the self.[49] According to Paul Tillich, man has nature at his command in the Western societies. The sympathetic attitude to the natural world that characterizes Gandhi's teaching, contrasts with the highly technological society of the western world. The technological control of nature which is found in the west has been interpreted as the fulfillment of God's command to Adam to exercise domination over all the earth and over every living thing.[50] How far these interpretations of Christianity are true it is difficult to say but one thing is certain that the reverence for the animal kingdom specially the cow is more prominent in the Hindu society and its offeshoots—Jainism and Buddism.

Tillich also refers to the control of nature when he discusses the relation between Christianity and Buddhism. He maintains that the main concepts of these two religions are the kingdom of God in Christianity and Nirvana in Buddhism. The Kingdom of God, according to him is characterized by the notion o "Participation', that is 'one participates in the kingdom of God as an individual'. The notion of Nirvana on the other hand is characterised by the feelings of identity. There can be no exploitation of nature by the presence of such a feelings of identity. The principles of identity as Tillich points out, as a principle of Hinduism finds expression in the prohibition of the killing of animals which is related to the belief that a man may be re-incarnated in animal form as a result of the operation of the Law karma, that is bad actions or karma in the past life leadus to a lower birth. This implies that a man desists from killing animals out of fear that he may be killing a reincarnated soul. But Gandhi's concept of identity is somewhat different that being simply a question of self interest. It stands for the essential unity of all beings which generates the feeling of compassion for the sub human world also.[51]

But though Gandhi advocated the principle of non-violence in every walk of life, it should not be thought that he carried out this ideal blindly. The question may arise: What should one do in case of venomous snakes, mosquitoes, disease carrying rats, fleas and so on? Gandhi here tried to solve the problem by holding that men's life is an aspiration towards perfection and in an imperfect world one has to make concession to human weakness. This does not however mean that Gandhi is trying to modify or make compromise with the ideal of non-violence. In certain situations one had to resort to violence for the welfare of the greater number. For example there is full justification for the use of violence against murderers and robbers; in order to protect the lives of others.

The ancient Hindu sages believed that the protection of the cow leads one to moksha or self-realisation. But Gandhi does not accept such a view. He says "I am not ready to believe that by merely protecting the animal cow, one can obtain Moksha. For moksha one must completely get rid of one's lower feelings like attachment, hatred, anger, jealousy etc. It follows therefore that the meaning of cow protection in terms of moksha must be much wider and far more comprehensive than is commonly supposed. The cow protection which can bring one moksha must from its very nature, include the protection of everything that feels. Therefore in my opinion, every little breach of the Ahimsa principle, like causing hurt by harsh speech to any one man, woman or child, to cause pain to the weakest and the most insignificant creature on earth would be a breach of the principle of cow protection."[52]

Gandhi was of the opinion that cow slaughter could not be stopped by law. Gandhi emphasised that there should be no prohibition of cow slaughter by legislation. Knowledge, education and the spirit of kindness towards cow alone can put an end to it. Gandhiji with his constructive mind laid various programmes of establishing Goshala, dairy farms, tanneries, pasture land an so on. In later times, Gandhi's emphasis on cow protection found expression at the hands of the framer of the constitution of India who have enshrined it in the Directive Principles of State Policy' under Article 48: "The state shall endevour to organise agriculture and animal husbandry in modern and scientific lines and shall, in particular, take steps for preserving and improving the breeds and prohibiting the slaughter of cows and calves and draught cattle." To Gandhi "Cow slaughter and man slaughter are the two sides of the same coin."[53]

THE STATUS OF WOMEN IN SOCIETY

No man in India has done more than Mahatma Gandhi to restore the dignity of women in society. In this respect also, as in other spheres of life Gandhi has been prompted by the ideals of truth, non-violence and sarvodaya.

The status of women at a stage in the evolution of Hindu society was not equal to that of men: women were regarded as being inferior in status to men as a result of which the women have developed a sort of inferiority complex. But though this is a picture of the general society, our ancient seers and learned men have realised the great potentialities in women. No wonder they have addressed her as 'sakti'—the source of all creation and strength. We find in the ancient Hindu scriptures that women were highly honoured. She was addressed as godess (devi), friend (sakhi), auspicious (Mangala) and who was joyfully welcomed as the empress (Samrajni)—the ruler of the husband's household. Women were always recognised as the better half. No religious ceremony in Hinduism is complete without the wife who is a 'dharma patni' to her husband. But then came a period of about thousand years which brought gloomy picture for women. She came to be looked upon as an object for pleasure. Gandhi, however, recognises the fact that physically there are vital differences between men and women. Hence their respective functions are different. Gandhiji therefore strongly disapproved the modern tendency in women to imitate men in every sphere. If the mother does not look after her children the race would become extinct. There is as much bravery in keeping one's house in order as there is in defending it against external enemies.

Thus Gandhi, having recognised the division of labour amongst men and women was of the opinion that the general qualities and culture required are same for both. He even encouraged those women who preferred to live an independent life of celibacy to devote their life to social service. But even though Gandhiji encouraged some women to follow celibacy, he believed in the ideal of marriage for women in general. He said — "it is no doubt an excellent thing for girls to remain unmarried for the sake of service, but the fact is that only one in a million is able to of so."[54] Gandhiji expressed the view that the real ornament of a women is her character and purity. Metals and stones can be no real ornaments. The names of Sita and Damayanti have become immortal not for their external jewellery but for their inner virtues. Therefore the asking of ornaments by Gandhiji in the form of donation had a much wider significance. Gandhi wrote "I wish to bring home to the women that real ornamentation is not in loading the body the metals and stones but in purifying the heart and developing the beauty of the soul."[55]

Gandhiji wanted women to take part in politics too and have independent thinking. Women should not merely live to carry out her parents or her husband's wishes. Women should be enrolled as voters and have practical education in any field of knowledge. As legislation is mainly the creation of men, they have been biased in framing the laws of society. Gandhiji maintained that women should work under no disability which is not suffered by men Gandhi devoted a great deal to the removal of many Indian customs that stood as a barrier for the free development of womanhood. Gandhiji vigorously opposed the system of purdah which was imposed on women, Originally purdah was on Islamic practice of veiling the faces of women and later on it came to be accepted by the Hindus. The main aim of the purdah system was to maintain the purity of women to protect their wives from other men. According to Gandhiji by such practices we reduce women to the status of slaves or property of their husbands. He considered it unjust on the part of men to consider himself as having the right to guard his wife's purity. If that be so, women should have the right to guard the purity of their husbands, Gandhiji considered it to be a fundamental mistake to assume that chastity was some kind of hot house plant to be protected by the walls of purdah. "Chastity was not something that could be imposed from without. It was something that grew from within."[56] Gandhiji realised that women as the embodiment of love and Ahimsa should participate in the day to day problems of the nation. According to Gandhi: "My contribution to the great problem lies in my presenting for acceptance truth and Ahimsa in every walk of life, whether for individuals or for nations. I have hugged the hope that in this women will be the unquestioned leader and having thus found her place in human evolution, will shed her inferiority complex. I have suggested in these column that women is the incarnation of Ahimsa. Ahimsa means infinite love which again means infinite capacity for suffering. Who but women, the mother of men shows this capacity in the largest measure? She shows it as she carries the infants and feeds it during nine months and derives joy in the suffering involved. What can beat the sufferings caused by the pangs of labour? But she forgets them in the joy of creation, who again suffers daily so that her babe may grow from day to day? Let her transfer that love to the whole of humanity.... It is given to her to teach the art of peace to the warring world. She can become the leader in satyagraha which does not require the learning that books give but does require the stout heart that comes from suffering and faith."[57]

The long struggle of Gandhi to establish the rights of women bore excellent fruits. How Indian women stood heroically by their menfolk,not only in he struggle for freedom, but also in the fight agaisnt caste, tyranny, superstition and against a multitude of social evils like drinking, child marriage etc. is a glaring proof of the success achieved in this respect.

BRAHMACHARYA

As has been discussed earlier in the 'Philosophical and religious principles of Gandhi', Brahmacharya means a way of life dedicated to or practice of brahma or God. But the word is generally used to mean life of self-restraint. Gandhi borrowed his idea of brahmacharya from the Hindu

Dharma shastras and adopted and modified it in his own way. Gandhiji realised that the great cause to which he and his followers dedicated themselves required a considerable amount of self-control. This self control can be acquired only if one has acquired control in other ways namely of thought, speech and action. In Gandhiji's words—"its root meaning may be given thus: that conduct which puts one in touch with God. The conduct consists in the fullest control over all the senses....popularly it has to come to mean mere physical control over the organ of generation. This narrow/meaning has debased brahmacharya and made its practice all but impossible. Control over the organ of generation is impossible without proper control of all the senses."[58]

Gandhiji's idea of brahmacharya is not as rigid as that of the Buddhist or Jaina thinkers. As Gandhiji says—"absolute renunciation, absolute Brahmacharya is the ideal state. If you dare not think of it, marry by all means, but even then live a life of self-control."[59] He realised that without self control one could not have true dedication. No worker who has not over comes lust can dedicate himself to the cause of Harijans, communal unity, Khadi, cow protection or village re-construction. "Great causes like these cannot be served by intellectual equipment alone, they call for spiritual effort or soul force. Soul force comes only through God's grace, and God's grace never descends upon a man who is slave to lust."[60] Marriage, according to Gandhi is a natural thing in life. But what is required is that one should live a life of self-restraint even within the married estate. The ideal of marriage is a spiritual union through the physical. The human love that marriage brings forth is a stepping stone to divine or universal love. Therefore he urged the married people to turn that human love into universal love through the practice of truth and non-violence.

The object of sexual relation, according to Gandhiji should be to have a issue when one intends to. He forbade sexual intercourse for the sake of mere pleasure. Slavery to passion makes moral and spiritual progress impossible. He also disapproves the modern tendencies in cinemas, magazine, pictures and music to rouse the sex instinct. To put it in his own words "Sex urge is a fine and noble things. There is nothing to be ashamed of in it. But it is meant only for the act of creation. Any other use of it is a sin against God and humanity. Contraceptives of a kind there were before and there will be hereafter, but the use of them was formerly regarded as sinful.... Let the young men and women of India beware of this and guard the treasure with which God blessed them and use it, if they wish, for the purpose for which it is intended."[61] Gandhiji himself practised brahmacharya after a certain age. Twice before he attempted to do so but could not succeed. But the third time he took a vow which was final. Gandhi remained a celibate from 1906, when he was thirty seven until his death. He believed that his celibacy was a response to the call of public duty and social service. Gandhi also had a sense of guilt about sex. When he was serving his father one night, he fell a victim to passion and went away to his wife, for which he could not be beside his father at the time of his father's death. "If passion has not blinded me, I should have been spared the torture of separation from my father during his last moments.... The share of my carnal desire at the critical moment of my father's death.... is a blot I shall never be able to efface or forget."[62] Gandhiji however seems to express paradoxical views regarding his attitude towards marriage and sex. Gandhiji holds marriage to be a sacrament. It is both a physical and spiritual union. Human love is a stepping stone to divine or universal love. The purpose of marriage should be friendship and companionship and not simply the gratification of the sexual desires.

Criticism

Gandhi goes too far when he says that in an ideal marriage there is no place for sexual satisfaction. According to Gandhi sexual intercourse should take place only when we desire to have an issue. But it is difficult to think of a sexual act without any reference to pleasure or satisfaction. Therefore it appears to be rather wrong when he maintains, for example, that 'The union is not meant for pleasure, but for bringing forth progeny. And union is a crime when the desire for progeny is absent.'[63] If this be so, then we cannot hold that sexual union is the culmination of the act of love between a man and a woman and is 'a stepping stone to divine universal love. Again how can sex be then conceived as a fine and noble thing, as Gandhi maintains without some amount of satisfaction? Gandhi also was against the use of contraceptives. In his view the use of contraceptive leads to an increase of vice with the loss of the power of self-restraint and results in the disillusion of the marriage bond but he does not explain clearly how the use of contraceptive is related to the break of the bond between two married people.

But in spite of the inconsistencies in his idea about sex and marriage, Gandhiji's contribution lies in recognizing the fact that excessive progagation of children should be stopped and he glorified the ancient Hindu practice of Brahmacharya. All the religions insist on some amount of self-restraint since without it men would degenerate to he level of animals. The *Kathopanishad* compares the senses to the horses and the sense objects to the spheres of their roving, the body to the chariot.[64] If the reins are not held firm, then the senses, like wicked horses, will become unmanageable, and if the individual has no control over his senses and mind, he will come to ruin. "Renunciation in Gandhiji's life redoubled his desire to work for human welfare. Greater control over the self gave him greater control over others." To be sure, storms continued to rage within him, but now he could harness them for the generation of more public power.'[65]

WIDOW REMARRIAGE AND CHILD MARRIAGE

Mahatma Gandhi's insistence on the right of remarriage for widow is a divergence from the long standing Hindu tradition according to which widows were bound to follow a life of strict celibacy, more so in the case of Brahmana widow. According to the custom of Sati, the widow has to burn herself along with her dead husband. Sometimes she was forced to do so by her relatives. Cases are on record when the woman out of fear used to jump out of fire but her body was again forcibly thrown back into the fire. This brutal act was stopped by legislation for the first time by Lord William Bentinck.

Though things had improved to some extent after that, a widow in India still had to face a very sorry plight. She had to undergo the tortures if she remained with her in-laws. Sometimes she became a burden to her parents. Gandhiji therefore gave all encouragement to widow remarriage. He believed that a women had an equal right to remmary as much as a man. In the words of Gandhi, "We cry out for cow protection in the name of religion, but we force widowhood upon our three lakhs of girl widows who could not understand the import of the marriage ceremony. To fórce widowhood upon little girls is a brutal crime for which we Hindus are paying dearly...voluntary widowhood consciously adopted by a woman, who has felt the affection of a patner adds grace and dignity to life, sanctifies the home and uplifts religion itself. Widowhood imposed by religion or custom is an intolerable yoke and defiles the home by secret vice and degrades religion. If we would be pure, if we want to save Hinduism, we must rid ourselves of this poison of enforced widowhood. the reform must begin by those who have girl widows, taking courage in both their hands and seeing that the child widows in their charge are duly and well married. They were really not married."[66] In Gandhiji's view, widow remarriage is no sin. Widowhood is an adornment to one who can observe it. But if she wished she has the full right to remmarry, just as a widower has. The statement that the widows attain moksha if they observe Brahmacharya has no foundation, according to Gandhiji, in experience. More things are necessary then mere brahmanarharya for the attainment of the final bliss. And brahmacharya that is superimposed carries no merit with it. Widow remarriage has nothing to do with the attainment of mukti. Gandhiji always was striving after mukti and it is the contemplation of his mukti which has given him the consciousness of the wrong done to maiden widow. Moreover "whilst there is, and very properly, glorification of real widowhood in Hinduism, there is so far to I am aware, no warrant for the belief that in the Vedic times there was any absolute ban upon the remarriage of widow. But my crusade is not against real widowhood. It is against its atrocious caricature ...... I therefore humbly but emphatically repeat the advice to every young Hindu to marry these maidens miscalled widows."[67]

Gandhiji also tried to abolish the custom of child marriage. In golden times it was considered to be a great social sin if girls attained puberty before marriage. According to Gandhiji the father is a guardian and not the owner of his children. It is therefore, undesirable, according to Gandhi to rid himself of the burden by giving her in marriage at a very early age.

THE DOWRY SYSTEM

The Dowry system is a great social evil which has plagued Indian society upto the modern times. Even today we hear of innumerable cases of young girls committing suicide being unable to bear the torture of her in-laws for failing to bring enough dowry. As Gandhiji said, "any young man who makes dowry a condition for marriage discredits his education and his country and dishonors womanhood.... A strong public opinion should be created in condemnation of this degrading practice of dowry, and young men who soil their fingers with such ill golden goods should be excommunicated from society."[68] Gandhiji wanted the parents to educate their daughters in such a way that they would refuse to marry one who wanted a price for marrying and would rather remain spinters than sit for marriage, Gandhiji believed on mutual love and mutual consent. Gandhiji condemned the evil of dowry in the following way: "Marriage must cease to be a matter of arrangement made by parents for money. The system is intimately connected with caste. So long as the choice is restricted to a few hundred young men or young women of a particular caste, the system will persist no matter what is said against it. The girls or boys or their parents will have to break the bonds of caste if the evil is to be eradicated. Then the age for marrying has also to be raised and the girls have to dare to remain spinsters if need be that is, if they do not get a suitable match. All this means education of a character that will revolutionise the mentality of the youth of a nation.[69]

PROHIBITION

According to Gandhiji, we must not live in order to eat, drink and be merry, but eat and drink in order to make our bodies temples of God and to use them for the service of men. Hence he condemns strongly the habit of drinking and smoking. The drinking habit destroys the soul of man and turns him into a beast. Gandhiji was well aware of the dangerous effect of wine not only on the user but on others as well. As he wrote in *Young India,*" As the Gita said, one had to shape one's conduct not merely accordingly to one's own requirement but also with an eye to the effect that it would have on others And if they saw the terrible havoc that this habit was causing among the working classes of India they would take a solemn vow not to touch liquor."[70]

Abstinence in India is a time honoured tradition from the days of the Vedas, the Upanishads, the Puranas and the Smritis up to Raja Ram Mohan Roy. The use of liquor has been too strongly condemned by them and Gandhi has also forbidden the use of liquor. According to Gandhi "Drink and drugs spoil the moral well being of those who are given to this habit."[71]

Lord Christ says, "he that eateh and drinketh unworthy, eateth and drinketh damnation to himself, not discerning the Lord's body."[72] The *Vinaya Pittaka* of the Buddhist declares, "He who drinks intoxicants commits grave offence." Abstinence is included in the five codes of Right conduct (panachasila).[73]

There are some people who use drinks and intoxicants in the name of religion. But Gandhiji does not encourage such a view. The Parsis have strongly supported the use of toddy. Toddy according to them is also a food and aids in digestion.

But according to Gandhi the use of such toddy was harmful. He expressed the view that drinks had been responsible for the destruction of even communities. Gandhiji said, "history records, that empires have been destroyed through that habit. The great community to which Srikrishna belonged was ruined by that habit. This monstrous evil was undaubteadly one of the contributory factors in the fall of Rome."[74] Gandhiji believed that cigarette smoking was as injurious as alcohol, similarly according to him one should not become a slave to even tea and coffee. Gandhiji once cited an example from Tolstoy's story in which a drunkard is hesitating to execute his design of murder so long as he has not smoked his cigar. But he puffs it, and then gets up smilling and saying, 'What a coward am I:' Takes the dagger and does the deed.[75]

Gandhiji is constant fight against drink and other intoxicants found expression in the section under the Directive Principles of State Policy' of our Indian Constitution. It expressed the states endevour to bring about prohibition, except for medicinal purposes. Thus Gandhiji's constant effort in respect of prohibition was a reform in the social sphere which naturally had a tremendous effect on the individual and consequently on the nation.

GANDHI'S ATTITUDE TOWARDS OTHER RELIGIONS

Mahatma Gandhi's attitude towards other religions seems to be an echo of the liberal attitude towards different forms of worship in Hindusim since the days of Rgveda.[76]

"Ekam sat vipra bahudha vadanti Agnim yamam matarisvanam ahuh."

"Truth is one, only th wise describe it is many ways. The spread of Hinduism is described in the epics of the *Ramayana* and the *Mahabharata*. Worship was paid to the supreme being under different names. According to the Bhagavadgita the supreme accepts us as we are, no matter how we approach Him, for all paths in which we wander are His. In the Mahimna stotram it is said that the faiths of men if they are dynamic and sincere, are like rivers which eventually went their way to the ocean, and when they reach it, all of them lose their separate identity.[77] The Puranas continue the tradition. The Supreme which is essentially one according to *Vishnu Purana* assumes the name of Brahma at the time of creation, of Vishnu while maintaining it and of Siva at the time of destruction. "Srististhitiyatakaranim brahmavisnusivabidhan Sa sajnam yati bhagavan eka eva janardanah"[78] This attitude of the Hindus is based on a definite philosophy of life which assumes that religion is a matter of personal realisation. The name by which we call God and the rite by which we approach him do not matter much. Many names have been given to the Absolute by the different learned men. It is called person by the Sankhya thinkers. Brahman by the Vedantists, pure and simple consciousness by the Vijnanvadins, Sunya by the Nihilists and so on. An enlightened Hindu is ready to accept any religious figure in whom the light of God has manifested. He is regarded as an avatar or an incarnaion of God. The *Bhagavadgita* says:

jada jada hi dharmasya glani bhavati bharata abhyutthanamadharmsya Tadathanam srijarmyaham[79]

["whenever righteousness declines and unrighteousness prevails I am born from age to age."]

Islam is called 'deen UI Haqq' or the religion of faith. According to the *Quran* 'there is one God and Muhammud is his prophet." Again the *Quran* says "We believe in God and the revelation given to us and to Abraham and Ishmail, Issac, Jacob, and that given to Moses and Jesus and that given to other apostles from their Lord. We make no difference between them.[80] The Sufis believe that just that it is the lustre of one sun that shines in the different sea waves and bubbles so it is one Truth that is expressed under the cover of different forms. Muhammud Ali in his translation of the *Quran* says: "It (Islam) requires them (men) to preach their own religion but not by assuming the religion of others....the religious freedom was established by Islam in a country like Arabia thirteen hundred years ago....It deserves to be noted that the lives of th Muslims are to be sacrificed not only to stop their own persecution by their opponents and to save churches, synagogues and cloisters as well—in fact to establish perfect religious freedom."[81]

Thus Gandhiji's religious toleration blossomed into a beautiful flower from the seed of toleration planted in him by the Hindu tradition. In a weekly letter written to the inmates of the Ashram at Sabarmati, written from Yeravada Central Prison in 1930, Gandhiji wrote: "Ahimsa teaches us to entertain the same respect for the religious faiths of others....This is made by the seeker of Truth, who follows the Law of Love. If we had attained the full vision of Truth,we would no longer be mere seekers but would have become one with God, for Truth is God. But being only seekers we prosecute our quest and are conscious of our imperfection. And if we are imperfect ourselves, religion as conceived by us must also be imperfect. Religion is always subject to a process of evolution and re-interpretation...Looking at all religions with an equal eye, we would not only hesitate, but would think to be our duty, to blend into our faith every acceptable feature of other faiths.[82] Gandhiji had used the analogy of the body and the soul to explain the existence of different faiths. The soul is one but the bodies which animates it are many, yet we recognise the unity of the soul. Again just as a single tree has many branches and roots similarly there is one true and perfect relgion, but it becomes many when it passes through the human medium. Hence the necessity of tolerance. Tolerance gives us spiritual insight and brings down the barrier between faith and faith.[83]

Mahatma Gandhi said: "I believe in the fundamental truth of all great religions of the world. I believe that they are all God given....And I believe that, if only we could read the scriptures of the different faiths from the standpoint of the followers of those faiths, we should find that they were at bottom all one an were all helpful to one another."[84] When Gandhiji went through the sacred books of different faiths like Christianity, Islam, Hinduism, Judaism and Zoroastrianism, he found that the different religions were beautiful flowers from the same garden.

The prayer at Gandhiji's Ashram at Phoenix in South Africa contained recitations from all religions and so also in India. Gandhiji was inspired in this line from his very childhood. As he says in his autobiography, "You have a knack of pleasing all Gods: said Sardar Patel on one occasion "Oh yes," said Gandhiji, "that was what my mother taught me. She would ask me to go to the Haveli, and also to the Siva temple, and you may be interested to hear that when we were married we were taken to worship not only to all the Hindu shrines but to a fakir's shrine as well."[85] The prayer meetings at Sabarmati too were attended by Hindus, Mussalmans and Christians as well. In the songs and the prayers, the name of Rama would sometimes be substituted for Ahuramazda. Sometimes the word 'Christian' would be used in place of Vaishanava, thus showing equal respect for all religions. Gandhiji always sang 'Rama Rahim', 'Krishna Karim' as well as "*Isvara Allah tere nam.*" In the Agakhan Palace at Poona in 1942 on the eve of the ramajan Idd, Gandhiji declared his intention to take only dates and milk on the next day, which were the prophets favourite articles of food and gave up bread and vegetables which were Gandhiji's favourites. Once in South Africa he kept Roza (fast) for the whole month.

The realisation of the need for unity in diversity, should not be mere toleration, for 'toleration' is a word which does not seem proper to Gandhiji. We should respect other faiths as our own. The world cannot be reduced to one religion, one culture and one language. It should be a federation of religion, cultures and languages, according to Gandhi.

The Jaina theory of anekantavada and Syadvada teaches us that every man is right from his own standpoint. Gandhiji tried his best to put this great philosophy into practice. He appreciatied the story of the seven blind men who gave seven different descriptions of the elephant They were all right from their respective points of view though partially. Gandhiji was greatly inspired by the doctrine of many sidedness of reality advocated by Jaina philosophy. To put in his own words "it is this doctrine that has taught me to judge a Mussalman from his own stand point and a Christian from his. Formerly I used to resent the ignorance of my opponents. Today I love them because I am gifted with the eye to see myself as others see me and vice versa. I want to take the whole world in the embrace of my love.'[86]

Gandhiji described how he derived comfort in difficult times from both the *Bhagavadgita* and the *New Testament*. He has also pointed out that these two scriptures also agree on various fundamental principles. He said "I have not been able to see any difference between *Sermon on the Mount* and the *Bhagavadgita*. I found nothing new in the Sermon on the Mount but the same idea which I had learnt in my childhood that "There is nothing much in giving a cup of water to on who gave you a cup of water or salute him who salutes you, but there is some virtue doing a good turn to one who had done a bad turn.'[87] Mahatma Gandhi's passionate love for religious unity made him oppose conversion. He saw no reason of conversion in from one faith to the other. In Gandhi's view there may be cases of voluntary conversion but nobody should be converted by forceful means. He objected to the mass conversion of Harijan and other poorer classes by the Christian missionaries. He did not allow some of his co-workers to give up their ancestral religion. For instance he wrote to one of them on 5th March, 1934 to a Jew who wanted to become a Hindu.

"You don't need to be a Hindu but a true Jews. If Judaism does not satisfy you no other faith will give your satisfaction for any length of time. I would advise you to remain a Jewess and appropriate the good of other faiths."[88] Gandhiji stated that the Christian missionaries would render true service to India, if they could persuade themselves to confine their activities to humanitarian service without the ultimate motive of converting India and her unsophisticated villagers. He believed that what is true in a particular religion will abide and what is untrue will fall to pieces without any regard to its number of followers. A life of service and simplicity commands out respect. Gandhi said that a rose does not need to preach. It simply spreads it fragrance. The fragrance is its own sermon. The fragrance of religious and spiritual life according to Gandhiji is far greater and finer.

Mahatma Gandhi therefore was the initiator of religious unity in the true sense although the germ of it can be traced back to a far ancient period. It is this sense of unity amongst different religious that has raised the status of India in the mind of the modern world and this was greatly result of the efforts of Mahatma Gandhi in this direction.

STEPS TAKEN BY GANDHI TO ESTABLISH HINDU-MUSLIM UNITY IN INDIA

Though India is essentially the land of the Hindus, many other religions have existed side by side of which the Muslims constitute a very large section of the total Indian population. In fact India had been under Muslim rule for a long period of time. Though rulers like Akbar and a few others tried their best to establish a strong bond between the two communities, history shows that at several times they were also at strife. Mahatma Gandhi's effort to establish Hindu-Muslim unity deserves special mention.

Mahatma Gandhi was very much pained to see the hatred in the minds of the Hindus and the Muslims against each other. Accordingly he devoted the entire issue of May 29, 1934 of *Young India* to his own 6,000 words article on "Hindu-Muslim tension; its cause and Cure." He undertook a twenty one days fast to restore the unity between the Hindus and the Muslims. On the twelft day of the fast, he wrote "Hitherto it has been a struggle and a yearning for a change of heart among Englishmen who compose the Government of India....But the struggle must for the moment be transformed to a change of heart amongst Hindus and Muslims. Before they can think of freedom, they must be brave enough to love one another, to tolerate one another's religion...This requires faith in oneself. And faith in oneself requires faith in God. If we have that faith we shall cease to fear one another."[89] It is interesting to note how, at all critical moments he ultimately appeals to God's help. Gandhi has an unflichig faith in Him.

On January 9, 1948, there had been a stabbing in Delhi. Rumours of all sorts of atrocities spread throughout the city and fanned the flames of religious hatred. Gandhiji was very such pained over the situation. He wanted to go to Pakistan especially to Sindh and Western Punjab to try to stop the riots and the ill treatment of the Hindus. But he had no moral justification to ask the Muslims in Pakistan to treat the Hindus as brother when the Hindus of Delhi and elsewhere did not treat the Muslism as brothers. His feelings of helplessness came to an end on January 12th, when it suddenly came to his mind that the should fast which was his last weapon in the place of a sword. Gandhiji made it clear that the fast would end when there would be a reunion of hearts of all the communities brought about without any outside pressure; but from an awakened sense of duty. The beginning of the fast was preceded by prayer and singing of the favourite devotional songs. The fast then commenced at 11 a.m. When a person heard of Gandhiji's fast, he wrote to him a note, pleading to withdraw it. Gandhiji replied "I had exhausted all resources and realised my utter helplessness. Here is the significance of my fast. If you read and ponder in your mind the epic of gajendra moksha (the story of the elephant) you must be able properly to appraise my step.... God sent me the fast. He alone will end it if and when he wills. In the meantimes it behoves us all to believe to the Good and we should act accordingly. Let our sole prayer be that God may vouchsafe me strength of spirit during the fast so that that temptation to live may not lead me into a hasty or premature termination of the fast."[90] The above is a clear evidence of Gandhi's absolute reliance on God on all important decisions.

In his second post prayer talk of the fast Gandhiji said "Before I ever knew anything of politics in my early youth, I dreamt the dream of communal unity in my heart. I shall jump in the evening of my life like a child, to feel that the dream has been realised in this life. The will for living the full span of life portrayed by the seers of old, and which they permit us to down at 125 years, will then revive. Who would not risk sacrificing his life for the realisation of such a dream? then we shall have real swaraj."[91] Mahatma Gandhi indeed sacrificed his life to this great cause.

On the fifth day of the fast Gandhi's condition deteriorated. He became too weak and felt nauseous. The doctors attending on him said that it was not advisable for Gandhi to continue the fast. That evening at the home of Dr. Rajendra Prasad, a widely representative group met to consider how to meet Gandhiji's conditions for breaking the fast. It has representations from various organizations and religious groups. After full discussion they decided to sign a seven point declaration to meet the terms Gandhi has set down. Dr. Rajendra Prasad read the pledge as Gandhi listened closely. It promised to protect the life, property and faith of the Muslims and assured that the incidents which had happened in Delhi would not happen again. Being completely assured, Gandhiji decided to break the fast. The breaking of the first was done with the usual ceremony of prayers. Taxts from the Japanese, Muslim and Parsi scriptures were recited. They were followed by the mantra.

Asato ma sadgamaya

tamaso ma jyotirgamaya

Mritorma amritam gamaya

Gandhi's favourite Christian hymn was also recited.

When I survey the wondrous cross..... Love so amazing, so divine, Demands my soul, my life, my all.

By such measures Gandhiji sought to establish Hindu-Muslim unity. He left no stone unturned to achieve this end. As he said "I am striving to become the best cement between the two communities. My longing is to be able to cement the two with my blood if necessary."[92] Gandhi again explained, "for good or for ill, the two communities are wedded to India; they are neighbours, sons of the same soil; they are destined to die here as they are born here. Nature will force them to live in peace come if they don't come together voluntarily."[93] Gandhiji wanted to create such a social atmosphere in which both the communities could live in peace and cooperation with mutual respect for each other.

GANDHIJI'S IDEAS ON EDUCATION

Mahatma Gandhi expressed his views on the ideal system of education that would be applicable to India. Through proper education Gandhi wanted to build up a strong man, not strong in the physical sense, but strong in character having high moral and religious virtues. The primary object of his socio-political-economic set up was to prevent a person from degenerating into a materialistic being and this he believed could be done only by a system of proper education.

Many people believe that Gandhiji had little or no

practical knowledge about the ancient or modern theories of education. Being too much pre-occupied in social and political matters he had no time to devote to educational matters. But this we find is largely a misconception. Like the greatest educational philosopher of the twentieth century, Prof. J. Dewy, Gandhi found opportunities to put his ideas to test at the Phoenix Settlement, the Tolstoy farm in Africa and Sabarmati Ashram in India. He also founded the Gujarat Vidyapith in 1920. He kept himself constantly in touch with students, teachers and educationists. As such the education system that he proposed for India is unique and practical.

Impact of Religion on Gandhi's Education

Mahatma Gandhi tried to frame his basic education in accordance with the ancient system of ashrama. Ashrama education is nothing but education with shrama or labour. The student in ancient ashrama learnt by rendering service to his "Guru' (teacher). He gathered fuel and water, cooked food and cleaned the surroundings. The student had to perform such functions as tending of cows (*gopalana*), tending of the sacrificial fire (*samidhaharan*) and gathering of fruits and roots (*phalamulaharan*). Similarly Gandhi's education had labour or shrama at the other side. Education and labour thus go hand in hand. The discipline laid down by Gandhiji for a student life reminds us of the ancient Yoga system of Philosophy. In student life as well as in ashrama life one was required to follow the Dwadasha Vrata prescribed by Gandhiji. These twelvefold vows were nothing but only a few spiritual principle to guide the student along the right path. The universal prayer of Gandhiji 'Vaishnava jana to, tena Kahiye' was to be recited by the student. The meaning behind it was that the qualities of a Vaishnava should be the qualities present in every student.

A study of the ancient Gurukul system of India proves that the aim of education is to develop the personality of the individual so as to make him a useful citizen of the society or country. Gandhi too wanted to train the students in such a way so that they may equip themselves properly in order to serve the country.

As we have seen that all the thoughts and activities of Gandhiji revolve round religion. In the field of education also his ideas revolved round God realisation. The primary aim of Gandhi's life was self realisation. He therefore wanted that the educational system should also be subservient to the aim. In his own words:

"The motto of the Gujarat Vidyapith (whose founder was Gandhi himself) is 'Sa Vidya Ya Vimuktaya." It means that is knowledge which is (leads to) salvation."[94] Purity of personal life is the one indispensable condition for building up sound education according to Gandhi. And this purity can only come when the Students are believers is God; that is Truth and Non-Violence, have a pure heart, lead a simple life and have faith in dignity of labour.

Education according to Gandhi is an all round drawing out of the man's body. Literacy not simply the end of education. Gandhiji believed that an all round development of the mind can be attained only when it goes with the education of the physical and spiritual faculties of the child. Gandhiji put more emphasis on the moral than on the intellectual aspect of education.

Mahatma Gandhi's belief in the essential unity of all mankind prompted him to work for the welfare of all human beings. Gandhi saw that one of the ways to fight for the suppressed classes was to secure for them the right of equal opportunity in the field of education also. He stood for the education of the total human being—mind, body and spirit. The mind or spirit should not be cultivated alone in isolation of the body. This reminds us of the educational theory of Plato who suggests gymnastics for the body and music for the soul to be included in any system of education. According to Gandhi also, the body must be kept fit, the intellect must be trained and the spirit must be properly cultivated since they constitute an indivisible whole. It is a mistake, therefore, to consider literacy as the 'be all and end all' of education.

In order to secure equal rights and opportunities for all Gandhiji insisted that free and compulsory primary education should be given to all boys and girls from 6 to 14 years of age.

Gandhi in his theory of basic education gives a unique approach to education. The foremost place, according to him should be given to handicrafts in the process of a child's education. This has two advantages, namely that it infuses the sense of creativity in a child and it also helps one to be self-supporting. Gandhi pointed out that subjects like history, geography, mathematics etc. could be taught side by side with handicrafts. In his view a child should not be overburdened with reading and writing from a very tender age. A child learning through the medium of oral communication learns better. As has been pointed out, the primary aim of education is the building up of a strong character. Intellectual education without character is like a wax statue, beautiful to look at but liable to melt by the application of a little heat.

Gandhiji was well aware of the importance of bread. he was therefore conscious of the dangers of higher education on the arts subjects without vocational training. Higher education without vocational training create students fit only for white collar jobs which are limited. It does not give them proper training to earn their livelihood and this is responsible for the unemployment problem which has become so acute in our country.

Gandhiji's firm conviction about the power of truth, love and Ahimsa made him base his education on these principles. Every person should be physically, mentally and spiritually trained to realise truth and love in every sphere of life. Gandhi was undoubtedly attracted to the ancient Indian culture and heritage but did not blindly accept anything without the test study and experiment to discover truth from different sources and bind them to a beautiful whole. Declaring the object of the National College

(Gujarat Vidya pith) he expressed his own ideal thus:

"The Gujarat Vidyapith does not propose to feed on, or repeat the ancient cultures. It rather hopes to build a new culture based on traditions of the past enriched by the experience of later times. It stands for synthesis of the different cultures that have come to stay in India, that have influenced Indian life, and that, in their turn have themselves been influenced by the spirit of the soil."[95] Gandhi also believed in the dictum 'An example is better than precept' which should be the guiding principle of a teacher. Gandhiji himself practised what he preached. In this sense Gandhi was a top educationist of his time.

On the question of the medium of instruction, Gandhi strongly opposed the use of English as the medium of instruction in schools. In his opinion it has caused severe loss to the students intellectually and morally. A child can easily grasp something that is taught in his mother tongue than through the medium of a foreign language. Gandhi had expressed this view out of his own experiences at high school when he spent half his time trying to master English before he tried to understand science or some art subjects. English has taken such dominance in our country that in some schools students speaking mother tongue during school hours are severely punished.

Imparting education through the medium of mother tongue according to Gandhi has also its moral and spiritual effects. English undermined the importance of the mother tongue. It also created a sort of the barrier between the students and the members of their own family who could not understand English and consequently it alienated them from their cultural heritage. Gandhiji recalled with serious repentance for not having adequate knowledge of Sanskrit. As a result he could not study the ancient text in original, like the *Gita* and others. And Gandhi felt that if he had spent those precious years in trying to acquire mastery over his mother tongue and Sanskrit, he would have been able to serve his country and his people better. Therefore,

Gandhi repeatedly insisted that one should never feel ashamed to express himself in his vernacular. The Indian people ought to build on their own cultural heritage but this does not mean that they should create a barrier between their culture and the cultures of the rest of the world. The diverse winds of culture should be allowed to be blown from all sides, but they should be experienced in our own cultural heritage. Gandhi's educational system is thus rooted in his fundamental belief in the nature of the self, the essential unity of mankind and the consequence of the belief in the unity of mankind. The way by which the welfare of the people could be secured depended to a large extent on the proper system of education.

There are some other important aspects of education on which Gandhi laid emphasis. The curriculum for the basic school according to him must include activities which laid stress on the need for cleanliness in the surrounding and proper civic sense. According to Gandhi children should themselves carry out cleaning and scavenging so that the prejudices against untouchables and scavengers would be removed. Gandhiji also emphasised the need for self sufficiency in the schools. A child should share some burden of the financial expenses by such means. He can grow some fruits within the compound for mid-day meal or produce some small furniture or whitewash the walls of the school rooms. The Gandhian system of education, therefore can solve some of the problems of present day society specially the problem of unemployment to some extent. Gandhiji thus proposes a system of education in accordance with the religious and ethical ideas of his religious tradition which can fulfill the needs of the people of India to a considerable degree.

CONCLUSION

Mahatma Gandhi dreamt of a social ideal which is very much similar to the inscriptions he read at the Delhi or Agra fort which reads: "If there is paradise on earth, it is here, it is here, it is here." Gandhiji said that he would love to see it inscribed on the gates of Pakistan and India. "In such paradise whether it is in the Indian Union or in Pakistan, there will be neither paupers, or beggars, neither high, nor low, neither millionaire employers, nor half starved employees, nor intoxicating drinks or drugs. There will be the same respect for women as vouchsafed to men and the chastity and purity of men and women will be jealously guarded. Where every woman except one's wife, will be treated by men of all religions as mother, sister or daughter according to her age. Where there will be no untouchability and where there will be equal respect for all faiths."[96]

A glance at Indian history shows that India from a long time had been choked by numerous evils resulting from social suppression. The society was hard hit by ritualism and orthodoxy. There is no doubt that from time to time great men tried to relieve the situation but few were successful in this difficult venture. Gandhiji tried to initiate important social reforms which have changed the very face of Indian society.

But some of the malpractices of society are still seen in present India. The dowry deaths for example are increasing in spite of the different legislative measures. Torture agaisnt Indian women is a common sight. The caste system in its rigid form is also prevalent in some interior parts of the country. Gandhiji's teachings can help us in doing away with such evils. What is needed at present in extensive education not merely in the form of University degrees, but education in the real sense which can help to change the very attitude of the people by broadening their mental horizon.

REFERENCES

1. *Harijan*, August 29, 1946.
2. *Gita*, Chapter 12, Sl. 4.
3. Mihir Kumar Sen, *Elements of Civics*, p. 3.

4. Dr. R. Shamsastry, *Kautilya Arthasastra,* Book I, Chapter XIII, p. 22-23.
5. *Ibid.*, April 13, 1962.
6. B.P. Kangle, *The Kautilya Arthasastra* part III, p. 119.
7. *Ibid.*, p. 146.
8. *Ibid.*, 3.20.16.
9. Dr. Rajendra Prasad's presidential speech at Sevagram from 13th to 15th March 1948 published in *Sarvodaya: its principles and programme,* p. 21.
10. *Harijan,* March 4, 1933, p.5.
11. *Dhammapada,* 393.
12. M.K. Gandhi, *In search of the Supreme,* Vol. III, p. 128.
13. *Harijan,* September 28, 1934, p. 260.
14. Sanyal and Mallick, *Sarvapalli Radhakrishnan,* cited in ' Social Philosophy', p. 241.
15. M.K. Gandhi, *An Autobiography,* pp. 171-4.
16. Sanyal and Mallick, A Quotation by Dr. Radhakrishnan, cited in *'Social Philosophy'* p. 241.
17. *Young India,* January 5, 1921.
18. M.K. Gandhi, *Varnasrama dharma,* Navajivan Trust, p. 6.
19. *Ibid.*, p. 14.
20. *Ibid,* pp. 15-17.
21. *Ibid,* p. 21.
22. Theodore de Bary, (ed.), *Sources of India Tradition,* Vol. I, p. 23.
23. *Rigveda* X. 90 from the Source Book in Indian Philosophy, p. 19.

24. *Gita* chapter IV, Sl. 13.
25. *Plato, The Republic* 100, section 415.
26. M.K. Gandhi, *Selections from Gandhi*, Vol. III, p. 161.
27. Louis Fischer, *The Essential Gandhi*, p. 252.
28. *Harijan*, February 11, 1933, p.2.
29. M.K. Gandhi, *In Search of the Supreme*, Vol. III, p. 161.
30. *Ibid.*, pp. 181-2.
31. *Ibid.*, pp. 81.
32. *Ibid*, pp. 168-69.
33. *Harijan*, August 24, 1934.
34. *Gita*, Chapter IX, Sl. 32.
35. *The Selected Works of Mahatma Gandhi*, vol. IV, p. 237.
36. M.K. Gandhi, *Autobiography*, p. 82.
37. Dr. Radhakrishnan, *Mahatma Gandhi*, p. 208.
38. M.K. Gandhi, *In Search of the Supreme*, Vol. III, p. 183.
39. *Young India*, 6th Oct., 1921.
40. M.K. Gandhi, *In Search of the supreme*, Vol. III, p.194.
41. M.K. Gandhi" *The Remvoal of Untouchabilty*, p. 81.
42. M.K. Gandhi, *In Search of the Supreme*, Vol. III, p. 202.
43. N.K. Bose, *Selections from Gandhi*, pp. 252-53.
44. *Young India*, June 8, 1921.
45. *Young India*, October 6, 1921.
46. Isaiah 66/3.
47. Romans 15/21.
48. Desai, Valji Govindji, *Glances at Islam*, footnote on, p. 14.

49. Surah II, Al bakhar, Ayat 286 of the Koran.
50. Paul Tillich, *Christianity and the Encounter of World Religons*, p. 69.
51. Glyn Richards, *The Philosophy of Gandhi*, p. 161.
52. *Young India*, January 29, 1925, p. 37.
53. *Collected works of Mahatma Gandhi*, Vol. XXV, p. 519.
54. *Harijan*, 22nd March, 1942.
55. *Harijan*, January 12, 1934.
56. M.K. Gandhi, *All Men are Brothers*, p. 161.
57. *Harijan* February 24, 1940, pp. 13-14.
58. N.K. Bose, *Selected from Gandhi*, pp. 248-161.
59. *Harijan*, Sep. 7, 35, p. 234.
60. *Harijan*, Nov. 21, 36, p. 231.
61. *Harijan*, March 28, 36.
62. M.K. Gandhi, *The story of my Experiements with Truth*, p. 22.
63. N.K. Bose, *Selected works of Mahatma Gandhi*, Vol. VI, p. 496.
64. *Kathaupanishad*, Chapter I. III 3-6.
65. Louis Fischer, *Gandhi: His Life and Message for the world*, p. 34.
66. *Young India*, August 5, 1926.
67. *Young India*, June 21, 28.
68. *Young India*, June 21, 28.
69. *Harijan*, May 23, 36.
70. *Young India*, February 28, 29.

71. *Young India,* April 11, 1929.
72. *New Testament,* I, Corin XI. 29.
73. *Diggha Nikaya Sutra,* 22.
74. *Young India,* April 11, 1929.
75. *Young India,* September 15, 1927.
76. *Rigveda* I. 164-46.
77. Mahimna Storam Sl. 7.
78. Sl. From *Vishnu Purana* quoted by Dr. Radhakrishnan in *Eastern Religion and Western Thought,* p. 310.
79. *Gita,* Chapter IV, Sl. 7&8.
80. *The Quran,* Chapter II, 136.
81. Muhammud Ali, *The Holy Quran* (translated into English), XV, Sl. 7&9.
82. M.K. Gandhi, From *Yeravda Mandir,* p. 26.
83. *Ibid,* p. 26.
84. *Harijan,* February 16, 1934, p. 5.
85. M.K. Gandhi, *Autobiography,* p. I, Chapter 10
86. *Young India,* January 21, 1926, p. 30.
87. V.B. Kher, (ed.), *In Search of the Supreme,* Vol. III, p. 37.
88. Chandrasekar Sukla; (ed.), Margaret Spiegels Artile in 'Reminscenes of Gandhiji'.
89. Louis Fischer, *Gandhi: His Life and Message for the World,* p. 77.
90. Gener Sharp, *Gandhi wields the Weappen of Moral Power,* p. 243.
91. Gandhi: *Non Violence in Peace and War,* p. 354.
92. *Young India,* September 29, 1927.

93. Dr. S. Radhakrishnan, *The Hindu View of Life*, p. 89.

94. *Young India*, March 20, 1930.

95. N.K. Bose, *Selectiosn from Gandhi*, p. 298.

96. Gandhi, *Non Violence in Peace and War*, p. 354.

6

RELEVANCE OF GANDHIAN CONCEPTS AND HIS CONTRIBUTION TO THE MODERN SOCIETY

The relevance of any thought or philosophy is measured in terms of its pragmatic value to the people and the society. If it offers genuine solutions to the problems faced by the society it is described as relevant. Again the question of relevance is related to the time factor. A certain theory or belief is relevant or may be relevant for the present and there may be concepts which are relevant for all times to come.

Mahatma Gandhi's ideas on different fields of human activity can be described as more or less relevant not during his times alone but even at the present with a few modification here and there and perhaps it would also be relevant for all times to come.

Gandhian thoughts are relevant basically because he was never rigoristic and conservative in his outlook. Like a scientist, Gandhi based his ideas on experiments. He repeatedly pointed out that his aim was not to be consistent with his previous statements but his aim was to be consistent with truth. So he himself confessed that he had "grown from truth to truth'. No wonder that his autobiography has been described as 'The Story of my experiment with Truth". It is clear, therefore, that Gandhi did not claim any finality for his conclusions. From Hind Swaraj to his prayer meetings in Delhi we are confronted with different opinions, and the the growth of his ideas are quite clear. He did not formulate a fixed system of laws like Marx, Lenin and other great thinkers. The only criteria to which every principle should conform are Truth and Ahimsa. Thus, we can formulate an economic principle or a political policy if it suits us provided it is based on Truth, justice, non-violence and the welfare of humanity.

The best gift which Gandhi presented to the world is his gift of non-violence. Though Gandhi was influenced by the ethical doctrines of Buddhism and Jainism in this respect, he gave ahimsa an active political content as an instrument for social action. By transforming the ethics of ahimsa from the individual to the social level he gave the doctrine of non-violence a revolutionary intent and direction. Gandhi's insistence on the resolution of all conflicts by peaceful means has become more relevant today when the world is torn by strife and oppression. The constant war going on in the borders of India and Pakistan on the Kashmir issue could have been solved long ago had the people of both the countries remained loyal to the yearnings of the Mahatma's heart. Gandhi was right when he said that war and violence never solve any problems. They sow the seeds of hatred that generate future wars. Dialogues and negotiations alone can settle disputes and the effects it produces are permanent. Hence it has been said that "the more of violence the less of revolution."

Gandhi's preaching of non-violence not only in case of individuals but in case of world peace seems to be an echo of the following Vedic verse.

"Sarve bhavantu sukhinah, Sarve santu niramaya Sarve bhadrani pasyantu ma Kascit dukh bhag bhavet."[1]

The Gandhian theory of politics with morality at the background will be like a fresh breath of air amidst a gloomy, polluted and dirty politics of the present times. The spiritualisation of politics as suggested by Gandhi is not merely a utopia but a living ideal towards which a nation should always strive. What form of government a country has and who are the leaders of a particular country, which political party comes to power is hardly important. What is important is the character of the people who form the government. Gandhiji had suggested the nature of the characters a satyagrahi should possess. The qualities prescribed by Gandhi for a satyagrahi should be the qualities of the individuals forming the government that is they should always be inspired by the qualities of truth, justice, honesty and sacrifice.

It is true that India today has witnessed several failures in the political system. There are various drawbacks in the system of parliamentary democracy. The Indian constitution laid down rules for free and fair elections but elections today are neither free nor fair. The system of false voting, booth capturing and a huge display of blackmoney have nullified the very purpose of election. The political parties are all functioning with anti-democratic ideals. Satyagraha of Gandhi which was means to resolve political conflicts has been replaced by violence. There is no true alternative to Gandhian principles to be followed for the success in politics.

Democracy has been defined as a government of the people, for the people and by the people but at present in India virtually this spirit of democracy is lost. The present political setup in India is neither capitalism nor socialism nor even the model prescribed by Gandhi. According to Pandit Jawaharlal Nehru India was fast becoming a socialistic pattern of society and the ideal of 'democratic Socialism' was the aim towards which India sought to move. The present political setup in India however is largely anti-socialistic and anti-democratic. Centralization took the place of decentralization and concentration of powers in hands of a few took the place of distribution of powers at the grass root level. Globalisation has replaced Gandhi's idea of 'Swadeshi.'

India had been saturated with the democratic feelings from the ancient times. Though in the past India was ruled by kings yet the king ruled by respecting the people's wishes. The epic *Ramayana*, which depicts the ideal system of government beautifully illustrates this aspect. No wonder that Gandhi visualised his state as Ramrajya. The daily life and social life of the people in ancient India was well organised and self regulated. So there was no need of external pressure. In contrast the democracy found in the west are external and artificial. The democracy adopted in the west was parliamentary democracy where importance lay only in the system of casting voters.

The functioning of Indian democracy at present is against Gandhiji's idea of 'Swaraj'. What India needs at present is decentralised democracy of Gandhi's dream with the village at the root. The panchayat should be the executive with committees which will carry out the true functions and they should be responsible and answerable to the villages. The plans and programmes to be carried out for the development of the villages should not wait for approval of the state or central governments. To put in Gandhi's own words "when people come into possession of political power, the interference with the freedom of the people is reduced to a minimum. In other words, a nation that runs its affairs smoothly and effectively without much state interference is truly democratic. Where such a condition is absent, the form of government is democratic only in name.'[2] This picture of democracy painted by Gandhi is what India desperately needs at present to end the political turmoil.

Gandhi's economy of "simple living and high thinking" does not seem to attract the present generation. Gandhi's ideas on economics seem to be too idealistic and impractical in the present trend of Globalisation. To improve the condition of the masses Gandhi introduced certain revolutionary techniques which are highly relevant for India today. The concept of bread labour, village self-sufficiency, decentralization, development of cottage and small scale industries, reliance on khadi, the spirit of Swadeshi, equal system of distribution and above all the maxim of the minimization of human wants are some of the innovative concepts which Gandhi presented to India for her rescue.

The present problem of poverty and unemployment can find its best solution by the Gandhian method. The primary aim of a welfare state like India is the 'Right to Live' and the 'Right to work for a living.' Unemployment of the people leads to a denial of this fundamental right. Gandhian economics is mostly labour oriented and not capital oriented. Hence individual with a small capital can set up a business and thus create facilities for self employment. Instead of looking for white collar jobs people can look for alternative meas of self employment.

The concentration of wealth in the hands of a few. the Gandhian theory of trusteeship seems to be superior to the Marxian method of socialization. Gandhi's novel outlook was responsible for finding out a new way to win over the capitalist class not by force but by voluntary method. Critics point out the defects inherent in the trusteeship theory where the honesty of the trustee may be doubted. But in such cases, Gandhi allows the use of non-violent coercion to force the trustee to come to terms

India has witnessed a long line of economic theories. But even amidst them Gandhiji's ideas on economics have a prominent role to play. To Gandhi economics was not an end in itself but only a means to a higher end namely self realization. To ignore Gandhiji's ideas in framing our economic policies would be to lead our economy to sheer destruction.

Gandhi's social philosophy too was rooted in the Oriental outlook. The Indian society at a particular period of its history was hard hit by ritualism and orthodoxy. Thousand of years of foreign rule in India supersede the Indian mind hampering the free growth of the mind and spirit. There is no doubt that from time to time saints and great men tried to restore the dead spirit. Gandhi tried to initiate a set of important social reforms which changed the very face of India.

Gandhiji's method of social revolution through satyagraha is unparalled in the whole world. In the early times 'revolution' referred merely to political revolution or a change in government. For example the French Revolution began with an aim to limit the power of the kind, the American revolution began with the slogan of "no taxation without representation" Gandhi was the initiator of a silent revolution totally different from the other kind. His revolution was not merely against the British government but a "total revolution" aimed at a drastic change in the life style of the masses as a whole. It was a thorough going change in the socio-economic life of the people. The aim of real revolution is to bring about a change in one's outlook, ideas and values of life. This change in one's outlook cannot be due to any external force or pressure as is conceived by Marx, Lenin and Engel. Coercion and violence can force people to behave in a particular way just as a master forces a slave or a dog to behave in the way he likes, but by no means can force change one's belief or outlook. Any social change involves change in the mind and heart of a human being. Violence creates an atmosphere of hatred, jealousy and bitterness. Violence also leads to greater violence. Gandhi very well realised this basic human nature and so he advocated a non-violent revolution as a means for social change. Not only Gandhi even a Marxist Professor A. Shishkin of the Soviet Academy of Sciences has remarked "The means which are demoralizing men and are cultivating cruelty, baseness etc. cannot serve the noble end of the liberation of the people.... we adopt the mean that are strengthening the moral consciousness of man."[3]

In Gandhi we have a fusion of social thought and social action. For example he once said "what I have done will endure, not what I have said or written". What Gandhi thought of, he did it at all costs. Albert Schweitzer held that Gandhi was wedded to the traditional Hindu philosophy of life negation, "the inactive ethics of perfecting the self alone" .... he implis that Hinduism implies harmlessness but not active love. Gandhi's active ahimsa is a refutation of Schweitzer's criticism. Gandhi has emphatically expressed his dislike for the life of a hermit or a recluse. He was sure about the fact that he could find God only amidst the suffering humanity. 'Manav dharma' or man's religion is another name of Hinduism. Gandhi made it clear that it is not advisable to run after other worldly ends. To Gandhi we can attain the spiritual life through the mundane life.

To Gandhi goes the credit of bringing about true national integration. Though "India is a unity in diversity from times immemorial, it was Gandhi who secured the political and administrative integration of India. The British tried to build the country together by improving the means of communication. But this was only an artificial integration. True integration lies in the hearts of man and this bond of unity was undoubtedly strengthened by the Father of the nation. There was no state in India, no village in any state, and no sect nor any race that did not take part in the freedom struggle.

India has presented the greatest contradiction when the woman in India is prayed as sakti—the goddess, the mother. But the other side of the picture is that she is dragged out of the husband's house, beaten and even murdered. Female foetecide, dowry deaths, prostitution nay even sati and the system of purdah are still seen in some of the remote Indian villages. Gandhi fought hard to remove such inhuman treatment towards woman. The implementation of Gandhi's precepts by legislation and practice can set right these evils. The womenfolk in India must remain ever grateful to Gandhi for initiating such reforms.

Gandhi displayed novelty and creativity also on his theory of education. His educational policy imbibes the best in all spheres—idealism, nationalism, pragmatism and so on. Education today has come to mean the addition of a set of university degrees. Gandhi had rightly emphasised that true education consists in the all round development of the individual—physical, mental and moral. Man is neither the body alone, nor the intellect alone nor the soul but the combination of all these three. In the harmonious combination and strengthening of all these faculties lies the true aim of education. For the true model of education Gandhi looked to our past tradition. The true light is the light of our self or the soul and the realization of this self is the aim of education. The relevance of Gandhi's ideas on education can hardly be over-estimated in modern times when the relation between the teacher and the taught is totally absent and when even after half a century of independence, a bulk of the people are still illiterate.

The impact of Gandhi's thoughts finds a clear manifestation in the framing of the constitution of India. The impact of his philosophy and religion is clearly evident from the preamble, the fundamental rights and Directive Principles of State Policy of the Indian constitution.

Gandhi's fight for the emancipation of the Harijans resulted in Article 17 of the Constitution of India for abolition of Untouchability and Article 46 of the Directive Principles of State Policy for promotion of educational and economic interests of the Scheduled caste, Scheduled Tribes and other weaker sections of the community to protect them from social injustice and all forms of exploitation. The promise to 'secure to all citizens of India Justice—social, economic and political, liberty of thought, expression, belief, faith and worship; equality of status and opportunity; and of promote among them all fraternity assuring the dignity of the individual and the unity of the nation" are basically the ideas emphasised by Gandhi.

The Fundamental Rights in part III of the constitution constitutes one of the areas approximate to Gandhian ideology to usher in an era of political democracy or swaraj. A code of written Civil Rights for the Indian citizens appeared as an innovation. Protection of minority interests, religious and cultural freedom were some of the items circulated by Gandhiji in the second session of the Second Round Table Conference. His views found place in the Right to Freedom of Religion (Arts 25-28) and Culture and Educational Rights (Art 29-30) in the constitution. His demand for equality and elimination of exploitation and discrimination resulted in Articles 15, 16, and Arts 23-24. His fight for the removal of untouchability resulted in Article 17.

For bringing about economic and social democracy, the Directive Principles of State Policy was a major step. It was to be brought about through village industries (Art. 43). Compuslory education for children (Art. 45), Prohibition (Art. 47), living wage for workers (Art. 43), ban on cow slaughter (Art 48) etc.

The incorporation of major Gandhian principle in the constitution was on the Panchayat. According to this directive: "The state shall take steps to organise village Panchayat and endow them with such powers and authority as may be necessary to enable them to function as units of self government" (Article 40). Articles 45 and 46 dealing with the provisions for the free and compulsory educational and economic interests of Scheduled castes, Scheduled tribes and other weaker sections of the community can be termed as Articles bearing perceptible vibration of Gandhian ideology.[4] Some writers however opine that a half hearted compromise had been achieved in framing the constitution of India by incorporation of some of the ideas and principles of Gandhi. These ideas and principles found prominent expression mostly in Part III and Part IV of the Indian Contitution—more in the the non-justiciable, non enforceable Directive Principles of State Policy than in the justiciable and legally enforceable Fundamental Rights.[5]

This does not however mean that Gandhi and his views lacked supporters but it was mainly due to some difference of opinion between Gandhi and the younger generation of intellectuals and socialistics of the Indian National Congress that his views couldn't find proper expression.

The mighty power of spirituality and religion in guiding human life is a well known fact. The political system that is guided by the forces of religion can withstand the most difficult circumstances. If any government, any organisation, any political power of social norm is to command respect it is imperative for it to be ruled by the virtues of religion such as love, sacrifice, humility, patience, fearlessness and so on. Love and not force is the basis of human life. A system which is based on force is short lived. The fate of Napoleon, the mighty emperor who died a prisoner in the deserted island of St. Helena is well known. Napoleon is remembered as a great historical figure, no doubt, but his achievements does not appeal to our heart as that of Gandhi. To conquer lands, to gain wars, to dominate people and attain power is one thing while to work for human welfare, to uplift the poor and down-trodden and to raise the moral standard of the people is another. Mahatma Gandhi stood in the second category and the success that he achieved in liberating the vast Indian empire from the mighty British yoke is a clear testimony to the success of one over the other. Mahatma Gandhi did not have great physical strength though he was energetic and healthy. He was not a rich man either. Professinally or intellectually he was not very brilliant. But what was that made him one of the world's greatest figures? It was certainly his unshakable faith in religion which pervaded every sphere of his activity. Gandhi was not a religious saint who preached his religion amongst the society through his 'sishyas' (disciples). But he infused religion in all affairs of life, including the state, commere and industries. Even today Gandhi shines as the brightest star in the firmament of Indian history with a heroism of soul that knew no bounds.*'Purusam Evadam Sarvam'*- says the Rigveda which means that 'Purusa' or the Great principle pervades the entire world. In place of 'Purusa', we say 'Dharmam evadam sarvam', that is religion pervaded every sphere of Gandhi's life.

The greatest contribution of Gandhi lay in transforming religion from a system of rituals into a practical code of conduct. The ancient religious texts no doubt emphasised the practical aspect of religion. As has been said in the Manu: "*Vedokhilo dharmamulam amsile cha tadvidam Acaraschaiva sadhu namatnastuti evacha.*"[6]

The source of dharma is the whole range of the Vedas and also the conduct and traditions of the persons who knows the vedas. Dharma (religion) can be learnt from what the good people do. People today seemed to have forgotten this great truth. The Hindu society had become excessively ritualistic. Gandhiji did much to remind us of this truth.

To put in his own words, "in the name of religion we Hindus have made a fetish of outward observances, and have degraded religion by making it simply a question of eating and drinking. Before the throne of the almighty we shall be judged not by what we have eaten nor whom we had been touched but to whom we have served and how.'[7] According to Gandhi the religious ideas should be practiced in all affairs of human life—social, political and economic. He himself gave a religious colour to every action. From a small deed of writing a letter to the launching of a great political movement, all formed a part of his religious and spiritual pursuit. "Manav Dharma" or man's religion is only another name of Hinduism. It is not advisable to run after other wordly ends. This is a new interpretation that he gave to religion. Gandhi's another great contribution in the spiritual fields was that he had reconciled the Hindu tradition of the East with the ideas of the West. He had thus bridged, the gulf between the east and the west proving that the common saying 'The east is east and the west is west and never the twin shall meet' to be false. He brought together the philosophic religion of the East with the ideas of civil and political liberty of the west and blended them into a beautiful whole. Mahatma Gandhi was one who rendered the greatest service to the cause of international understanding. Gandhi also brought about a beautiful synthesis between science and spirituality. Gandhi synthesized science and spirituality in his metaphysics, epistemology, morality and so on. In the realms of reality which he expressed as 'Truth' he maintained that reality is neither wholly material nor wholly spiritual but a combination of both. At the same time it is universal in and through the particular. This is clear when he says that all the particular religions are so many different roads to the one perfect and universal Religion. Like an anekantavadin, Gandhi says that it is not possible for a finite and limited being to know the whole Truth just as it is not possible for a blind man to give a true description of an elephant. In his metaphysics, Gandhi at times behaves like an advaitin and at other times he speaks in the manner of a Jaina pluralist, though there is no contradiction in his scheme of ideas.

In the religious stand point Gandhi successfully synthesized theism and atheism when he declared the reality as 'Truth'. The term 'truth' was acceptable not only to a theist but also to the atheist. In the realm of epistemology Gandhi recognized the value of different sources of knowledge like perception, inference, testimony, intuition etc. and brought about a beautiful synthesis between them. People make a distinction between the outer world of experience and reason and the inner world which can be best realised through faith, intuition and testimony. Gandhi also recognized the power of one's inner voice or conscience in matters of conflict. According to Gandhi the inner voice combines in itself both intuition and reason. "There is something within me, which never deceives me, tells me how you have to stand againt the whole world"—says Gandhi. This view, however, is not anti-rational or irrational.

In the field of morality and values Gandhi sought to bring about a synthesis between the ends and means. Self realisation which is the highest ideal for Gandhi is spiritual no doubt but which is realised by and through the means of a material life. According to Gandhi it is impossible to concentrate on spiritual matters without the minimum bodily comfort. Freedom for Gandhi includes freedom in all the spheres—economic—political, social, moral, religious and spiritual. In Gandhi's philosophy there is no dichotomy between science and spirituality. This is exactly what modern physics is heading towards that is the progress of the world is heading towards a spiritualistic trend. To quote Dr. R.K. Pandey, "the deepest mystery that quantum physics revealed is that the man of science in the larger interest of the whole humanity must atone for his initial fault of banishing his soul into eternal exile."[8]

Gandhi, as has already been mentioned, did not derive his ideas from any religion or scripture. It assimilated all that was the best of every religion. The lofty principles preached by the different religions lost its brilliance while passing through different periods. The task of Mahatma Gandhi was only to remind the people of the ancient virtues. No doubt this was a Herculean task, to infuse morality and religion to a nation which was so long under suppression and moral degradation. But India was fortunate to have great persons from time to time who came to her rescue, reminding us of the famous sloka of the *Gita*.

"Yada yada hi dharmasya glani bhavati Bharata Abhyutthanamadharmsya Tadathanam srjarmyaham[9] ["Whenever righteousness declines and unrighteousness rises; I creat myself."]

Mahatma Gandhi was indeed born to fight against unrighteousness and establish righteousness. Today the entire humanity is facing a crisis. The world has become too materialistic resulting in a loss of spiritual values. Everyone is lost in the mad race for money, power and glory. The powerful nations are trying to swallow up the smaller nations. A reign of terror, chaos, confusion, oppression and exploitations surrounds. The greatest remedy for all these evils lies is religion. In our times we have seen that the development of science and technology failed to satisfy human minds. The people in the west are now in search of a life which can bring peace and happiness. Many are running after the spiritual life of the East. This is a clear indication of the fact that only religion is the answer to the present catastrophe. Though religion reigns supreme in India, at present it has become only a myth. Violence, anarchism, disunity and untruthful behaviour are seen everywhere in India. In the words of Dr. Radhakrishnan, "if civilization is to survive we must accept that its essence does not consist in power, glory, strength, wealth and prestige but in free activity of the human mind, in the increase of moral virtue, in the cultivation of good taste and skill in the art of living."[10] If the world is to be saved the religious ideals should be given the place of highest value for which Mahatmaji always fought so much so that he died crying out *'He Ram'* which is another name for his religion. The importance of religion is accepted by even other thinkers who belong to disciplines other than religion. Some thinkers of the west are convinced that the salvation of Europe wouldn't be possible without a spiritual revaluation. A great psychoanalyst, Jung, has remarked, "I have treated many hundreds of patients. Among them all - in the second half of my life-there has not be one patient, whose problem in the last analysis was not a problem of finding a religious outlook of life. It is safe to say that everyone of my patients fell ill because he had lost a spiritual ideal. No one was really healed, who did not regain his spiritual outlook."[11]

In a book called *Future Shock*, an American novelist Alvin Toffler has pointed out the horrors that the industrialisation and mechanization of life has brought about in the modern age. The author has visualised that the world of future has to embrace things of the spirit and slow down the pace of technology if it is to attain peace and prosperity. To quote Alvin Toffler, "Can one live in a society that is out of control? that is the question posed for us by the concept of "Future Shock'. For that is the situation we find ourselves in... Urbanization, ethnic conflict, migration, population, crime—a thousand example spring to our mind, of field in which our efforts to shape change seem increasingly inept and futile."[12]

Even the communist leaders like Lenin and Marx, who in principles reject religion unconsciously believe in some form of religion. Their appeals to the virtues of equality, justice and brotherhood are nothing but reference to religious principles at the root. These are only religion in disguise. The appreciation and adoration of Lenin and Marx is promoted by the religious urge sleeping in their mind.

If we want to build up a society in the Gandhian model religion is the first necessity. Gandhi gave his precious suggestions in almost every field of human activity. We have already discussed the relevance of some of his important ideas. All of those ideas may not be fully applicable in the present day society but they do indicate a direction towards which we should move. He infused morality in the dirty field of politics and made it clear that the first and foremost consideration of the Government lay in the welfare of the individuals forming the society. He strove to improve the condition of the poor by glorifying the concept of bread labour. To him goes the credit of the destruction of many evils that poisoned Hindu life and society. It may be necessary, no doubt, to modify some of his ideals in the light of the present day society. Gandhiji did not claim any rigidity for his methods and politics. He was not against modification of some of his principles to suit the conditions of any situation provided the direction remained the same. It is for the present day thinkers and politicians to examine his ideas and make the best use of them. For successful implementation of Gandhiji's ideas, a total moral transformation of the people is necessry. For example if the theory of trusteeship is to be successful in the economic field, the honesty of the trustee is an indispensable condition. In matters of politics if the best form of Government is that which governs the least, the people under that Government should be fit enough to be their own Governor. If untouchability is to be completely eradicated and social equality is to be maintained, every one should have a faith in the maxim "All men are brothers." To be brief, the success of Gandhiji's ideas today would depend on how much the people have progressed ethically.

By showing the impact of religion on the thoughts of a great leader like Mahatma Gandhi, we can safely point out that if the leaders of today are influenced by similar virtues of religion, it will go a long way in reducing the present crisis in India. Political life as we find today stands blind to all religious values. Our society is spiritually sapped. Our age needs politicians who are not merely motivated by the considerations of power and economic gains but by human considerations. Gandhiji tried to emphasise this particular point to bring about a peaceful condition of human existence. It is expected that the Gandhian technique will bring about a revolution in the near future if not immediately. Since the end of the World War-II the world has shown many examples of the success of ahimsa against tyranny and injustice. The negroes of the United States is a glaring example. This non-violence may be like a few tiny drops in the vast ocean of violence. There is no doubt, that these drops, however, tiny they might be is sure to create mighty inluence and is a way to the great renaissance of the human world. We are proud of the fact that it is India, where, Gandhi who taught such a great gospel was born and largely because it is the Indian religion and teaching which is at the background.

REFERENCES

1. *Rigveda,* Chap
2. M.K. Gandhi, *Harijan* 11.1. 1936.
3. Shishkin, 'Contemporary Philosophy and Social Revaluation' Proc. Philosophical Congress (1957) P. 188.
4. K.C. Markandan, *Directive Principle son the Indian Constitution,* p. 95-III.
5. V.T. Patil, (ed.), *Studies of Gandhi 'The essay on Gandhi and the making of the Indian Constitution'* p. 79.
6. *Man,* Chapter II Sl. 6.

7. M.K. Gandhi, *Hindu Dharma*, p. 13.
8. P.K. Pandey, *Temper of Modern Science and Indian Meta Physics*
9. *Bhagavadgita*, Chapter IV Sl. 7.
10. S. Radhakrishnan,. *Religion and Society*, p. 66.
11. T.L. Vaswani, *Gandhi: The Man of Age*, p.13.
12. Alvin Toffler, *Future Shock*, p. 466.

SELECT BIBLIOGRAPHY

WORKS BY GANDHI: PRIMARY SOURCES

Gandhi, M.K., *All Men are Brothers,* UNESCO Publication.

Gandhi, M.K., *An Autobiography,* Navajivan Publishing House, Ahmedabad.

Gandhi, M.K., *Ashram Observances in Action,* Navajivan Publishing House, Ahmedabad

Gandhi, M.K., *Bapu's Letters to Mira,* Navajivan Publishing House, Ahmedabd.

Gandhi, M.K., *Bread Labour,* Navajivan Publishing House, Ahmedabad.

Gandhi, M.K., *Cent Per Cent Swadeshi,* Navajivan Publishing House, Ahmedabad.

Gandhi, M.K., *Collected Works of Mahatma Gandhi,* Vol.1.

Gandhi, M.K., *Communism and Communists,* Navaivan Publishing House, Ahmedabad.

Gandhi, M.K., *Communism and Communists,* Navajivan Publishing House, Ahmedabad.

Gandhi, M.K., *Congress and its Future,* Navajivan Publishing House, Ahmedabad.

Gandhi, M.K., *Constructive Programmes—Its Meaning and Place,*

Gandhi, M.K., *Co-operation,* Navajivan Publishing House, Ahmedabad.

Gandhi, M.K., *Correspondence with the Government 1947-47,* Navajivan Publishing House, Ahmedabad.

Gandhi, M.K., *Delhi Diary*, Navajivan Publishing House, Ahmedabad.

Gandhi, M.K., *Economic and Industrial Life and Relation*, Vols. I, II, and III, Navajivan Publishing House, Ahmedabad.

Gandhi, M.K., *From Yeravada Mandir*, Navajivan Publishing House, Ahmedabad.

Gandhi, M.K., *Gandhiji Expects*, Navajivan Publishing House, Ahmedabad.

Gandhi, M.K., *Gita - My Mother*, edt. By Anand T. Hingorani, Bharatiya Vidya Bhavan, Bombay, 1965.

Gandhi, M.K., *Gokhale-My Political Guru*, Navajivan Publishing House, Ahmedabad.

Gandhi, M.K., *Harijan*

Gandhi, M.K., *Hind Swaraj*, Navajivan Publishing House, Ahmedabad.

Gandhi, M.K., *Hindu Dharma*, Navajivan Publishing House, Ahmedabad

Gandhi,M.K., *In Search of the Supreme*, Vol.I, II and III, edt. By V.B. Kher, Navajivan Publishing House, Ahmedabad

Gandhi, M.K., *In Search of the Supreme*, Vol. I, II and III, edt. By V.B. Kher, Navajivan Publishing House, Ahmedabad.

Gandhi, M.K., *India of My Dreams* Complied by R.K. Prabhu, Navajivan Publishing House, Ahmedabad.

Gandhi, M.K., *Jawaharlal Nehru—The Jewel of India*, Pearl Publication Pvt. Ltd., Bombay.

Gandhi, M.K., *Khadi-Why and How*, Navajivan Publishing House, Ahmedabad.

Gandhi,M.K., *Letters to Raj Kumari Amrit Kaur*, Navajivan Publishing House, Ahmedabad.

Gandhi, M.K., *Letters to Sardar Vallabhbhai Patel*, Navajivan

Publishing House, Ahmedabad.

Gandhi, M.K., *My God*, Navajivan Publishing House, 1962 Complied by R.K. Prabhu.

Gandhi, M.K., *My Non Violence*, Navajivan Publishing House, Ahmedabad.

Gandhi, M.K. *My Philosophy of Life*, ed. by Anand T. Hingarani, Pearl Publication, Bombay, 1961.

Gandhi, M.K., *My Picture of Free India*, Bharatiya vidya Bhavan, Bombay.

Gandh, M.K., *My Socialism*, Navajivan Publishing House, Ahmedabad.

Gandhi,M.K., *My Religion*, Navajivan Publishing House, Ahmedabad, 1955, edt. By Bharatan Kumaarappa

Gandhi, M.K., *Pen Portraits and Tributes*, National Book Trust, 1969.

Gandhi, M.K., *Ruskin's Unto this Last-aparaphrase*, Navajivan Publishing House, Ahmedabad 1968.

Gandhi, M.K., *Sarvodaya*, Navajivan Publishing House, Ahmedabad 1954.

Gandhi, M.K., *Satyagraha in South Africa*, Navajivan Publishing House, Ahmedabad, 1961.

Gandhi, M.K., *Socialism of My Conception*, Bharatiya Vidya Bhavan, 1966.

Gandhi, M.K., *Selecton from Gandhi*, N.K.Bose, edt. Navajivan Publishing House, Ahmedabad.

Gandhi, M.K., *Strikes*, Navajivan Publishing House, Ahmedabad, 1961.

Gandhi, M.K., *The Message of Mahatma Gandhi*, Etd. Mohan Rao U.s. publication Division 1968.

Gandhi, M.K., *The Nature Cure*, Bharatiya Vidya Bhavan, Bombay, 1966.

Gandhi, M.K. *To Students*, Navajivan Publishing House, Ahmedabad.

Gandhi, M.K., *Towards Non Violence Socialism*, Navajivan Publishing House, ahmedabad 1962.

Gandhi, M.K., *Trusteeship*, Navajivan Publishing House, Ahmedabad, 1969.

Gandhi, M.K., *Trust is God*, Navajivan Publishing House, Ahmedabad, 1969.

Gandhi, M.K., *Varnasrama Dharma*, Navajivan Publishing House, Ahmedabad, 1962.

Gandhi, M.K., *Village Industries*, Navajivan Publishing House, Ahmedabad, 1963.

Gandhi, M.K., *Voluntary Poverty*, Navajivan Publishing House, Ahmedabad, 1961.

Gandhi, M.K., *What Jesus means to Me*, Navajivan publishing House, Ahmedabad, 1959.

Gandhi, M.K., *Wit and Wisdom of M. Gandhi*, ed. by N.B. Sen, New Book Society of India, New Delhi, 1960.

Gandhi, M.K., *Young India*, 1919-1922 (1922); 1924-1926 (1927); 1927-1928 (1935), Madras, S. Ganesan.

II SECONDARY SOURCES

Books on Gandhi and Gandhian Thought

Agarwal, S.N., *Gandhian Constitution of Free India*, Kitabistan, Allabahad, 1946.

Ahluwalia, B.K., *Facets of Gandhi*, Luxmi Book Store, New Delhi, 1968.

Aiyer, N. Chandra Sekhara: *Gandhi's View of Life*, Bharatiya Vidya Bhavan, Bombay.

Andres, C.F., *Mahatma Gandhi's Ideas*, Asia Publishing House, 1947.

Ashe, Jeoffrey, *Gandhi, A Study in Revolution*, Asia Publishing House, 1968.

Kumar, R. (ed.), *Essays on Gandhian Politics*, Oxford University Press, London, 1971.

Kumorappa, J.C., *Gandhian Economic Thought*, Akhil Bharat Sarva Seva Sangha, Varanasi, 1962.

———, *Gandhian Way of Life*, Maganvadi, Wardha, 1952.

Mahadevan, T.K., *Truth and Non Violence*, Gandhi Peace Foundation, New Delhi, 1970.

Malkani, N.R., *Ramblings and Renaisances of Gandhi*, Navajivan Publishing House, Ahmedabad, 1970.

Mashruwala, K.G., *Gandhi and Marx*, Navajivan Publishing House, Ahmedabad, 1960.

Mathur, J.S., *Essays on Gandhian Economic*, Chaitanya Publishing house, 1959.

Maurer, H., *Great Soul*, Orient Longmans, 1969.

Merchant, Vijay, *Trusteeship Management*, The Indian Centre for Encouraging Excellence, Bombay, 1969.

Ministry of Education, Govt. of India, *Gandhian Outlook and Technique*, 1953.

Munishi, K.M., *Reconstruction of Society Through Trusteeship*, Bharatiya Vidya Bhavan, Bombay.

Mazumdar, H.T., *Mahatma Gandhi, A Prophetic Voice*, Navajivan Publishing House, Ahmedabad, 1963.

Narayana, J.P., *A Picture of Sarvodaya Social Order*, Sarvodaya Publication, 1961.

Narayan, Sriman, *Letters from Gandhi*, Nehru, vinoba, Asia Publishing House, 1968.

Nehru, J., *Mahatma Gandhi*, Asia Publishign House,1966.

Prabhu, R.K. and Rao, U. R., *The Mind of Mahatma Gandhi*, Oxford University Press, 1946.

Prasad, Mahadeo, *Social Philosophy of Mahatma Gandhi*, Visvavidyalay Prakashan, Gorokhpur, 1958.

Prasad, Rajendra, *At the feet of Mahatma Gandhi*, Asia Publishing House, Calcutta, 1961.

———, *Satyagraha in Champran*, Navajivan Publishing House, Ahmedabad, 1949.

Publication Division

New Delhi, *The Collected Works of Mahatma Gandhi*, Vol. I to 90.

Pyareral, *Mahatma Gandhi*, The Early Phase Navajivan Publishing House, Ahmedabad, 1965.

———, *Mahatma Gandhi, The last Phase*, Vol. II Navajivan Publishign House, Ahmedabad, 1958.

Radhakrishnan, S., *Mahatma Gandhi-Essays and Reflections*, Jaico Publishing House, Bombay, 1956.

———, *Mahatma Gandhi, 100 Years*, Gandhi Peace Foundation, New Delhi, 1968.

Rajagopalachari, C., *Gandhiji's Teachings and Philosophy* Bharatiya Vidya Bhavan, Bombay, 1967.

Ramachandran G and Mahadevan, T.K., *Gandhi: His Relevance for our Times*, Gandhi Peace Foundation 1967.

Rao, M.B., (ed.), *The Mahatma*, People's Publishing House, 1969.

Rao, V.K.R., *The Gandhian Alernative to Western Socialism*, Bhavan's Book, 1970.

Rolland, Romain, *Mahatma Gandhi*, Publications Division, 1968.

Sharp, Gene, *Gandhi Wields the Weapon of Moral Power*, Navajivan, 1901.

Sheean, Vincent, Lead, *Kindly Light*, Jaico Publishing House, Bombay, 1949.

Sheean vincent: Mahatma Gandhi, *A Great life in Brief*, Publication Divison, Government of India, 1968.

Shukla, C.S., *Coversations of Gandhiji*, Vora & Co., Bombay, 1940.

——, *Incidents of Gandhiji's Life*, Vora & Co., Bombay, 1949.

——, *Gandhiji's View of Life*, Bharatiya Vidya Bhavan, 1968.

——, *Reminiscenes of Gandhiji*, Vora & Co., Bombay, 1951.

Sinha, M.P., *Contemporary Relevance of Gandhi*, Nachiketa Publication, Bombay, 1970.

Tendulkar, D.G., *Mahatma Vol. I-VIII.*, Publications Division, Government of India, 1957.

Verma, V.P., *Political Philosophy of Mahatma Gandhi & Sarvodaya*, Lakshmi Narayan Agarwal, 1965.

Watson, F., *Taling of Gandhiji*, Gandhi Smarak Nidhi, New Delhi, 1965.

Other Books

Acharya, R.M.N., *Philosophy of Religion*, J.N. Ghose and Sons, Calcutta.

Advaita Ashrama, Calcutta, *Selections from Swami Vivekananda*

Cowell and Couch, *Sarava Darsana Samgraha*, Chowkhamba Sans. series.

Dutta, D.M., *The Chief Currents of Contemporary Philosphy*, Calcutta University Press, Calcutta.

Dutta & Chatterjee, *An Introduction to Indian Philosophy*.

Edwards, D. Miall, *Philosophy of Religion*, Progressive Publishers, Calcutta.

Encyclopaedias, *Relevant atricles of Encyclopaedia Britanica, Encyclopaedia of Philosophy Encyclopaedia of Religion and Ethics* by Hastings.

Mahadevan, T.M.P., *Outlines of Hinduism*, Chetana Publication, Bomaby.

Radhakrishnan, S., *An idealist View of Life*, George Allent Unwin.

——, *Eastern Religion and Western Thought,* Oxford unviersity Press, London.

——, *Recovery of Faith,* An Orient Paperback, New Delhi.

Radhakrishnan, S, & Muirhead J.H. (ed.), *Contemporary Indian Philosophy,* Muirhead Library of Philosophy

Sharma, C.D., *A Criticla Survey of Indian Philosophy,* Matilal Banarsidass, Delhi.

Srivastava, R.S., *Contemporary Indian Philosophy,* Oriental Publishers, Delhi.

Thilly Frandk, *A History of Philosophy,* Central Book deppt. allahabad.

Trevor, Ling , *A History of Religions East and West,* MacMillan & Co. Ltd.

Vidyarthi, P.B. Early Indian Religious Thought, Orienal Publishers, New Delhi.

INDEX